ALL

"Once they paint orange on you,
it never washes off."
—HARVEY ROBINSON

TRIUMPH
B O O K S

Table of Contents

Introduction

During halftime of the 1953 Mississippi State game, a competition was held to determine the official mascot of the Tennessee football team.

One by one, several coonhounds were introduced to the fans, who voted with applause. The last dog, a blue tick named Blue Smokey, let out a loud, distinctive bark after being cheered. As the pleased crowd grew more vocal and egged him on, he responded in kind.

Needless to say, Blue Smokey won the job.

The coonhounds who have served as Blue Smokey have had a colorful and checkered history.

Getty Images

Getty Images

35

Tennessee has led the SEC in attendance for 35 consecutive seasons.

The Volunteers have been just as colorful over the years, and not because of the bright orange uniforms that stand out like few others. The line of mascots has been kidnapped, injured, mixed it up with other animal mascots, and even gotten its teeth on a handful of opposing players.

The orange and white have won national championships, been a regular contender in the conference most college football aficionados admit is the toughest in the nation, and produced the likes of Peyton Manning, Reggie White, and Doug Atkins.

But Tennessee football is about a lot more, reflected in *Sports Illustrated on Campus* naming Knoxville the best college football weekend. There's the massive house that mythic coach General Neyland built, "Rocky Top", the Pride of the Southland band forming the T, the Vol Walk, the Third Saturday in October, quarterbacks leading the marching band in celebration, checkerboard end zones, the Volunteer Navy, and a whole heap of tradition and victories along the way.

Yes, there is nothing ordinary about Tennessee football. ■

SEASON PREVIEW

The biggest question facing the 2009 Tennessee Volunteers doesn't have to do with Lane Kiffin's age, or lack of experience as a collegiate head coach.

Rather, it's whether following a legend is tougher than working for one, because UT fans are desperately hoping that's not the case.

Before he was named the 21st head coach in Tennessee football history on December 1, 2008, Kiffin was primarily known for being the youngest coach in the NFL's modern history when he took the reigns of the Oakland Raiders at the age of 31.

That occurred in January 2007. The honeymoon proved to be a lot shorter than even most critics expected after Kiffin developed a rocky relationship with owner Al Davis, who fired him September 30, 2008, for what he said was insubordination.

Kiffin had a 5-15 record with the Raiders. He filed a grievance with the NFL to claim salary he maintains he's owed by the team.

However, the demands and expectations figure to be equally high at Tennessee, especially after replacing Phillip Fulmer, who won a national championship in 1998. Athletics director Mike Hamilton even said as much, and set the bar high, when introducing the new addition to the Tennessee coaching fraternity.

Lane Kiffin has not backed off the aggressive tone he set upon his hiring. If nothing else, his passion has energized a weary Volunteers fan base.

"Tennessee football history is made up of great coaches and great players who have shaped who we are today," he said. "Choosing a coach to fall in the line of Gen. Neyland, Bowden Wyatt, Doug Dickey, Johnny Majors, Phillip Fulmer, among others, is no small task."

The son of longtime NFL defensive coordinator Monte Kiffin, who left the Tampa Bay Buccaneers to join him in Knoxville, has a pretty strong pedigree himself, to go with an impressive resume.

Kiffin spent seven seasons as an assistant at Southern California under coach Pete Carroll, including two as recruiting and offensive coordinator.

During his three years as recruiting coordinator, each recruiting class was ranked as the nation's best by at least one recruiting service.

Meanwhile, in 2006, the Trojans finished first in the Pac-10 in passing efficiency, averaging 142.8

Getty Images

The Volunteers faithful have a lot to cheer about as the Kiffin era begins in 2009.

Getty Images

yards per game, and produced two 1,000-yard receivers (Dwayne Jarrett with 1,105 and Steve Smith at 1,083) and a 3,000-yard passer (John David Booty, 3,347).

But following Fulmer, who had only two losing seasons, won't be easy.

"I view this guy as a legend in this profession, a guy that so many people have looked up to in Coach Fulmer," Kiffin said. "He's done an unbelievable job here and I can't even imagine what he's gone through giving 35 years of his life to this university.

"I'm extremely honored to follow him. I'm not trying to be him, all I'm trying to do is carry on some of the things he's done. In my opinion, the University of Tennessee football program wouldn't be anywhere near where it is today without Coach Fulmer. As long as I am here, as long as you guys will have me here, my arms will always be open to Coach Fulmer and his entire family. Our doors will be open because he is a special part of this university. There's no way we'd be here today without him." ■

Offense

Gerald Jones

Offense

There's just no way to describe the 2008 Tennessee offense other than not good.

The Volunteers played three different quarterbacks, none of whom was able to effectively, or consistently, move coordinator Dave Clawson's West Coast-styled offense. Consequently, Tennessee finished the season ranked 115th out of 119 teams in total offense. It scored 14 or fewer points seven times.

There wasn't a reliable go-to playmaker. Sophomore wide receiver Gerald Jones came closest with four touchdown catches, but fans were left hoping, almost begging, for safety sensation Eric Berry to take some snaps on offense (which did happen).

Granted, that was then, but it doesn't take a genius to figure out that Lane Kiffin will make some wide-ranging changes on offense, even for the returning players.

"We'll have highly competitive practices that they'll be involved with and they've got to show us what they're going to do, because in the fall, the first shots that are going to come, we're going to give them to our newcomers," Kiffin said shortly after being hired. "We've got to find out if the great players we go and recruit, can they help us right away."

Utilizing playmakers, once he has them, is something Kiffin has experience with.

Not only did he begin his coaching career at

Fresno State under the direction of Pat Hill and offensive coordinator Jeff Tedford (now the head coach at Cal), Kiffin worked under Sonny Lubick at Colorado State, and Tom Coughlin and Dom Capers with the Jacksonville Jaguars.

When he was an assistant for Pete Carroll (2001-06), Kiffin served as Southern California's passing game coordinator in 2004, and was both the offensive coordinator and recruiting coordinator in 2005-06. During that stretch, the Trojans had back-to-back Heisman Trophy winners with Matt Leinart (2004) and Reggie Bush (2005).

"I have no doubt that Lane will do great things at UT," Carroll said. "He handled all of our national recruiting at USC and brought us great players during our championship seasons. While serving as our offensive coordinator, USC had the best offense in the history of football in 2005. The Tennessee fans and alumni will be very happy with the way Lane will embrace Coach (Phillip) Fulmer and the tradition at UT."

Getty Images

The pro-style design will surely ignite what had become a dormant Tennessee offense.

Defense

Defense

If there's one aspect of Tennessee football that isn't expected to change much in 2009, at least in terms of results, it's the defense.

Last year's unit, under the direction of coordinator John Chavis, wasn't just good, but borderline exceptional. Led by sophomore safety Eric Berry, who had seven interceptions for 265 return yards, the Volunteers ranked fourth nationally in total defense.

Had the offense done anything, UT easily could have won eight or nine games, played in a decent bowl game, and probably saved head coach Phillip Fulmer's job.

However, one of the initial, if not the first, phone calls Lane Kiffin made regarding the Tennessee job was to his father, Monte Kiffin, who quickly signed on to be his defensive coordinator.

"I don't think this could have happened anywhere else because he never said, 'I'm going with you wherever you go,'" Lane Kiffin told the *Knoxville News*. "It had to be a special place. He doesn't want to come here to be mediocre. He wants to come here to win national championships."

Lane Kiffin also had to sell his father on the job some in order to pry him away from the warm weather of Florida, where he was enjoying his 13th year with the Tampa Bay Buccaneers, and 28th in

10

Number of times Monte Kiffin's defense ranked in the NFL top 10 in the past 12 seasons.

the National Football League. The longest tenured defensive coordinator in the league, Monte Kiffin is considered by most football aficionados to be nothing short of a defensive legend.

Among his accomplishments, Monte Kiffin's defense was the key to the Buccaneers' Super Bowl championship in 2002. Not only was Tampa Bay the first team since the 1985 Chicago Bears to lead the league in total defense (252.8 yards), but they also let in fewest points allowed (196) and total interceptions (31).

At its peak, the unit included linebacker Derrick Brooks, cornerback Ronde Barber, defensive tackle Warren Sapp, and defensive end Simeon Rice. But safety John Lynch may have been the key.

In Monte Kiffin's famous "Tampa Cover 2" scheme, speed is emphasized over size and the attacking philosophy hinges on a bend-but-don't-break attitude. It's also set up to essentially funnel everything toward one player in the middle, the safety.

"I think I remember John Lynch the best as number 47," Kiffin said when Lynch retired at the end of the 2008 season. "Those were the days when we had what we called the "Lynch Rule." When we called the Lynch Rule, that meant 47 was going to be in the box. He was going to be the eighth guy in the box. Nobody could play it any better than John Lynch. He would light you up."

Imagine what he might duo with the best safety in college football.

Player to watch: Eric Berry

Considering what he's already done, one has to wonder what safety Eric Berry has left to accomplish.

In 2008, he led the nation with seven interceptions. His 265 return yards set both Tennessee and Southeastern Conference records (244 yards by Florida's Joe Brodsky, 1956), leaving him just 14 short of Terrell Buckley's NCAA record of 501 interception return yards (1989-91, Florida State). That was despite his first two pickoffs resulting, combined, in one return yard.

For his career, Berry's made 12 interceptions for 487 return yards and three touchdowns—through his sophomore season.

"He's a special player," former coach Phillip Fulmer said.

Not surprisingly, Berry's haul of 2008 postseason awards could only be described as impressive.

He was a unanimous All-American, just the 12th in Tennessee history and first since offensive lineman Antone Davis in 1990. Both the coaches and

Eric Berry should have another dominant season—perhaps on both sides of the ball?

media named him SEC defensive player of the year.

The only thing he missed out on was the Jim Thorpe Award for the nation's best defensive back, which instead went to Ohio State senior cornerback Malcolm Jenkins—though critics claimed the primary reason was due to age.

But missing was something Berry rarely did in 2008, even while tackling. While he was third on the Volunteers with 72, some of his hits were more than highlight-reel material.

Among them, his punishing blow on Georgia tailback Knowshown Moreno, and sending Alabama receiver Marquis Maze spinning almost completely around before landing hard on the turf.

There was also his impressive sack of Florida quarterback Tim Tebow, not to mention taking some snaps on offense.

Did we mention he didn't turn 20 until the offseason?

Getty Images

While Berry can cover receivers like a blanket, it is his thunderous hits that make offenses fear him.

Berry was a unanimous All-American, just the 12th in Tennessee history and first since offensive lineman Antone Davis in 1990. Both the coaches and media named him SEC defensive player of the year.

It makes one wonder if he might have a legitimate shot to be the first defensive player to win the Heisman Trophy since Michigan's Charles Woodson edged quarterback Peyton Manning in 1997.

"It kind of flashes through my head a little bit, like 'Wow, Eric Berry wins the Heisman Trophy,'" Berry told the *Knoxville News-Sentinel*. "But the type of game that football is today, I think it would be hard for me to even become a finalist for the Heisman Trophy. It's so offensive minded.

"People want to see points scored, they want to see a lot of yardage and big runs. That would probably be a tough thing to accomplish next season."

What he can focus on as a junior is improving his one-on-one coverage, open-field tackling, and being a team leader. Berry was named one of six captains during his sophomore season.

Combined with a new head coach in Lane Kiffin and recovering from offseason arthroscopic shoulder surgery, there's plenty to focus on in 2009.

"Just buy in to what he has to offer and what he wants to do with the team," Berry said. "We just can't have any, I guess you could say, rejecting of it because he's the new coach. You can't look at what happened to Coach Fulmer or anything like that. You have to focus on the future, you can't just be down in the dumps." ■

Player to watch: Gerald Jones

With the departures of running back Arian Foster and offensive lineman Anthony Parker, arguably Tennessee's two best offensive players in 2008, there were major questions at nearly every position during the off season.

About the closest thing to an exception can be found among an otherwise-thin group of wide receivers: Gerald Jones, the Volunteers' version of Mr. Versatility. Not only is he the top returning receiver with 30 catches for 323 yards, but Jones also averaged 10.0 and 38.3 return yards on punts and kicks, respectively.

Considering Jones was followed on the statistics page by Austin Rogers, with 14 catches for 180 yards, and only two other returning wideouts had a catch last year, Jones will be heavily counted on while a talented group of freshmen find its way.

Jones was Oklahoma's Gatorade Player of the Year for 2006 as a quarterback and defensive player at Millwood High School in Oklahoma City. As a Tennessee freshman he had crucial touchdown and first-down catches in overtime in a 52–50 win over Kentucky. He's lined up a few times behind center with the Vols as well.

"We've got to establish our running game and our personality," Coach Lane Kiffin said. "We've got to be a physical offense and it starts up front, how you go about the running game. We've got to learn who we are.

"In the passing game, we have to get a connection between our quarterback and our receivers. Everyone is involved in the passing game, but the passing game we want is wide-receiver dominated." ■

Getty Imag

With an impressive 2009 recruiting class lured by Kiffin's NFL experience, fans should be in for a show at Rocky Top for years to come.

2009 National Signing Day Class

Jerod Askew, LB, 6-1, 230, Oscar Smith HS, Chesapeake, Va.

Bryce Brown, RB, 6-0,215, Wichiat East HS. Wichita, Kan.

Mike Edwards, DB, 5-10, 170, Glenville Academic Campus, Cleveland, Ohio

Eric Gordon, DB, 5-10, 187, Hillsboro HS, Nashville, Tenn.

James Green, WR, 6-2, 190, Leon HS, Tallahassee, Fla.

Janzen Jackson, DB, 6-0, 174, Barbe HS, Lake Charles, La.

Arthur Jeffery, DT, 6-4, 285, Booker HS, Sarasota, Fla.

Greg King, LB, 6-3, 200, Melrose HS, Memphis, Tenn.

Nigel Mitchell-Thornton, LB, 6-2, 228, Stephenson HS, Stone Mountain, Ga.

Darren Myles, DB, 6-1, 190, Carver HS, Atlanta, Ga.

Robert Nelson, LB, 6-0, 205, Stone Mountain (Ga.) HS

David Oku, RB, 5-10, 186, Lincoln East HS, Lincoln, Neb.

Nyshier Oliver, ATH, 5-10, 180, Saint Peter's Prep, Jersey City, N.J.

Kevin Revis, OL, 6-4, 265, Rhea County HS, Evensville, Tenn.

Nu'Keese Richardson, WR, 5-10, 165, Pahokee (Fla.) HS

Zach Rogers, WR, 6-2, 170, David Lipscomb HS, Nashville, Tenn.

JerQuari Schofield, OL, 6-6, 315, South Aiken HS, Aiken, S.C.

Rae Sykes, DE, 6-4, 240, Coffeyville (Kan.) CC

Marsalis Teague, ATH, 5-10, 180, Henry County HS, Paris, Tenn.

Marlon Walls, LB, 6-2, 225, Hargrave (Va.) Military Academy

Toney Williams, RB, 6-1, 235, Milton HS, Alpharetta, Ga.

University of Tennessee

Location: Knoxville, Tennessee
Founded: 1794
Enrollment: 26,802
Nickname: Volunteers
Colors: Orange and white
Mascot: Smokey

Stadium: Neyland Stadium/Shields-Watkins Field (104,079)

Tickets: 800-332-VOLS (8657) or 865-656-1200

Website: http://www.utsports.com

National Championships (2): 1951, 1998

The "Other" Four: Tennessee has also been named national champions in 1938, 1940, 1950, and 1967.

SEC Championships (13): 1938, 1939, 1940, 1946, 1951, 1956, 1967, 1969, 1985, 1989, 1990, 1997, 1998

Other Conference Championships (3): SIAA 1914; Southern 1927, 1932

Bowl Appearances: 47 (25-22)

First Season: 1891

T

2008 SEASON REVIEW

GAME 1: UCLA 27, No. 18 Tennessee 24

PASADENA | Making his first start, junior quarterback Kevin Craft shook off four first-half interceptions to help lead an upset victory in Rick Neuheisel's coaching debut at UCLA.

The Bruins took the lead with 27 seconds left in regulation only to see Tennessee's Daniel Lincoln make a 47-yard field goal as time expired. In overtime, Kai Forbath made his 42-yard attempt, but Lincoln missed from 34 yards.

Craft had 66 yards in the first half, but went 18-of-25 for 193 yards and one touchdown in the second half.

	1st Qtr	2nd Qtr	3rd Qtr	4th Qtr	OT	Final
Tennessee (18)	0	14	0	10	0	**24**
UCLA	7	0	3	14	3	**27**

SCORING PLAYS

UCLA-TD, S Westgate 17 YD BLOCKED PUNT RETURN (K Forbath KICK) 13:45 1st Qtr

TENN.-TD, M Hardesty 11 YD RUN (D Lincoln KICK) 3:02 2nd Qtr

TENN.-TD, N McKenzie 61 YD INTERCEPTION RETURN (D Lincoln KICK) 14:37 2nd Qtr

UCLA-FG, K Forbath 41 YD 13:45 3rd Qtr

UCLA-TD, R Carter 3 YD RUN (K Forbath KICK) 8:09 4th Qtr

TENN.-TD, M Hardesty 20 YD RUN (D Lincoln KICK) 13:06 4th Qtr

UCLA-TD, R Moya 3 YD PASS FROM K Craft (K Forbath KICK) 14:33 4th Qtr

TENN.-FG, D Lincoln 47 YD 15:00 4th Qtr

UCLA-FG, K Forbath 42 YD 1st OT

GAME STATISTICS

	TENN. (18)	UCLA
First Downs	20	20
Yards Rushing	34-177	31-29
Yards Passing	189	259
Sacks–Yards Lost	1-8	1-9
Passing Efficiency	19-42-1	25-43-4
Punts	7-33.4	6-46.8
Fumbles-Lost	2-1	0-0
Penalties-Yards	9-55	2-25
Time of Possession	29:51	30:09

2008 Review

INDIVIDUAL STATISTICS: RUSHING

TENN.—Arian Foster 13-96, Montario Hardesty 12-66, Gerald Jones 2-11, Jonathan Crompton 6-3, Kevin Cooper 1-1. UCLA-Raymond Carter 15-14, Kahlil Bell 5-11, Chane Moline 6-5, Kevin Craft 4-1, - Team 1-MINUS 2.

INDIVIDUAL STATISTICS: PASSING

TENN.—Jonathan Crompton 19-41-189- 1, - Team 0-1-0- 0, E.J. AbramsWard 0-0-0- 0. UCLA-Kevin Craft 25-43-259- 4.

INDIVIDUAL STATISTICS: RECEIVING

TENN.—Josh Briscoe 1-41, Gerald Jones 4-40, Lucas Taylor 3-37, Kevin Cooper 4-27, Austin Rogers 1-16, Arian Foster 4-12, Luke Stocker 1-11, Brandon Warren 1-5. UCLA-Ryan Moya 7-65, Taylor Embree 4-53, Dominique Johnson 4-51, Terrence Austin 5-37, Logan Paulsen 1-18, Marcus Everett 1-17, Nelson Rosario 1-14, Trevor Theriot 1-5, Kahlil Bell 1-MINUS 1.

ATTENDANCE: 68,546

GAME 2: Tennessee 35, UAB 3

KNOXVILLE | Tennessee recorded 548 offensive yards as UAB had little success slowing the Volunteers down.

Lucas Taylor led UT with 132 receiving yards on nine catches, and Arian Foster has 100 rushing yards on 12 carries. Lennon Creer added 93 rushing yards and touchdown runs of 45 and 3 yards.

Tennessee had an announced attendance of 98,205, well below capacity (102,038).

	1st Qtr	2nd Qtr	3rd Qtr	4th Qtr	Final
UAB	0	0	3	0	**3**
Tennessee	14	0	14	7	**35**

SCORING PLAYS

TENN.-TD, G Jones 20 YD PASS FROM J Crompton (D Lincoln KICK) 10:25 1st Qtr

TENN.-TD, G Jones 14 YD PASS FROM J Crompton (D Lincoln KICK) 13:55 1st Qtr

UAB-FG, S Waters 47 YD 5:25 3rd Qtr

TENN.-TD, M Hardesty 6 YD RUN ((D Lincoln KICK) 7:52 3rd Qtr

TENN.-TD, L Creer 45 YD RUN (D Lincoln KICK) 13:19 3rd Qtr

TENN.-TD, L Creer 3 YD RUN (D Lincoln KICK) 4:10 4th Qtr

TENNESSEE FOOTBALL

GAME STATISTICS

	UAB	TENNESSEE
First Downs	14	25
Yards Rushing	26-108	41-266
Yards Passing	167	282
Sacks–Yards Lost	1-7	1-9
Passing Efficiency	19-34-3	20-33-2
Punts	6-38	2-34.5
Fumbles-Lost	1-0	0-0
Penalties-Yards	9-79	8-65
Time of Possession	28:46	31:14

INDIVIDUAL STATISTICS – RUSHING
UAB-Joseph Webb 14-78, Rashad Slaughter 8-21, Aaron Johns 1-8, Justin Brooks 2-4, Justin Johnson 1-MINUS 3. TENN.-Arian Foster 12-100, Lennon Creer 8-93, Tauren Poole 9-43, Montario Hardesty 7-28, Nick Stephens 1-5, Jonathan Crompton 4-MINUS 3.

INDIVIDUAL STATISTICS – PASSING
UAB-Joseph Webb 19-34-167- 3. TENN.-Jonathan Crompton 19-31-240- 2. Nick Stephens 1-2-42- 0.

INDIVIDUAL STATISTICS – RECEIVING
UAB-Frantrell Forrest 8-83, Jeffrey Anderson 2-28, Mark Ferrell 2-19, Jim Mitchell 2-11, Justin Brooks 2-10, Rashad Slaughter 1-9, Zach Lankford 2-7. TENN.-Lucas Taylor 9-132, Brandon Warren 2-48, Gerald Jones 3-39, Arian Foster 1-22, Luke Stocker 2-16, Josh Briscoe 1-12, Denarius Moore 1-12, Kevin Cooper 1-1.

ATTENDANCE: 98,205

GAME 3: No. 4 Florida 30, Tennessee 6

KNOXVILLE | Florida took advantage of three turn-overs and Brandon James had his fourth career punt return for a touchdown as the Gators beat Tennessee for the fourth straight time.

Defending Heisman Trophy winner Tim Tebow was held to 122 total yards, but still had two touchdown passes. The Volunteers fumbled at the 2-yard line and had a pass intercepted in the end zone during the first half.

Florida coach Urban Meyer improved to 8-1 against the Gators' three biggest rivals: Tennessee, Georgia, and Florida State. He also joined Steve Spurrier as the only coach to beat Phillip Fulmer four straight seasons.

	1st Qtr	2nd Qtr	3rd Qtr	4th Qtr	Final
Florida (4)	17	3	7	3	30
Tennessee	0	0	0	6	6

SCORING PLAYS

FLORIDA-TD, A Hernandez 2 YD PASS FROM T Tebow (J Phillips KICK) 4:45 1st Qtr

FLORIDA-FG, J Phillips 39 YD 7:25 1st Qtr

FLORIDA-TD, B James 78 YD PUNT RETURN (J Phillips KICK) 10:18 1st Qtr

FLORIDA-FG, J Phillips 40 YD 10:17 2nd Qtr

FLORIDA-TD, P Harvin 15 YD PASS FROM T Tebow (J Phillips KICK) 10:31 3rd Qtr

TENN.-TD, J Crompton 1 YD RUN 0:42 4th Qtr

FLORIDA-FG, J Phillips 27 YD 5:31 4th Qtr

TENNESSEE FOOTBALL

GAME STATISTICS

	FLORIDA (4)	TENN.
First Downs	16	16
Yards Rushing	39-147	31-96
Yards Passing	96	162
Sacks–Yards Lost	1-2	0-0
Passing Efficiency	8-15-0	18-28-1
Punts	1-57	4-37.5
Fumbles-Lost	0-0	2-2
Penalties-Yards	9-57	9-95
Time of Possession	29:58	30:02

INDIVIDUAL STATISTICS – RUSHING
FLORIDA-Emmanuel Moody 9-55, Chris Rainey 9-37, Percy Harvin 6-31, Tim Tebow 12-26, - Team 3-MINUS 2. TENN.-Arian Foster 14-37, Jonathan Crompton 7-22, Gerald Jones 4-18, Montario Hardesty 5-15, Lennon Creer 1-4.

INDIVIDUAL STATISTICS – PASSING
FLORIDA-Tim Tebow 8-15-96- 0. TENN.-Jonathan Crompton 18-28-162- 1.

INDIVIDUAL STATISTICS – RECEIVING
FLORIDA-Percy Harvin 2-49, Louis Murphy 2-18, Aaron Hernandez 2-15, Kestahn Moore 1-9, Riley Cooper 1-5. TENN.-Gerald Jones 5-40, Luke Stocker 3-25, Lucas Taylor 2-24, Josh Briscoe 1-22, Arian Foster 2-19, Denarius Moore 1-13, Brandon Warren 2-12, Montario Hardesty 2-7.

ATTENDANCE: 106,138

2008 Review

GAME 4: No. 15 Auburn 14, Tennessee 12

AUBURN | Auburn only needed two touchdowns, one on offense and one on defense, to send Tennessee to its worst start since 1994.

While quarterback Jonathan Crompton passed for only 67 yards, Auburn's Jake Ricks recovered a fumble in the end zone for a 14-6 lead with 7:06 left in the second quarter.

The Tigers won their fourth straight against Tennessee for the first time since 1961-64.

	1st Qtr	2nd Qtr	3rd Qtr	4th Qtr	Final
Tennessee	0	6	0	6	12
Auburn (15)	7	7	0	0	14

SCORING PLAYS

AUBURN-TD, R Dunn 18 YD PASS FROM C Todd (W Byrum KICK) 12:09 1st Qtr

TENNESSEE-FG, D Lincoln 47 YD 0:52 2nd Qtr

TENNESSEE-FG, D Lincoln 35 YD 5:58 2nd Qtr

AUBURN-TD, J Ricks RECOVERED FUMBLE IN END ZONE (W Byrum KICK) 7:54 2nd Qtr

TENNESSEE-TD, M Hardesty 2 YD RUN 0:07 4th Qtr

GAME STATISTICS

	TENN.	AUBURN (15)
First Downs	9	15
Yards Rushing	33-124	38-97
Yards Passing	67	129
Sacks – Yards Lost	2-5	2-10
Passing Efficiency	8-24-0	18-29-1
Punts	10-39.9	9-43.7
Fumbles-Lost	1-1	1-0
Penalties-Yards	3-35	9-59
Time of Possession	27:15	32:45

INDIVIDUAL STATISTICS: RUSHING
TENN.-Montario Hardesty 10-35, Arian Foster 8-30, Gerald Jones 4-25, Lennon Creer 4-19, Jonathan Crompton 7-15. AUBURN-Ben Tate 19-70, Mario Fannin 4-18, Kodi Burns 8-16, Chris Todd 2-6, Eric Smith 2-0, -Team 2-MINUS 6, Robert Dunn 1-MINUS 7.

INDIVIDUAL STATISTICS – PASSING
TENN.-Jonathan Crompton 8-23-67- 0, Gerald Jones 0-1-0- 0. AUBURN-Chris Todd 14-23-93- 1. Kodi Burns 4-6-36- 0.

INDIVIDUAL STATISTICS – RECEIVING
TENN.-Austin Rogers 1-14, Gerald Jones 1-14, Lennon Creer 1-9, Luke Stocker 1-8, Josh Briscoe 1-7, Lucas Taylor 1-6, Montario Hardesty 1-5, Arian Foster 1-4. AUBURN-Robert Dunn 6-54, Mario Fannin 3-29, Tommy Trott 3-19, Montez Billings 3-16, Rodgeriqus Smith 2-7, Ben Tate 1-4.

ATTENDANCE: 87,451

2008 Review

GAME 5: Tennessee 13, Northern Illinois 9

KNOXVILLE | Trying to spark the anemic offense, Tennessee started Nick Stephens at quarterback. His 52-yard touchdown pass to Denarius Moore in the third quarter gave the Volunteers a 10-point lead and was the longest offensive play of the season.

However, UT barely outgained Northern Illinois, 225-194, converted three of 13 third downs, and only had nine first downs.

"We're still very much a work in progress," Coach Phillip Fulmer said. "I thought we made some strides in running the offense at times."

	1st Qtr	2nd Qtr	3rd Qtr	4th Qtr	Final
Northern Illinois	3	0	6	0	**9**
Tennessee	0	3	10	0	**13**

SCORING PLAYS

NORTHN ILLINOIS-FG, M Salerno 25 YD 12:07 1st Qtr

TENN.-FG, D Lincoln 36 YD 8:10 2nd Qtr

TENNESSEE-FG, D Lincoln 34 YD 2:23 3rd Qtr

TENN.-TD, D Moore 52 YD PASS FROM N Stephens
(D Lincoln KICK) 5:11 3rd Qtr

NORTHN ILLINOIS-FG, M Salerno 24 YD 10:15 3rd Qtr

NORTHN ILLINOIS-FG, M Salerno 25 YD 13:29 3rd Qtr

GAME STATISTICS

	NORTH ILLINOIS	TENN.
First Downs	12	9
Yards Rushing	34-76	32-69
Yards Passing	118	156
Sacks–Yards Lost	4-10	3-28
Passing Efficiency	15-27-1	10-18-0
Punts	5-39.6	4-36.5
Fumbles-Lost	1-0	2-2
Penalties-Yards	7-90	6-45
Time of Possession	33:11	26:49

2008 Review

INDIVIDUAL STATISTICS: RUSHING

NORTHN ILLINOIS-DeMarcus Grady 15-47, Meco Brown 8-14, Chad Spann 2-9, Justin Anderson 4-6, Dan Nicholson 4-1, Ryan Morris 1-MINUS 1. TENN.-Arian Foster 18-75, Montario Hardesty 7-20, Gerald Jones 1-2, - Team 1-MINUS 2, Nick Stephens 5-MINUS 26.

INDIVIDUAL STATISTICS: PASSING

NORTHN ILLINOIS-Dan Nicholson 10-15-83- 1, DeMarcus Grady 4-10-39- 0, Ryan Morris 0-1-0- 0, Greg Turner 1-1-MINUS 4- 0. TENN.-Nick Stephens 10-17-156- 0. Gerald Jones 0-1-0- 0.

INDIVIDUAL STATISTICS: RECEIVING

NORTHN ILLINOIS-Landon Cox 3-40, Willie Clark 1-35, Nathan Palmer 5-22, Reed Cunningham 2-21, Marcus Perez 2-13, Jason Schepler 1-6, Meco Brown 1- MINUS 19. TENN.-Denarius Moore 3-65, Gerald Jones 2-50, Josh Briscoe 2-22, Austin Rogers 2-14, Luke Stocker 1-5.

ATTENDANCE: 99,539

GAME 6: No. 10 Georgia 26, Tennessee 14

ATHENS | After being outscored by a combined 49 points the previous two meets, Georgia got even with a dominating victory.

Not only did the Bulldogs outgain the Volunteers on the ground 148-1, quarterback Matthew Stafford passed for 310 yards and a touchdown.

Overall, Georgia tallied 458 yards on 81 plays, compared to 209 yards on 45 plays for Tennessee, and had a 29-10 advantage in first downs and 42:09 to 17:51 in time of possession.

	1st Qtr	2nd Qtr	3rd Qtr	4th Qtr	Final
Tennessee	0	7	7	0	**14**
Georgia (10)	10	10	0	6	**26**

SCORING PLAYS

GEORGIA-TD, B Southerland 1 YD RUN (B Walsh KICK) 7:44 1st Qtr

GEORGIA-FG, B Walsh 34 YD 11:48 1st Qtr

GEORGIA-FG, B Walsh 20 YD 2:06 2nd Qtr

TENN.-TD, G Jones 2 YD PASS FROM N Stephens (D Lincoln KICK) 12:37 2nd Qtr

GEORGIA-TD, M Massaquoi 9 YD PASS FROM M Stafford (B Walsh KICK) 14:51 2nd Qtr

TENN.-TD, L Taylor 12 YD PASS FROM N Stephens (D Lincoln KICK) 9:23 3rd Qtr

GEORGIA-FG, B Walsh 41 YD 0:05 4th Qtr

GEORGIA-FG, B Walsh 28 YD 12:11 4th Qtr

GAME STATISTICS

	TENN.	GEORGIA (10)
First Downs	10	29
Yards Rushing	15-1	45-148
Yards Passing	208	310
Sacks–Yards Lost	2-15	0-0
Passing Efficiency	13-30-0	25-36-2
Punts	6-48	2-54
Fumbles-Lost	1-0	0-0
Penalties-Yards	10-97	11-76
Time of Possession	17:56	42:04

INDIVIDUAL STATISTICS: RUSHING
TENN.-Montario Hardesty 6-20, Arian Foster 3-3, Lennon Creer 2-2, - Team 1-MINUS 1, Gerald Jones 1-MINUS 8, Nick Stephens 2-MINUS 15. GEORGIA-Knowshon Moreno 27-101, Caleb King 9-18, Matthew Stafford 5-15, Shaun Chapas 2-10, Richard Samuel 1-3, Brannan Southerland 1-1.

INDIVIDUAL STATISTICS: PASSING
TENN.-Nick Stephens 13-30-208- 0. GEORGIA-Matthew Stafford 25-36-310- 2.

INDIVIDUAL STATISTICS: RECEIVING
TENN.-Gerald Jones 4-68, Denarius Moore 1-60, Lucas Taylor 4-47, Luke Stocker 1-25, Arian Foster 3-8. GEORGIA-Mohamed Massaquoi 5-103, Shaun Chapas 3-64, A.J. Green 7-53, Demiko Goodman 3-50, Kenneth Harris 4-19, Knowshon Moreno 1-14, Brannan Southerland 1-10, Caleb King 1-MINUS 3.

ATTENDANCE: 92,746

2008 Review

GAME 7: Tennessee 34, Mississippi State 3

KNOXVILLE | With his 72-yard interception return for a touchdown, sophomore safety Eric Berry became the SEC's career interception return leader with 397 yards (Bobby Wilson, Ole Miss, 379, 1946-49).

The Volunteers had 101 interception return yards in the game.

Berry's pick sparked a 21-point fourth quarter, including a 12-play, 51-yard drive in which Lennon Creer got the ball on every snap, and scored on a 1-yard run.

	1st Qtr	2nd Qtr	3rd Qtr	4th Qtr	Final
Mississippi State	0	3	0	0	**3**
Tennessee	0	6	7	21	**34**

SCORING PLAYS

TENN.-FG, D Lincoln 36 YD 3:43 2nd Qtr

MISSISSIPPI ST-FG, A Carlson 43 YD 8:26 2nd Qtr

TENN.-FG, D Lincoln 28 YD 13:51 2nd Qtr

TENN.-TD, M Hardesty 1 YD RUN (D Lincoln KICK) 5:00 3rd Qtr

TENN.-TD, E Berry 72 YD INTERCEPTION RETURN (D Lincoln KICK) 4:23 4th Qtr

TENN.-TD, D Morley 32 YD INTERCEPTION RETURN (D Lincoln KICK) 5:50 4th Qtr

TENN.-TD, L Creer 1 YD RUN (D Lincoln KICK) 12:21 4th Qtr

GAME STATISTICS

	MISS. STATE	TENN.
First Downs	13	16
Yards Rushing	30-69	39-139
Yards Passing	120	136
Sacks–Yards Lost	5-30	1-3
Passing Efficiency	13-30-3	10-21-0
Punts	6-39.3	4-44
Fumbles-Lost	2-0	0-0
Penalties-Yards	3-24	1-8
Time of Possession	30:55	29:05

2008 Review

INDIVIDUAL STATISTICS: RUSHING
MISSISSIPPI ST-Anthony Dixon 15-46, Christian Ducr 6-19, Wesley Carroll 1-5, Wade Bonner 1-1, Tyson Lee 7-MINUS 2. TENN.-Lennon Creer 17-68, Arian Foster 11-40, Nick Stephens 3-17, Montario Hardesty 6-15, Tauren Poole 2-MINUS 1.

INDIVIDUAL STATISTICS: PASSING
MISSISSIPPI ST-Tyson Lee 12-23-114- 3, Wesley Carroll 1-7-6- 0. TENN.-Nick Stephens 10-20-136- 0. Arian Foster 0-1-0- 0.

INDIVIDUAL STATISTICS: RECEIVING
MISSISSIPPI ST-Brandon McRae 2-28, Anthony Dixon 3-27, Arnil Stallworth 1-15, Aubrey Bell 2-13, Brandon Henderson 1-12, Nelson Hurst 1-7, Co-Eric Riley 1-6, Delmon Robinson 1-6, Christian Ducr 1-6. TENN.-Denarius Moore 1-45, Austin Rogers 2-23, Lucas Taylor 2-23, Arian Foster 1-19, Montario Hardesty 1-12, Kevin Cooper 1-9, Brandon Warren 1-3, Lennon Creer 1-2.

ATTENDANCE: 98,239

GAME 8: No. 2 Alabama 29, Tennessee 9

KNOXVILLE I After Tennessee's defense yielded just two rushing touchdowns all season, Alabama scored three to record its first back-to-back wins in the series since 1991-92.

"It's just a special rivalry and a special game to all of us involved in it in different ways," Coach Phillip Fulmer said. "I'll be back up tomorrow. I'm not down. I just got a lot on my mind right now."

Tennessee fell to 6-14 against ranked teams over the previous four seasons, and 1-9 at home against top 10 foes since 2000.

	1st Qtr	2nd Qtr	3rd Qtr	4th Qtr	Final
Alabama (2)	6	7	9	7	**29**
Tennessee	3	0	0	6	**9**

SCORING PLAYS

ALABAMA-FG, L Tiffin 39 YD 4:42 1st Qtr

TENN.-FG, D Lincoln 31 YD 8:32 1st Qtr

ALABAMA-FG, L Tiffin 43 YD 13:23 1st Qtr

ALABAMA-TD, G Coffee 3 YD RUN (L Tiffin KICK) 12:19 2nd Qtr

ALABAMA-FG, L Tiffin 30 YD 4:32 3rd Qtr

ALABAMA-TD, J Wilson 1 YD RUN 13:22 3rd Qtr

ALABAMA-TD, R Upchurch 4 YD RUN (L Tiffin KICK) 5:17 4th Qtr

TENN.-TD, J Briscoe 10 YD PASS FROM N Stephens 7:34 4th Qtr

GAME STATISTICS

	ALABAMA (2)	TENN.
First Downs	23	10
Yards Rushing	43-178	21-36
Yards Passing	188	137
Sacks–Yards Lost	0-0	2-16
Passing Efficiency	17-24-0	16-28-0
Punts	3-38	7-43.7
Fumbles-Lost	1-1	0-0
Penalties-Yards	3-35	7-60
Time of Possession	35:32	24:28

INDIVIDUAL STATISTICS: RUSHING
ALABAMA-Roy Upchurch 14-86, Glen Coffee 19-78, Terry Grant 4-11, John Parker Wilson 2-2, Mark Ingram 4-1. TENN.-Arian Foster 6-21, Montario Hardesty 8-12, Lennon Creer 3-7, Nick Stephens 4-MINUS 4.

INDIVIDUAL STATISTICS: PASSING
ALABAMA-John Parker Wilson 17-24-188- 0. TENN.-Nick Stephens 16-28-137- 0.

INDIVIDUAL STATISTICS: RECEIVING
ALABAMA-Julio Jones 6-103, Nick Walker 3-24, Will Oakley 1-14, Roy Upchurch 2-13, Mike McCoy 1-13, Brad Smelley 1-8, Nikita Stover 1-6, Glen Coffee 1-4, Marquis Maze 1-3. TENN.-Josh Briscoe 4-46, Arian Foster 3-32, Luke Stocker 2-30, Austin Rogers 2-17, Brandon Warren 2-8, Lucas Taylor 1-4, Eric Berry 1-3, Denarius Moore 1-MINUS 3.

ATTENDANCE: 106,138

2008 Review

GAME 9: South Carolina 27, Tennessee 6

COLUMBIA | South Carolina quarterback Stephen Garcia passed for 139 yards and two touchdowns before being sidelined by a knee injury in the third quarter.

It was only South Carolina's fourth victory against Tennessee, and first win at home since 1992.

UT quarterbacks were sacked six times, and the Volunteers were held to fewer than 10 points for the third time in the season. Tennessee had minus-2 rushing yards in the first half, and finished with just 34.

	1st Qtr	2nd Qtr	3rd Qtr	4th Qtr	Final
Tennessee	0	0	6	0	**6**
South Carolina	7	14	3	3	**27**

SCORING PLAYS

SO. CAROLINA-TD, M Davis 12 YD PASS FROM S Garcia (R Succop KICK) 7:01 1st Qtr

SO. CAROLINA-TD, S Woodson 68 YD INTERCEPTION RETURN (R Succop KICK) 0:15 2nd Qtr

SO. CAROLINA-TD, K McKinley 4 YD PASS FROM S Garcia (R Succop KICK) 4:43 2nd Qtr

SO. CAROLINA-FG, R Succop 31 YD 7:27 3rd Qtr

TENN.-TD, A Foster 1 YD RUN 10:51 3rd Qtr

SO. CAROLINA-FG, R Succop 31 YD 11:48 4th Qtr

TENNESSEE FOOTBALL

GAME STATISTICS

	TENN.	SO. CAROLINA
First Downs	11	11
Yards Rushing	28-34	44-101
Yards Passing	173	154
Sacks–Yards Lost	6-40	1-6
Passing Efficiency	15-32-1	10-20-1
Punts	9-45.3	8-45
Fumbles-Lost	2-2	1-0
Penalties-Yards	3-15	3-35
Time of Possession	27:30	32:30

INDIVIDUAL STATISTICS: RUSHING
TENN.-Arian Foster 14-56, Lennon Creer 3-9, Kevin Cooper 2-3, - Team 1-MINUS 2, Jonathan Crompton 2-MINUS 14, Nick Stephens 6-MINUS 18. SOUTH CAROLINA-Mike Davis 26-58, Eric Baker 7-22, Bobby Wallace 4-16, Stephen Garcia 6-11, Chris Smelley 1-MINUS 6.

INDIVIDUAL STATISTICS: PASSING
TENN.-Nick Stephens 10-24-134- 1, Jonathan Crompton 5-8-39- 0. SOUTH CAROLINA-Stephen Garcia 9-19-139-1. Chris Smelley 1-1-15- 0.

INDIVIDUAL STATISTICS: RECEIVING
TENN.-Austin Rogers 3-72, Arian Foster 3-33, Lucas Taylor 1-27, Josh Briscoe 3-18, Gerald Jones 2-13, Luke Stocker 1-8, Brandon Warren 1-3, Lennon Creer 1-MINUS 1. SOUTH CAROLINA-Kenny McKinley 4-50, Weslye Saunders 2-42, Eric Baker 1-31, Mike Davis 2-25, Moe Brown 1-6

ATTENDANCE: 81,731

2008 Review

GAME 10: Wyoming 13, Tennessee 7

KNOXVILLE | Five days after Phillip Fulmer agreed to step down as head coach effective the end of the season, Wyoming, despite being the lowest scoring team in major college football (11.7 points per game), shocked the Volunteers at homecoming.

"Many fans have been supportive. Some have been angry. All of us are disappointed," Fulmer said at his resignation press conference. "I'm proud that the accomplishments over the last 17 years have been part of such high expectations.

"Our Tennessee family is united in its goals, but divided in the right path to get there. I love Tennessee too much to let her stay divided."

	1st Qtr	2nd Qtr	3rd Qtr	4th Qtr	Final
Wyoming	7	6	0	0	13
Tennessee	0	0	7	0	7

SCORING PLAYS

WYOMING-TD, G Genho 4 YD PASS FROM C Stutzriem (J Scott KICK) 2:56 1st Qtr

WYOMING-TD, W Dobbs 24 YD INTERCEPTION RETURN (TWO-POINT CONVERSION FAILED) 5:57 2nd Qtr

TENN.-TD, G Jones 8 YD PASS FROM J Crompton (D Lincoln KICK) 4:52 3rd Qtr

GAME STATISTICS

	WYOMING	TENN.
First Downs	15	15
Yards Rushing	48-167	31-101
Yards Passing	99	118
Sacks–Yards Lost	0-0	3-27
Passing Efficiency	9-17-0	14-36-2
Punts	5-35.2	6-39.8
Fumbles-Lost	1-1	1-0
Penalties-Yards	1-15	2-15
Time of Possession	31:14	28:46

2008 Review

INDIVIDUAL STATISTICS – RUSHING
WYOMING-Devin Moore 32-98, Wynel Seldon 12-40, Chris Stutzriem 3-21, Brandon Stewart 1-8. TENN.-Lennon Creer 16-82, Tauren Poole 11-44, Nick Stephens 2-MINUS 9, Jonathan Crompton 2-MINUS 16.

INDIVIDUAL STATISTICS – PASSING
WYOMING-Chris Stutzriem 8-16-95- 0, Karsten Sween 1-1-4- 0. TENN.-Jonathan Crompton 11-27-91- 0. Nick Stephens 3-9-27- 2.

INDIVIDUAL STATISTICS – RECEIVING
WYOMING-Chris Johnson 1-26, David Leonard 1-23, Brandon Stewart 1-14, Greg Bolling 1-11, Devin Moore 2-9, Chris Sundberg 1-7, Travis Burkhalter 1-5, Greg Genho 1-4. TENN.-Gerald Jones 5-37, Lucas Taylor 3-32, Austin Rogers 2-17, Denarius Moore 1-14, Luke Stocker 1-11, Josh Briscoe 1-8, Tauren Poole 1-MINUS 1.

ATTENDANCE: 99,489

GAME 11: Tennessee 20, Vanderbilt 10

NASHVILLE | Sophomore safety Eric Berry returned his seventh interception of the season for a touchdown to help Tennessee beat in-state rival Vanderbilt.

The pickoff was the 12th of his career, giving him 265 interception return yards for the season, and 487 for his career.

Philip Fulmer lost once in 16 games against Vanderbilt, a 28-24 decision in Knoxville in 2005, his only other losing season.

	1st Qtr	2nd Qtr	3rd Qtr	4th Qtr	Final
Tennessee	0	20	0	0	**20**
Vanderbilt	0	0	10	0	**10**

SCORING PLAYS

TENN.-TD, M Hardesty 8 YD RUN (D Lincoln KICK) 3:35 2nd Qtr

TENN.-FG, D Lincoln 25 YD 7:15 2nd Qtr

TENN.-TD, E Berry 45 YD INTERCEPTION RETURN (D Lincoln KICK) 9:04 2nd Qtr

TENN.-FG, D Lincoln 24 YD 14:56 2nd Qtr

VANDERBILT-FG, B Hahnfeldt 31 YD 3:53 3rd Qtr

VANDERBILT-TD, R Langford 42 YD INTERCEPTION RETURN (B Hahnfeldt KICK) 10:40 3rd Qtr

GAME STATISTICS

	TENN.	VANDERBILT
First Downs	15	16
Yards Rushing	51-222	28-25
Yards Passing	21	188
Sacks–Yards Lost	2-7	6-40
Passing Efficiency	4-9-2	19-44-2
Punts	6-37.5	7-37.6
Fumbles-Lost	1-1	2-1
Penalties-Yards	6-29	5-42
Time of Possession	35:14	24:46

INDIVIDUAL STATISTICS: RUSHING
TENN.-Lennon Creer 13-80, Arian Foster 11-53, Montario Hardesty 7-41, B.J. Coleman 7-17, Eric Berry 4-11, Gerald Jones 6-11, Kevin Cooper 2-6, Jonathan Crompton 1-3. VANDERBILT-Jeff Jennings 7-19, Jared Hawkins 2-9, Mackenzi Adams 9-4, D.J. Moore 1-0, Chris Nickson 9-MINUS 7.

INDIVIDUAL STATISTICS: PASSING
TENN.-B.J. Coleman 4-8-21- 1, Jonathan Crompton 0-1-0- 1. VANDERBILT-Mackenzi Adams 18-38-192- 1. -Team 0-1-0- 0. Chris Nickson 1-5-MINUS 4- 1.

INDIVIDUAL STATISTICS: RECEIVING
TENN.-Austin Rogers 1-7, Gerald Jones 1-7, Kevin Cooper 1-5, Denarius Moore 1-2. VANDERBILT-George Smith 5-46, D.J. Moore 2-32, Sean Walker 3-30, Justin Wheeler 2-25, Jeff Jennings 3-23, Gaston Miller 1-16, Brandon Barden 3-16.

ATTENDANCE: 38,725

2008 Review

GAME 12: Tennessee 28, Kentucky 10

KNOXVILLE | Phillip Fulmer was given the game ball and carried off the field by his players after finishing his career at Tennessee 152-52.

Tennessee had 210 rushing yards and avoided a school-record eighth loss. It also extended the nation's longest active winning streak by one team over another to 24 games.

"We've had a great run," Fulmer said. "I wasn't really ready for it to end, but it probably ended as well as it could."

	1st Qtr	2nd Qtr	3rd Qtr	4th Qtr	Final
Kentucky	3	0	0	7	**10**
Tennessee	0	7	7	14	**28**

SCORING PLAYS

KENTUCKY-FG, L Seiber 40 YD 10:00 1st Qtr

TENN.-TD, J Crompton 1 YD RUN (D Lincoln KICK) 15:00 2nd Qtr

TENN.-TD, D Moore 63 YD PASS FROM J Crompton (D Lincoln KICK) 1:16 3rd Qtr

TENN.-TD, L Creer 5 YD RUN (D Lincoln KICK) 0:36 4th Qtr

TENN.-TD, G Jones 2 YD RUN (D Lincoln KICK) 9:16 4th Qtr

KENTUCKY-TD, A Smith 1 YD RUN (L Seiber KICK) 11:16 4th Qtr

TENNESSEE FOOTBALL

GAME STATISTICS

	KENTUCKY	TENN.
First Downs	11	16
Yards Rushing	38-96	53-210
Yards Passing	97	101
Sacks–Yards Lost	1-12	2-12
Passing Efficiency	9-14-0	6-8-0
Punts	6-38.2	4-44.8
Fumbles-Lost	0-0	0-0
Penalties-Yards	8-52	2-20
Time of Possession	25:42	34:18

INDIVIDUAL STATISTICS: RUSHING
KENTUCKY-Tony Dixon 15-48, Randall Cobb 11-22, Alfonso Smith 8-20, John Conner 2-5, Moncell Allen 2-1. TENN.-Gerald Jones 5-67, Arian Foster 21-59, Eric Berry 3-26, Lennon Creer 6-24, Montario Hardesty 8-19, Jonathan Crompton 8-17, - Team 2-MINUS 2.

INDIVIDUAL STATISTICS: PASSING
KENTUCKY-Mike Hartline 5-7-74- 0, Randall Cobb 4-7-23- 0. TENN.-Jonathan Crompton 6-8-101- 0.

INDIVIDUAL STATISTICS: RECEIVING
KENTUCKY-E.J. Adams 1-35, Alfonso Smith 2-21, T.C. Drake 1-18, Tony Dixon 1-10, Eric Adeyemi 1-8, Maurice Grinter 1-4, Kyrus Lanxter 2-1. TENN.-Denarius Moore 1-63, Arian Foster 1-17, Gerald Jones 3-15, Brandon Warren 1-6.

ATTENDANCE: 102,388

Offensive line tandem Ramon Foster and Anthony Parker
carry Phillip Fulmer off the field after his 152nd—and
final—win. The victory over Kentucky also extended the
Volunteers' winning streak over the Wildcats to 24
games, the longest active streak in the nation.

Starting Lineups

Opener (UCLA)

OFFENSE
LT 79 Chris Scott
LG 75 Anthony Parker
C 50 Josh McNeil
RG 65 Jacques McClendon
RT 78 Ramon Foster
TE 88 Luke Stocker
TE 1 Brandon Warren
WR 4 Gerald Jones
WR 12 Lucas Taylor
QB 8 Jonathan Crompton
TB 27 Arian Foster

DEFENSE
DE 94 Wes Brown
DT 98 Demonte' Bolden
DT 55 Dan Williams
DE 91 Robert Ayers
SLB 48 Adam Myers-White
MLB 35 Ellix Wilson
WLB 5 Rico McCoy
CB 24 DeAngelo Willingham
CB 41 Dennis Rogan
FS 7 Demetrice Morley
SS 14 Eric Berry

Last Game (Kentucky)

OFFENSE
LT 79 Chris Scott
LG 51 Vladimir Richard
C 50 Josh McNeil
RG 75 Anthony Parker
RT 78 Ramon Foster
TE 88 Luke Stocker
WR 21 Austin Rogers
WR 4 Gerald Jones
WR 12 Lucas Taylor
QB 8 Jonathan Crompton
TB 27 Arian Foster

DEFENSE
LE 94 Wes Brown
DT 98 Demonte' Bolden
RT 55 Dan Williams
RE 91 Robert Ayers
SLB 20 Nevin McKenzie
MLB 35 Ellix Wilson
WLB 5 Rico McCoy
LCB 24 DeAngelo Willingham
RCB 41 Dennis Rogan
FS 7 Demetrice Morley
SS 14 Eric Berry

2008 Review

Final Statistics

TEAM STATISTICS	UT	OPP
SCORING	208	201
Points Per Game	17.3	16.8
FIRST DOWNS	172	195
Rushing	86	75
Passing	70	100
Penalty	16	20
RUSHING YARDAGE	1475	1237
Yards Gained Rushing	1747	1514
Yards Lost Rushing	272	277
Rushing Attempts	409	444
Average Per Rush	3.6	2.8
Average Per Game	122.9	103.1
TDs Rushing	14	6
PASSING YARDAGE	1750	1925
Att-Comp-Int	309-153-9	332-186-17
Average Per Pass	5.7	5.8
Average Per Catch	11.4	10.3
Average Per Game	145.8	160.4
TDs Passing	8	8
TOTAL OFFENSE	3225	3162
Total Plays	718	776
Average Per Play	4.5	4.1
Average Per Game	268.8	263.5
KICK RETURNS: #-Yards	44-1037	39-820
PUNT RETURNS: #-Yards	28-212	20-251
INT RETURNS: #-Yards	17-478	9-193
KICK RETURN AVERAGE	23.6	21.0
PUNT RETURN AVERAGE	7.6	12.6

INT RETURN AVERAGE	28.1	21.4
FUMBLES-LOST	12-9	9-3
PENALTIES-Yards	66-539	70-539
Average Per Game	44.9	44.9
PUNTS-Yards	69-2819	64-2643
Average Per Punt	40.9	41.3
Net Punt Average	34.9	37.0
TIME OF POSSESSION/Game	28:33	31:26
3RD-DOWN Conversions	58/167	69/186
3rd-Down Pct.	35%	37%
4TH-DOWN Conversions	5/14	7/14
4th-Down Pct.	36%	50%
SACKS BY-Yards	23-135	25-170
MISC YARDS	0	0
TOUCHDOWNS SCORED	26	20
FIELD GOALS-ATTEMPTS	10-19	21-25
ONSIDE KICKS	0-0	0-0
RED-ZONE SCORES	28-37 76%	27-35 77%
RED-ZONE TOUCHDOWNS	19-37 51%	14-35 40%
PAT-ATTEMPTS	22-22 100%	18-19 95%
ATTENDANCE	710136	369199
Games/Avg Per Game	7/101448	5/73840
Neutral Site Games	0	0

	1st Qtr	2nd Qtr	3rd Qtr	4th Qtr	OT	Final
Tennessee	17	63	58	70	0	**208**
Opponents	67	50	41	40	3	**201**

2008 Review

Individual Statistics

RUSHING	GP	ATT	GAIN	LOSS	NET	AVG	TD	LONG	AVG/G
Arian Foster	11	131	597	27	570	4.4	1	41	51.8
Lennon Creer	11	73	392	4	388	5.3	4	45	35.3
M. Hardesty	11	76	289	18	271	3.6	6	27	24.6
Gerald Jones	11	23	148	22	126	5.5	1	55	11.5
Tauren Poole	12	22	87	1	86	3.9	0	19	7.2
Eric Berry	12	7	44	7	37	5.3	0	23	3.1
J. Crompton	8	37	107	80	27	0.7	2	15	3.4
B.J. Coleman	3	7	24	7	17	2.4	0	10	5.7
Kevin Cooper	12	5	10	0	10	2.0	0	4	0.8
TEAM	6	5	0	7	-7	-1.4	0	0	-1.2
Nick Stephens	7	23	49	99	-50	-2.2	0	18	-7.1
Total	12	409	1747	272	1475	3.6	14	55	122.9
Opponents	12	444	1514	277	1237	2.8	6	23	103.1

PASSING	GP	EFFIC	CMP-ATT-INT	PCT	YDS	TD	LNG	AVG/G
J. Crompton	8	98.13	86-167-5	51.5	889	4	63	111.1
Nick Stephens	7	108.28	63-130-3	48.5	840	4	60	120.0
B.J. Coleman	3	47.05	4-8-1	50.0	21	0	7	7.0
Gerald Jones	11	0.00	0-2-0	0.0	0	0	0	0.0
TEAM	6	0.00	0-1-0	0.0	0	0	0	0.0
Arian Foster	11	0.00	0-1-0	0.0	0	0	0	0.0
Total.	12	99.81	153-309-9	49.5	1750	8	63	145.8
Opponents.	12	102.44	186-332-17	56.0	1925	8	37	160.4

RECEIVING	GP	NO.	YDS	AVG	TD	LONG	AVG/G
Gerald Jones	11	30	323	10.8	4	43	29.4
Lucas Taylor	11	26	332	12.8	1	48	30.2
Arian Foster	11	19	166	8.7	0	26	15.1
Austin Rogers	12	14	180	12.9	0	49	15.0
Josh Briscoe	12	14	176	12.6	1	41	14.7
Luke Stocker	12	13	139	10.7	0	26	11.6
Denarius Moore	12	11	271	24.6	2	63	22.6
Brandon Warren	12	10	85	8.5	0	42	7.1
Kevin Cooper	12	7	42	6.0	0	9	3.5
M. Hardesty	11	4	24	6.0	0	12	2.2
Lennon Creer	11	3	10	3.3	0	9	0.9

Eric Berry	12	1	3	3.0	0	3	0.2
Tauren Poole	12	1	-1	-1.0	0	0	-0.1
Total	12	153	1750	11.4	8	63	145.8
Opponents	12	186	1925	10.3	8	37	160.4

PUNT RETURNS	NO.	YDS	AVG	TD	LONG
Gerald Jones	15	150	10.0	0	40
Dennis Rogan	13	62	4.8	0	10
Total	28	212	7.6	0	40
Opponents	20	251	12.6	2	78

INTERCEPTIONS	NO.	YDS	AVG	TD	LONG
Eric Berry	7	265	37.9	2	72
D. Willingham	3	2	0.7	0	5
D. Morley	2	32	16.0	1	32
Nevin McKenzie	1	61	61.0	1	61
Dennis Rogan	1	38	38.0	0	38
Robert Ayers	1	8	8.0	0	8
Ellix Wilson	1	3	3.0	0	3
Brent Vinson	1	69	69.0	0	69
Total	17	478	28.1	4	72
Opponents	9	193	21.4	3	68

KICK RETURNS	NO.	YDS	AVG	TD	LONG
Dennis Rogan	28	698	24.9	0	43
Lennon Creer	6	104	17.3	0	31
Gerald Jones	3	115	38.3	0	43
Brandon Warren	2	34	17.0	0	18
Denarius Moore	2	49	24.5	0	27
Eric Berry	2	32	16.0	0	21
Luke Stocker	1	5	5.0	0	5
Total	44	1037	23.6	0	43
Opponents	39	820	21.0	0	67

FUMBLE RETURNS	NO.	YDS	AVG	TD	LONG
Total	0	0	0.0	0	0
Opponents	2	42	21.0	1	38

2008 Review

SCORING	TD	FGS	PATS KICK	RUSH	RCV	PASS	DXP	SAF	PTS
Daniel Lincoln	0	10-18	22-22	0-0	0	0-0	0	0	52
M. Hardesty	6	0-0	0-0	0-0	0	0-0	0	0	36
Gerald Jones	5	0-0	0-0	0-0	0	0-0	0	0	30
Lennon Creer	4	0-0	0-0	0-0	0	0-0	0	0	24
Eric Berry	2	0-0	0-0	0-0	0	0-0	0	0	12
J. Crompton	2	0-0	0-0	0-0	0	0-2	0	0	12
Denarius Moore	2	0-0	0-0	0-0	0	0-0	0	0	12
Nevin McKenzie	1	0-0	0-0	0-0	0	0-0	0	0	6
Lucas Taylor	1	0-0	0-0	0-0	0	0-0	0	0	6
Josh Briscoe	1	0-0	0-0	0-0	0	0-0	0	0	6
Arian Foster	1	0-0	0-0	0-0	0	0-0	0	0	6
D. Morley	1	0-0	0-0	0-0	0	0-0	0	0	6
B. Colquitt	0	0-1	0-0	0-0	0	0-0	0	0	0
Nick Stephens	0	0-0	0-0	0-1	0	0-1	0	0	0
Total	26	10-19	22-22	0-1	0	0-3	0	0	208
Opponents	20	21-25	18-19	0-0	0	0-1	0	0	201

TOTAL OFFENSE	G	PLAYS	RUSH	PASS	TOTAL	AVG/G
J. Crompton	8	204	27	889	916	114.5
Nick Stephens	7	153	-50	840	790	112.9
Arian Foster	11	132	570	0	570	51.8
Lennon Creer	11	73	388	0	388	35.3
M. Hardesty	11	76	271	0	271	24.6
Gerald Jones	11	25	126	0	126	11.5
Tauren Poole	12	22	86	0	86	7.2
B.J. Coleman	3	15	17	21	38	12.7
Eric Berry	12	7	37	0	37	3.1
Kevin Cooper	12	5	10	0	10	0.8
TEAM	6	6	-7	0	-7	-1.2
Total	12	718	1475	1750	3225	268.8
Opponents	12	776	1237	1925	3162	263.5

Daniel Lincoln celebrates the field goal that sent the 2008 game at UCLA into overtime. Lincoln led the 2008 Tennessee squad in scoring, hitting on 10 field goals and making all 22 of his extra-point attempts.

FIELD GOALS

FGM-FGA		PCT	01-19	20-29	30-39	40-49	50-99	LG	BLK
Daniel Lincoln	10-18	55.6	0-0	3-3	5-9	2-3	0-3	47	0
B. Colquitt	0-1	0.0	0-0	0-0	0-0	0-0	0-1	0	0

FG SEQUENCE	TENNESSEE	OPPONENTS
UCLA	51,55,[47],34	[41],[42]
UAB	-	[47]
Florida	-	[39],[40],[27]
Auburn	[47],[35]	35
Northern Illinois	[36],[34],32	46,[25],[24],[25]
Georgia	-	[34],[20],[41],[28]
Mississippi State	[36],[28],34	39,[43]
Alabama	[31],51,43	[39],[43],[30]
South Carolina	-	[31],[31]
Wyoming	-	31
Vanderbilt	[25],56,[24]	[31]
Kentucky	31	[40]

Numbers in (parentheses) indicate field goal was made.

PUNTING	NO.	YDS	AVG	LONG	TB	FC	I20	BLKD
Britton Colquitt								
	42	1821	43.4	71	5	15	13	0
Chad Cunningham								
	25	988	39.5	57	3	6	11	0
TEAM	2	10	5.0	10	0	0	0	2
Total	69	2819	40.9	71	8	21	24	2
Opponents	64	2643	41.3	57	3	8	15	1

ALL PURPOSE	G	RUSH	REC	PR	KOR	IR	TOT	AVG/G
Dennis Rogan	12	0	0	62	698	38	798	66.5
Arian Foster	11	570	166	0	0	0	736	66.9
Gerald Jones	11	126	323	150	115	0	714	64.9
Lennon Creer	11	388	10	0	104	0	502	45.6
Eric Berry	12	37	3	0	32	265	337	28.1
Lucas Taylor	11	0	332	0	0	0	332	30.2
Denarius Moore	12	0	271	0	49	0	320	26.7
M. Hardesty	11	271	24	0	0	0	295	26.8
Austin Rogers	12	0	180	0	0	0	180	15.0
Josh Briscoe	12	0	176	0	0	0	176	14.7
Luke Stocker	12	0	139	0	5	0	144	12.0
Brandon Warren	12	0	85	0	34	0	119	9.9
Tauren Poole	12	86	-1	0	0	0	85	7.1
Brent Vinson	8	0	0	0	0	69	69	8.6
Nevin McKenzie	12	0	0	0	0	61	61	5.1
Kevin Cooper	12	10	42	0	0	0	52	4.3
D. Morley	11	0	0	0	0	32	32	2.9
J. Crompton	8	27	0	0	0	0	27	3.4
B.J. Coleman	3	17	0	0	0	0	17	5.7
Robert Ayers	12	0	0	0	0	8	8	0.7
Ellix Wilson	11	0	0	0	0	3	3	0.3
D. Willingham	12	0	0	0	0	2	2	0.2
TEAM	6	-7	0	0	0	0	-7	-1.2
Nick Stephens	7	-50	0	0	0	0	-50	-7.1
Total	12	1475	1750	212	1037	478	4952	412.7
Opponents	12	1237	1925	251	820	193	4426	368.8

Arian Foster had his best season as a junior, rushing for 1,139 yards and scoring 14 total touchdowns.

| | | |—————Tackles—————| | | |
DEFENSIVE LEADERS	GP	SOLO	AST	TOTAL	TFL/YDS
35 Ellix Wilson	11	47	42	89	4.5-16
5 Rico McCoy	12	38	49	87	3.5-8
14 Eric Berry	12	44	28	72	8.5-21
41 Dennis Rogan	12	32	21	53	1.0-19
20 Nevin McKenzie	12	30	23	53	10.0-46
91 Robert Ayers	12	34	15	49	15.5-63
55 Dan Williams	12	23	25	48	8.5-19
7 D. Morley	11	22	20	42	1.0-1
24 D. Willingham	12	24	18	42	1.0-1
94 Wes Brown	12	18	19	37	5.5-18
98 Demonte' Bolden	12	25	10	35	6.0-10
48 A. Myers-White	12	20	6	26	3.0-14
95 Walter Fisher	11	13	7	20	3.0-18
99 Ben Martin	12	13	5	18	2.0-9
56 Nick Reveiz	12	9	9	18	.
43 Savion Frazier	12	8	10	18	0.5-1
84 Chris Walker	11	13	2	15	4.0-22
13 Brent Vinson	8	6	7	13	1.0-4
57 Gerald Williams	10	8	4	12	0.5-2
31 M. Johnson	11	8	3	11	.
42 L. Thompson	12	5	5	10	.
33 J. Williams	11	6	3	9	.
46 Andre Mathis	6	3	4	7	.
87 Quintin Hancock	12	4	2	6	.
28 Tauren Poole	12	2	3	5	.
6 Denarius Moore	12	2	2	4	.
53 Morgan Cox	12	1	3	4	.
9 Daryl Vereen	8	.	3	3	.
37 Antonio Gaines	7	3	.	3	.
96 Chad Cunningham	12	.	2	2	.
45 Kevin Cooper	12	1	.	1	.
44 Josh Hawkins	4	.	1	1	.
21 Austin Rogers	12	1	.	1	.
12 Lucas Taylor	11	1	.	1	.
78 Ramon Foster	12	1	.	1	.
2 M. Hardesty	11	.	1	1	.
75 Anthony Parker	12	1	.	1	.
Total	**12**	**466**	**352**	**818**	**79-292**
Opponents	**12**	**406**	**392**	**798**	**67-275**

NO-YDS	INT-YDS	BRUP	QBH	RCV-YDS	FF	KICK	SAF
	I-Sacks-I	**I—Pass Def—I**		**I—Fumbles—I**		**I—Blkd—I**	
1.0-9	1-3	2	3	1-0	.	.	.
1.0-1	.	3	2	.	.	.	.
3.0-11	7-265	6	.	.	.	.	.
.	1-38	5	.	2-0	.	.	.
5.0-30	1-61	5	1	.	.	.	.
3.0-29	1-8	.	6	.	.	.	.
1.5-7	.	1	8	.	.	.	.
.	2-32	2	.	.	.	.	.
.	3-2	4	.	.	.	.	.
2.5-12	.	.	9	.	.	.	.
.	.	1	4	.	.	.	.
.	.	2	1	.	.	.	.
2.0-14	.	.	.	.	1	.	.
1.0-3	.	.	5	.	1	.	.
.	.	.	.	.	.	.	.
.	.	.	.	.	.	.	.
3.0-19	.	.	1	.	2	.	.
.	1-69	1	.	.	.	.	.
.	.	1	1	.	.	.	.
.	.	3	.	.	.	.	.
.	.	.	.	.	1	.	.
.	.	.	.	.	1	.	.
.	.	.	.	.	.	.	.
.	.	.	.	.	.	.	.
.	.	.	.	.	.	.	.
.	.	.	.	.	.	.	.
.	.	.	.	.	.	.	.
.	.	.	.	.	.	.	.
.	.	.	.	.	.	.	.
.	.	.	.	.	.	.	.
.	.	.	.	.	.	.	.
.	.	.	.	.	.	.	.
.	.	.	.	.	.	1	.
.	.	.	.	.	.	.	.
23-135	**17-478**	**36**	**41**	**3-0**	**6**	**1**	**.**
25-170	**9-193**	**53**	**16**	**9-42**	**8**	**2**	**.**

2008 SEC Conference Standings

	SEC				OVERALL		
EASTERN DIVISION							
W-L	**PCT.**	**PF**	**PA**	**W-L**	**PCT.**	**PF**	**PA**
*^Florida							
7-1	.875	359	100	12-1	.923	587	167
Georgia							
6-2	.750	215	214	9-3	.750	385	307
Vanderbilt							
4-4	.500	144	174	6-6	.500	233	241
South Carolina							
4-4	.500	163	186	7-5	.583	260	243
Tennessee							
3-5	.375	129	149	5-7	.417	208	201
Kentucky							
2-6	.250	143	238	6-6	.500	269	260
WESTERN DIVISION							
W-L	**PCT.**	**PF**	**PA**	**W-L**	**PCT.**	**PF**	**PA**
#Alabama							
8-0	1.000	255	115	12-1	.923	405	169
Ole Miss							
5-3	.625	208	149	8-4	.667	370	213
LSU							
3-5	.375	207	254	7-5	.583	364	311
Arkansas							
2-6	.250	167	248	5-7	.417	263	374
Auburn							
2-6	.250	93	149	5-7	.417	208	216
Mississippi State							
2-6	.250	97	204	4-8	.333	183	296

Eastern Division Champion; # Western Division Champion; ^ SEC Champion

Future Schedules

2009

Sept. 5	Western Kentucky	Knoxville
Sept. 12	UCLA	Knoxville
Sept. 19	Florida	Gainesville
Sept. 26	Ohio	Knoxville
Oct. 3	Auburn	Knoxville
Oct. 10	Georgia	Knoxville
Oct. 24	Alabama	Tuscaloosa
Oct. 31	South Carolina	Knoxville
Nov. 7	Memphis	Knoxville
Nov. 14	Ole Miss	Oxford
Nov. 21	Vanderbilt	Knoxville
Nov. 28	Kentucky	Lexington

2010

Sept. 4	UT Martin	Knoxville
Sept. 11	Oregon	Knoxville
Sept. 18	Florida	Knoxville
Sept. 25	UAB	Knoxville
Oct. 2	LSU	Baton Rouge
Oct. 9	Georgia	Athens
Oct. 23	Alabama	Knoxville
Oct. 30	South Carolina	Columbia
Nov. 6	Memphis	Memphis
Nov. 13	Ole Miss	Knoxville
Nov. 20	Vanderbilt	Nashville
Nov. 27	Kentucky	Knoxville

THROUGH
THE YEARS

1891
0-1

Nov. 21	Sewanee	Chattanooga	L	24-0
Coach: None				24-0

Tennessee's first game was played in the mud against formidable Sewanee. ... The program didn't have a head coach during its first five seasons.

1892
2-5

Oct. 15	Maryville	Maryville	W	25-0
Oct. 21	Vanderbilt	Nashville	L	22-4
Oct. 24	Sewanee	Sewanee	L	54-0
Nov. 2	Sewanee	Knoxville	L	10-0
Nov. 12	Chattanooga A.C.	Chattanooga	W	16-6
Nov. 17	Vanderbilt	Knoxville	L	12-0
Nov. 24	Wake Forest	Knoxville	L	10-6
Coach: None				51-114

Tennessee recorded its first victory in the season opener against Maryville. ... Robert Reese Neyland was born February 17 in Greenville, Texas.

1893
2-4

Oct. 21	Kentucky A&M	Knoxville	L	56-0
Nov. 3	Wake Forest	Winston-Salem	L	64-0
Nov. 4	Trinity	Durham	L	70-0
Nov. 7	North Carolina	Chapel Hill	L	60-0
Nov. 18	Maryville	Knoxville	W	32-0
Nov. 30	Asheville Athletics	Knoxville	W	12-6
Coach: None				44-256

From 1859-1924, Duke University was known as Trinity College. The University of Kentucky was known as Kentucky A&M from 1878-1907.

Robert Neyland, seen here in 1932, was born in 1892, the same year that Tennessee recorded the first victory in school history. The 1892 Tennessee squad finished 2-5, losing twice to both Sewanee and Vanderbilt.

1894

2-0-2 (unofficial)

Nov. 3	Maryville	Knoxville	T	0-0
Nov. 10	Knoxville A.C.	Knoxville	T	8-8
Nov. 29	Knoxville YMCA	Knoxville	W	12-4
Dec. 7	Carson-Newman	Jefferson City	W	18-0
Coach: None				38-12

Only two athletes returned to campus after the 1893 season, or admitted that they had been on the team, and the practice field was being graded and improved during this time. After the university's athletic association dropped football, W.B. Stokley, a transfer from Wake Forest, formulated a club team which played a four-game schedule. Because football was not recognized by the university, the results are not included in either the official school or NCAA statistics and records.

1895

3-2-1 (unofficial)

Oct. 19	Knoxville YMCA	Knoxville	W	4-0
Nov. 2	Maryville	Knoxville	T	6-6
Nov. 4	Bingham School	Asheville	W	12-0
Nov. 14	Fort McPherson	Atlanta	L	28-0
Nov. 28	Saint Alban's	Bristol	L	38-0
Nov. 30	Tenn. Medical Unit	Knoxville	W	40-0
Coach: None				128-6

Because football was not recognized by the university during the 1984-95 seasons, called "The Lost Years" by school officials, the results are not included in either the official Tennessee or NCAA statistics and records.

Through the Years

1896
4-0

Oct. 22	Williamsburg Institute	Knoxville	W	10-6
Oct. 24	Chattanooga A.C.	Chattanooga	W	4-0
Nov. 14	Virginia Tech	Knoxville	W	6-4
Nov. 26	Central University	Knoxville	W	30-0
				50-10

Football officially returned as a recognized sport at the university. ... Tennessee joined the Southern Intercollegiate Athletic Association, and would play in the conference through the 1920 season.

1897
4-1

Oct. 15	King	Knoxville	W	28-0
Oct. 23	Williamsburg Institute	Knoxville	W	6-0
Nov. 8	North Carolina	Knoxville	L	16-0
Nov. 25	Virginia Tech	Roanoke	W	18-0
Nov. 26	Bristol A.C.	Bristol	W	12-0
Coach: None				64-16

The Vols only loss in 1897 was to their only SIAA opponent, North Carolina. The four wins were all non-conference.

1899
5-2

Oct. 11	King	Knoxville	W	11-5
Oct. 21	Virginia Tech	Knoxville	L	5-0
Oct. 28	Sewanee	Sewanee	L	51-0
Nov. 4	Kentucky A&M	Knoxville	W	12-0
Nov. 11	Georgia	Knoxville	W	5-0
Nov. 23	Washington & Lee	Knoxville	W	11-0
Nov. 30	Kentucky University	Knoxville	W	41-0
Coach: J.A. Pierce				80-61

Tennessee didn't field a team in 1898 due to the Spanish-American War. When it returned, the university's athletic association hired J.A. Pierce to serve as its first full-time football coach. Over two seasons, his teams compiled a 9-4-1 record. ... Kentucky University later became Transylvania University, and the University of Tennessee at Chattanooga was known as Grant University from 1889-1906.

1900
3-2-1

Oct. 10	King	Knoxville	W	22-0
Oct. 22	Vanderbilt	Nashville	T	0-0
Nov. 1	North Carolina	Knoxville	L	22-5
Nov. 10	Auburn	Birmingham	L	23-0
Nov. 27	Grant	Knoxville	W	28-0
Dec. 1	Georgetown	Knoxville	W	12-6
Coach: J.A. Pierce				67-51

All-Southern Conference: Bill Newman

The tie vs. Vanderbilt was the first in school history. The UT yearbook had a football theme on the cover.

1901
3-3-2

Oct. 12	King	Knoxville	W	8-0
Oct. 19	Clemson	Knoxville	T	6-6
Oct. 26	Nashville	Nashville	L	16-5
Nov. 2	Kentucky University	Knoxville	L	6-0
Nov. 9	Vanderbilt	Nashville	L	22-0
Nov. 16	Georgetown	Knoxville	W	12-0
Nov. 23	Kentucky A&M	Knoxville	W	5-0
Nov. 28	Alabama	Birmingham	T	6-6
Coach: George Kelley				42-56

Kelley was the first of two former Princeton players to coach the Volunteers in consecutive years.

1902
6-2

Oct. 11	King	Knoxville	W	12-0
Oct. 21	Maryville	Knoxville	W	34-0
Oct. 25	Vanderbilt	Knoxville	L	12-5
Nov. 1	Sewanee	Knoxville	W	6-0
Nov. 7	Nashville	Nashville	W	10-0
Nov. 15	Ole Miss	Memphis	W	11-10
Nov. 22	Georgia Tech	Atlanta	W	10-6
Nov. 27	Clemson	Knoxville	L	11-0
Coach: H.F. Fisher				88-39

All-Southern Conference: Nash Buckingham, Joey Beane

Tennessee enjoyed its first victory against Sewanee, which had been a region power. ... The football team was informally referred to as the Volunteers for the first time.

1903

4-5

Oct. 3	Maryville	Knoxville	W	17-0
Oct. 10	Carson-Newman	Knoxville	W	38-0
Oct. 17	Vanderbilt	Nashville	L	40-0
Oct. 29	South Carolina	Columbia	L	24-0
Oct. 31	Nashville	Nashville	W	10-0
Nov. 7	Georgia	Knoxville	L	5-0
Nov. 14	Sewanee	Knoxville	L	17-0
Nov. 21	Georgia Tech	Knoxville	W	11-0
Nov. 26	Alabama	Birmingham	L	24-0
Coach: H.F. Fisher				76-110

H.F. Fisher was 10-7 during his two seasons as head coach.

1904

3-5-1

Oct. 1	Maryville	Knoxville	W	17-0
Oct. 15	Nashville	Knoxville	T	0-0
Oct. 22	Georgia Tech	Atlanta	L	2-0
Oct. 29	Sewanee	Knoxville	L	12-0
Nov. 5	Vanderbilt	Nashville	L	22-0
Nov. 12	Clemson	Knoxville	L	6-0
Nov. 16	Cincinnati	Knoxville	L	35-0
Nov. 19	Grant	Chattanooga	W	23-0
Nov. 24	Alabama	Birmingham	W	5-0
Coach: S.D. Crawford				45-77

Tennessee enjoyed its first victory against Alabama.

The Tennessee-Vanderbilt rivalry dates back to the early 1900s, with the Volunteers usually beating up the Commodores—as they did here in the 2007 edition of the game.

1905

3-5-1

Sept. 30	TN School for Deaf	Knoxville	W	16-6
Oct. 7	American Univ.	Knoxville	W	104-0
Oct. 14	Clemson	Clemson	T	5-5
Oct. 21	Vanderbilt	Knoxville	L	45-0
Oct. 28	Sewanee	Sewanee	L	11-6
Nov. 4	Georgia Tech	Atlanta	L	45-0
Nov. 18	Centre	Knoxville	W	31-5
Nov. 30	Alabama	Birmingham	L	29-0
Dec. 3	Grant	Chattanooga	L	5-0
Coach: J.D. Depree				162-151

Tennessee began officially calling itself the Volunteer state, and the school subsequently took up the nickname.

1906

1-6-2

Oct. 6	American Univ.	Knoxville	W	10-0
Oct. 13	Maryville	Knoxville	L	11-0
Oct. 20	Centre	Knoxville	L	6-0
Oct. 25	American Univ.	Harriman	T	5-5
Nov. 3	Sewanee	Knoxville	L	17-0
Nov. 10	Kentucky A&M	Lexington	L	21-0
Nov. 19	Clemson	Clemson	L	16-0
Nov. 21	Georgia	Athens	T	0-0
Nov. 29	Alabama	Birmingham	L	51-0
Coach: J.D. Depree				15-127

Three-time captain Roscoe Word served as an assistant coach for J.D. Depree, who went 4-11-3 during his two seasons.

1907
7-2-1

Oct. 5	TN Military Institute	Knoxville	W	30-0
Oct. 12	Georgia	Athens	W	15-0
Oct. 19	Georgia Tech	Atlanta	L	6-4
Oct. 21	Clemson	Clemson	W	4-0
Oct. 26	Maryville	Knoxville	W	34-0
Nov. 2	Chattanooga	Knoxville	W	57-0
Nov. 9	Kentucky A&M	Knoxville	T	0-0
Nov. 16	Mississippi A&M	Memphis	W	11-4
Nov. 18	Arkansas	Little Rock	W	14-2
Nov. 28	Alabama	Birmingham	L	5-0

Coach: George Levene   169-17

**All-Southern Conference: Walker Leach,
N.W. Dougherty, Roscoe Word**

**The seven wins were a program record. ...
George Levene played at Penn. ... Mississippi
State was known as Mississippi A&M until 1932.
... Organized cheerleading was introduced to
Tennessee by R.C. "Red" Matthews.**

1908
7-2

Oct. 3	North Carolina	Knoxville	W	12-0
Oct. 10	Maryville	Knoxville	W	39-5
Oct. 17	Kentucky State	Knoxville	W	7-0
Oct. 24	Georgia	Knoxville	W	10-0
Oct. 31	Georgia Tech	Atlanta	W	6-5
Nov. 7	Vanderbilt	Nashville	L	16-9
Nov. 14	Clemson	Knoxville	W	6-5
Nov. 21	Chattanooga	Knoxville	W	35-6
Nov. 26	Alabama	Birmingham	L	4-0

Coach: George Levene   124-41

**All-Southern Conference: Walker Leach,
N.W. Dougherty**

1909
1-6-2

Oct. 2	Centre	Knoxville	T	0-0
Oct. 9	North Carolina	Knoxville	L	3-0
Oct. 16	Kentucky State	Lexington	L	17-0
Oct. 23	Georgia	Knoxville	L	3-0
Oct. 30	Georgia Tech	Knoxville	L	29-0
Nov. 6	Vanderbilt	Nashville	L	51-0
Nov. 13	Alabama	Knoxville	L	10-0
Nov. 20	Chattanooga	Chattanooga	T	0-0
Nov. 25	Transylvania	Knoxville	W	11-0
Coach: George Levene				11-113

Nathan Dougherty's career as a guard came to an end. He was 6-2, 185-pounds, and his nickname was "Big'n." Dougherty returned to Tennessee to teach in 1916 and was dean of the engineering college from 1940-56. A building at the engineering college was named for him in 1964. He served on the university's athletic council for 40 years, was president of the Southern Conference, a founder of the Southeastern Conference, acting commissioner of the Southeastern Conference, and vice-president of the NCAA.

1910
3-5-1

Oct. 1	Centre	Knoxville	L	17-2
Oct. 8	Mooney School	Knoxville	W	7-0
Oct. 15	Vanderbilt	Nashville	L	18-0
Oct. 22	Georgia	Athens	L	35-5
Oct. 29	Howard	Birmingham	W	17-0
Oct. 31	Mississippi A&M	Starkville	L	48-0
Nov. 5	Kentucky State	Knoxville	L	10-0
Nov. 12	Maryville	Knoxville	W	13-0
Nov. 19	Chattanooga	Knoxville	T	6-6
Coach: Andrew A. Stone				50-134

Andrew Stone was the seventh coach in 11 years.

1911

3-4-2

Oct. 7	Mooney School	Knoxville	W	27-0
Oct. 14	Georgia Tech	Atlanta	L	24-0
Oct. 21	Maryville	Knoxville	W	22-5
Oct. 28	N Carolina State	Raleigh	L	16-0
Nov. 4	Centre	Knoxville	T	0-0
Nov. 11	Virginia Tech	Blacksburg	L	36-11
Nov. 18	Southwestern	Knoxville	W	22-0
Nov. 25	TN Medical School	Memphis	T	0-0
Nov. 30	Kentucky State	Lexington	L	12-0
Coach: Z.G. Clevenger				82-93

Z.G. Clevenger's straight T formation gave Tennessee's offense a distinct identity.

1912

4-4

Oct. 5	King	Knoxville	W	101-0
Oct. 12	Maryville	Knoxville	W	38-0
Oct. 19	TN Medical School	Memphis	W	62-0
Oct. 26	Sewanee	Chattanooga	L	33-6
Nov. 2	Centre	Knoxville	W	67-0
Nov. 9	Mercer	Macon	L	27-14
Nov. 16	Kentucky State	Knoxville	L	13-6
Nov. 28	Alabama	Birmingham	L	7-0
Coach: Z.G. Clevenger				294-80

Tennessee ended its three-year run of losing seasons. However, it was still winless in Southern Intercollegiate Athletic Association play.

1913
6-3

Sept. 27	Carson-Newman	Knoxville	W	58-0
Oct. 4	Athens	Knoxville	W	95-0
Oct. 11	Maryville	Knoxville	W	75-0
Oct. 18	Sewanee	Chattanooga	L	17-6
Oct. 25	Davidson	Knoxville	W	9-0
Nov. 1	Chattanooga	Knoxville	W	21-0
Nov. 8	Vanderbilt	Nashville	L	7-6
Nov. 14	Alabama	Tuscaloosa	L	6-0
Nov. 27	Kentucky State	Lexington	W	13-7
Coach: Z.G. Clevenger				283-37

All-Southern Conference: Mush Kerr

Tennessee snapped its losing streak in SIAA play, which was entering its fifth season, and had its first winning season in five years. ... When the Alabama game lasted into the evening hours, spectators with automobiles were asked to circle the field and turn on their headlights so play could continue.

1914
9-0, SIAA Champions

Sept. 26	Carson-Newman	Knoxville	W	89-0
Oct. 3	King	Knoxville	W	55-3
Oct. 10	Clemson	Knoxville	W	27-0
Oct. 17	Louisville	Louisville	W	66-0
Oct. 24	Alabama	Knoxville	W	17-7
Oct. 31	Chattanooga	Knoxville	W	67-0
Nov. 7	Vanderbilt	Nashville	W	16-14
Nov. 14	Sewanee	Chattanooga	W	14-7
Nov. 26	Kentucky State	Knoxville	W	23-6
Coach: Z.G. Clevenger				374-37

All-Southern Conference: Alonzo Carroll, Farmer Kelly, Mush Kerr, Russ Lindsay

Tennessee won its first conference title, and also recorded the first victory in school history against Vanderbilt.

Tennessee and Florida first met on the gridiron in 1916, though it would take seven decades for the rivalry to blossom with SEC realignment. The Vols won the first matchup via shutout, 24-0.

1915
4-4

Sept. 25	Carson-Newman	Knoxville	W	101-0
Oct. 2	Tusculum	Knoxville	W	21-0
Oct. 9	Clemson	Knoxville	L	3-0
Oct. 16	Centre	Knoxville	W	80-0
Oct. 23	Cumberland	Knoxville	W	101-0
Oct. 30	Vanderbilt	Nashville	L	35-0
Nov. 13	Mississippi A&M	Knoxville	L	14-0
Nov. 25	Kentucky State	Lexington	L	6-0
Coach: Z.G. Clevenger				303-58

All-Southern Conference: Graham Vowell

Clevenger (26-15-2), a former Indiana player, eventually returned to his alma mater in 1923 and stayed there until his retirement.

1916
8-0-1

Sept. 30	Tusculum	Knoxville	W	33-0
Oct. 7	Maryville	Knoxville	W	32-6
Oct. 14	Clemson	Clemson	W	14-0
Oct. 21	South Carolina	Knoxville	W	26-0
Oct. 28	Florida	Tampa	W	24-0
Nov. 4	Chattanooga	Chattanooga	W	12-7
Nov. 11	Vanderbilt	Knoxville	W	10-6
Nov. 18	Sewanee	Chattanooga	W	17-0
Nov. 30	Kentucky State	Knoxville	T	0-0
Coach: John Bender				168-19

All-Southern Conference: Graham Vowell, Morris Vowell, Lloyd Wolfe

John Bender came to Tennessee from Kansas State. ... Tennessee held its first homecoming and defeated Vanderbilt, 10-6.

1917
0-3 (unofficial)

Nov. 3	11th U.S. Infantry	Knoxville	L	21-6
Nov 10	Bat. B Va. Field Artillery	Chattanooga	L	35-0
Nov. 16	Camp Gordon	Atlanta	L	38-0

6-94

With the majority of players called into military service for World War I, varsity football was suspended by the University of Tennessee Athletic Council, chaired by Professor Nathan W. Dougherty. Meanwhile, two unofficial squads were formed from Army recruits and students, a training unit called the Fighting Mechanics and the Student Army Training Corps. The results listed are from the SATC team.

1918
3-2 (unofficial)

Nov. 2	Sewanee	Knoxville	L	68-0
Nov. 9	Vanderbilt	Nashville	L	76-0
Nov. 16	Maryville	Knoxville	W	9-7
Nov. 23	Milligan	Knoxville	W	32-0
Nov. 28	TN Military Instit.	Knoxville	W	46-0

87-151

While varsity play was suspended due to World War I, results listed are from the Student Army Training Corps team. ... In addition to many of his players, Coach John R. Bender enlisted into the military and was an instructor at Camp John Sevier in Greenville, S.C.

1919

3-3-3

Sept. 27	Tusculum	Knoxville	W	29-6
Oct. 3	Maryville	Knoxville	W	32-2
Oct. 11	Vanderbilt	Nashville	T	3-3
Oct. 18	Mississippi A&M	Knoxville	L	6-0
Oct. 25	Clemson	Clemson	L	14-0
Nov. 1	North Carolina	Knoxville	T	0-0
Nov. 8	South Carolina	Columbia	T	6-6
Nov. 15	Cincinnati	Knoxville	W	33-12
Nov. 27	Kentucky	Lexington	L	13-0
Coach: John Bender				103-62

All-Southern Conference: W.O. Lowe

1920

7-2

Sept. 25	Emory & Henry	Knoxville	W	45-0
Oct. 2	Maryville	Knoxville	W	47-0
Oct. 9	Vanderbilt	Knoxville	L	20-0
Oct. 16	Chattanooga	Chattanooga	W	35-0
Oct. 23	Clemson	Knoxville	W	26-0
Oct. 30	Mississippi A&M	Starkville	L	13-7
Nov. 6	Transylvania	Knoxville	W	49-0
Nov. 13	Sewanee	Chattanooga	W	20-0
Nov. 25	Kentucky	Knoxville	W	14-7
Coach: John Bender				243-40

All-Southern Conference: Buck Hatcher

Tennessee enjoyed its 100th victory against Transylvania.

The history of the majestic stadium that is Neyland Stadium began in 1921 at tiny Shields-Watkins Field. One of the finest in the world for sport, more historic moments than one can count occurred on the site.

1921

6-2-1

Sept. 24	Emory & Henry	Knoxville	W	27-0
Oct. 1	Maryville	Maryville	W	7-0
Oct. 8	Chattanooga	Knoxville	W	21-0
Oct. 15	Dartmouth	Hanover	L	14-3
Oct. 22	Florida	Knoxville	W	9-0
Oct. 29	Vanderbilt	Nashville	L	14-0
Nov. 5	Mississippi A&M	Memphis	W	14-7
Nov. 12	Sewanee	Knoxville	W	21-0
Nov. 24	Kentucky	Lexington	T	0-0
Coach: M.B. Banks				102-35

All-Southern Conference: Graham Vowell, Roe Campbell

The Emory & Henry victory was the first game at Shields-Watkins Field (capacity 3,200), named in honor of the donor and his wife. Previously, home games were played at the corner of 15th Street and Cumberland. ... Tennessee joined the Southern Conference

The Sewanee Bulldogs were one of college football's earliest powers, putting together dominant seasons in the late 1800s. Though they were charter members of the SEC in 1932, by the 1920s the program had declined measurably.

1922
8-2

Sept. 23	Emory & Henry	Knoxville	W	50-0
Sept. 30	Carson-Newman	Knoxville	W	32-7
Oct. 7	Maryville	Knoxville	W	21-0
Oct. 14	Camp Benning	Columbus	W	15-0
Oct. 21	Georgia	Athens	L	7-3
Oct. 28	Ole Miss	Knoxville	W	49-0
Nov. 4	Vanderbilt	Knoxville	L	14-6
Nov. 11	Mississippi A&M	Memphis	W	31-3
Nov. 18	Sewanee	Chattanooga	W	18-7
Nov. 30	Kentucky	Knoxville	W	14-7
Coach: M.B. Banks				239-45

All-Southern Conference: Tarzan Holt, Roe Campbell, Roy Striegel, Rufe Clayton

Tennessee wore orange jerseys for the first time against Emory & Henry, a 50-0 victory. The color was inspired by the American daisy, which grew on the hill north of the stadium. Previously, the team wore black.

1923
5-4-1

Sept. 29	Army	West Point	L	41-0
Oct. 6	Maryville	Knoxville	T	14-14
Oct. 13	Georgetown	Knoxville	W	13-6
Oct. 20	Georgia	Knoxville	L	17-0
Oct. 27	Mississippi A&M	Memphis	W	7-3
Nov. 3	Tulane	Knoxville	W	13-2
Nov. 10	Vanderbilt	Nashville	L	51-7
Nov. 17	VMI	Knoxville	L	33-0
Nov. 24	Ole Miss	Knoxville	W	10-0
Nov. 29	Kentucky	Lexington	W	18-0
Coach: M.B. Banks				82-167

Guard Estes Kefauver went on to serve in the United States Senate from 1948 until his death in 1963, and was the Democratic vice-presidential nominee in the 1956 election.

1924
3-5

Oct. 4	Emory & Henry	Knoxville	W	27-0
Oct. 11	Maryville	Knoxville	W	28-10
Oct. 18	Carson-Newman	Knoxville	W	13-0
Oct. 24	Mississippi A&M	Memphis	L	7-2
Nov. 1	Georgia	Athens	L	33-0
Nov. 8	Centre	Knoxville	L	32-0
Nov. 15	Tulane	New Orleans	L	26-7
Nov. 27	Kentucky	Knoxville	L	27-6
Coach: M.B. Banks				83-135

All-Southern Conference: Roe Campbell

1925
5-2-1

Oct. 3	Emory & Henry	Knoxville	W	51-0
Oct. 10	Maryville	Knoxville	W	13-0
Oct. 17	Vanderbilt	Nashville	L	34-7
Oct. 24	Louisiana State	Knoxville	T	0-0
Oct. 31	Georgia	Knoxville	W	12-7
Nov. 7	Centre	Danville	W	12-0
Nov. 14	Mississippi A&M	Knoxville	W	14-9
Nov. 26	Kentucky	Lexington	L	23-20
Coach: M.B. Banks				129-73

All-Southern Conference: J.G. Lowe

Banks (27-15-3), who was known for his winged-T offense, stepped down as head coach after becoming ill, and took the same job at Central High School. It should be noted, though, that Banks was 0-4 against then state–power Vanderbilt, and at that point Tennessee was 2-17-2 in the series. ... Robert R. Neyland (pronounced NEE-land) arrived on campus as ROTC commandant and served as a backfield coach. ... For the first time, the Beer Barrel trophy was awarded to the winner in the Kentucky series.

Through the Years

1926

8-1

Sept. 25	Carson-Newman	Knoxville	W	13-0
Oct. 2	North Carolina	Knoxville	W	34-0
Oct. 9	Louisiana State	Baton Rouge	W	14-7
Oct. 15	Maryville	Knoxville	W	6-0
Oct. 23	Centre	Knoxville	W	30-7
Oct. 30	Mississippi A&M	Starkville	W	33-0
Nov. 6	Sewanee	Knoxville	W	12-0
Nov. 13	Vanderbilt	Nashville	L	3-20
Nov. 25	Kentucky	Knoxville	W	6-0
Coach: Robert R. Neyland				151-34

All-Southern Conference: John Barnhill

Tennessee promoted Robert R. Neyland, the most successful coach in Volunteers history, who brought the single-wing offense to Tennessee. One of his initial directives was to beat Vanderbilt, which he didn't do his first season, but did the following season. UT has dominated the series since.

1927

8-0-1, Southern Conference champions

Sept. 24	Carson-Newman	Knoxville	W	33-0
Oct. 1	North Carolina	Chapel Hill	W	26-0
Oct. 8	Maryville	Knoxville	W	7-0
Oct. 15	Ole Miss	Knoxville	W	21-7
Oct. 22	Transylvania	Knoxville	W	57-0
Oct. 29	Virginia	Knoxville	W	42-0
Nov. 5	Sewanee	Knoxville	W	32-12
Nov. 12	Vanderbilt	Knoxville	T	7-7
Nov. 24	Kentucky	Lexington	W	20-0
Coach: Robert R. Neyland				245-26

All-Southern Conference: John Barnhill, Dick Dodson, Dave McArthur

In just his second season, Coach Robert R. Neyland notched both his first undefeated season, and conference title.

Then-Major Robert Neyland was promoted to the head coaching job in 1926, and the Tennessee program has been among college football's elite ever since. The Volunteers won their first seven games that season, falling only to rival Vanderbilt.

1928

9-0-1

Sept. 29	Maryville	Knoxville	W	41-0
Oct. 6	Centre	Knoxville	W	41-7
Oct. 13	Ole Miss	Knoxville	W	13-12
Oct. 20	Alabama	Tuscaloosa	W	15-13
Oct. 27	Washington & Lee	Knoxville	W	26-7
Nov. 3	Carson-Newman	Knoxville	W	57-0
Nov. 10	Sewanee	Knoxville	W	37-0
Nov. 17	Vanderbilt	Nashville	W	6-0
Nov. 29	Kentucky	Knoxville	T	0-0
Dec. 8	Florida	Knoxville	W	13-12
Coach: Robert R. Neyland				249-51

All-Southern Conference: Gene McEver

Sophomore Gene McEver's 98-yard kick return on the opening play led to an upset against Alabama, and escalated the rivalry between the teams. Before the kickoff, Coach Robert R. Neyland asked Crimson Tide coach Wallace Wade if they could end the game early if it got out of hand. ... The young team was nicknamed the "Flaming Sophomores." ... In many ways, 1928 was considered the breakthrough year for the football program, which was making its first lasting impressions on the national scene.

1928 was Gene McEver's first as an All-Southern Conference performer. He was recognized three times by the conference and was a 1954 inductee to the College Football Hall of Fame.

1929

9-0-1

Sept. 28	Centre	Knoxville	W	40-6
Oct. 5	Chattanooga	Chattanooga	W	20-0
Oct. 12	Ole Miss	Knoxville	W	52-7
Oct. 19	Alabama	Knoxville	W	6-0
Oct. 26	Washington & Lee	Roanoke	W	39-0
Nov. 2	Auburn	Knoxville	W	27-0
Nov. 9	Carson-Newman	Knoxville	W	73-0
Nov. 16	Vanderbilt	Knoxville	W	13-0
Nov. 28	Kentucky	Lexington	T	6-6
Dec. 7	South Carolina	Knoxville	W	54-0

Coach: Robert R. Neyland   330-19

All-American: Gene McEver
All-Southern Conference: Gene McEver, Bobby Dodd, Paul Hug, Fritz Brandt

Although guard Herman Hickman initially reported as a 205-pound 17-year-old, he bulked up to 225 pounds and became known as one of the greatest linemen to ever play the game. Known for his quickness and mobility, Tennessee lost only one game during his three varsity seasons. ... Halfback Gene McEver led the nation in scoring with 130 points. "The best player I ever coached...the best I ever saw," Coach Robert R. Neyland said.

130

The number of points Gene McEver scored during the 1929 season—still a Tennessee single-season record.

1930
9-1

Sept. 27	Maryville	Knoxville	W	54-0
Oct. 4	Centre	Knoxville	W	18-0
Oct. 11	Ole Miss	Knoxville	W	27-0
Oct. 18	Alabama	Tuscaloosa	L	18-6
Oct. 25	North Carolina	Knoxville	W	9-7
Nov. 1	Clemson	Knoxville	W	27-0
Nov. 8	Carson-Newman	Knoxville	W	34-0
Nov. 15	Vanderbilt	Nashville	W	13-0
Nov. 27	Kentucky	Knoxville	W	8-0
Dec. 6	Florida	Jacksonville	W	13-6
Coach: Robert R. Neyland				209-31

All-American: Bobby Dodd
All-Southern Conference: Bobby Dodd, Harry Thayer, Buddy Hackman

The Bobby Dodd era at quarterback came to a close, during which Tennessee went 27-1-2 and fans proudly boasted "In Dodd we trust." Edwin Camp of the *Atlanta Journal* called him "the greatest football player ever developed in the South." Dodd went on to serve Georgia Tech for 57 years, including 22 seasons as head football coach. He compiled a 165-64-8 record and his team once went 31 straight games without a defeat. ...The loss to Alabama snapped a 33-game unbeaten streak. ... Halfback Gene McEver missed the season due to a knee injury.

Bobby Dodd had no time off once he was done with school: he was hired as a Georgia Tech assistant before graduating from UT. He was elected to the College Football Hall of Fame as both a player and coach and Georgia Tech's stadium now bears his name.

1931
9-0-1

Sept. 26	Maryville	Knoxville	W	33-0
Oct. 3	Clemson	Knoxville	W	44-0
Oct. 10	Ole Miss	Knoxville	W	38-0
Oct. 17	Alabama	Knoxville	W	25-0
Oct. 24	North Carolina	Chapel Hill	W	7-0
Oct. 31	Duke	Knoxville	W	25-2
Nov. 7	Carson-Newman	Knoxville	W	31-0
Nov. 14	Vanderbilt	Knoxville	W	21-7
Nov. 26	Kentucky	Lexington	T	6-6
Dec. 5	New York Univ.	Charity Bowl	W	13-0
Coach: Robert R. Neyland				243-15

All-American: Herman Hickman
All-Southern Conference: Herman Hickman, Ray Saunders, Gene McEver

Beattie Feathers scored touchdowns of 60, 75, and 80 yards vs. Ole Miss, 70 vs. Kentucky, 65 vs. Duke, and 65 vs. New York University. ... The victory against NYU was in the New York Charity Game. ... After his final season, guard Herman Hickman went from pro football to pro wrestling and was known as the "The Tennessee Terror." He later became the head coach at Yale and was a staff writer in the early years of *Sports Illustrated*. ... Halfback Gene McEver finished his varsity career with a 27-0-3 record, with all three ties against Kentucky. "I'm still trying to figure out those Wildcat games," he said years later.

The number of points scored by Gene McEver during his career—the most ever by a non-kicker in the program's history.

Former Tennessee star Beattie Feathers (left) went on to become the first NFL running back to be credited with rushing for 1,000 yards in a season. After his playing days, he served as the head coach at four different colleges.

1932

9-0-1, Southern Conference champions

Sept. 24	Chattanooga	Chattanooga	W	13-0
Oct. 1	Ole Miss	Knoxville	W	33-0
Oct. 8	North Carolina	Knoxville	W	20-7
Oct. 15	Alabama	Birmingham	W	7-3
Oct. 22	Maryville	Knoxville	W	60-0
Oct. 29	Duke	Knoxville	W	16-13
Nov. 5	Mississippi A&M	Knoxville	W	31-0
Nov. 12	Vanderbilt	Nashville	T	0-0
Nov. 24	Kentucky	Knoxville	W	26-0
Dec. 3	Florida	Jacksonville	W	32-13
Coach: Robert R. Neyland				238-36

All-Southern Conference: Beattie Feathers, Van Rayburn

Beattie Feathers helped lead the Volunteers to another unbeaten season. He scored impressive touchdowns of 54 yards vs. North Carolina, and 33 vs. Ole Miss, and averaged 46 yards on 23 punts in a driving rain against Alabama. "Beattie didn't think in terms of first downs, only in terms of touchdowns," teammate Freddie Moses said.

4

National championships won by the Volunteers during Robert Neyland's 21 seasons as head coach.

Through the Years

1933

7-3

Sept. 30	Virginia Tech	Knoxville	W	27-0
Oct. 7	Mississippi State	Knoxville	W	20-0
Oct. 14	Duke	Durham	L	10-2
Oct. 21	Alabama	Knoxville	L	12-6
Oct. 28	Florida	Knoxville	W	13-6
Nov. 4	George Washington	Washington, D.C.	W	13-0
Nov. 11	Ole Miss	Knoxville	W	35-6
Nov. 18	Vanderbilt	Knoxville	W	33-6
Nov. 30	Kentucky	Lexington	W	27-0
Dec. 9	LSU	Baton Rouge	L	0-7

Coach: Robert R. Neyland 176-47

Captain: Talmadge Maples
All-American: Beattie Feathers
All-SEC: Beattie Feathers, Sheriff Maples

Beattie Feathers finished his career with 32 touchdowns in 30 games, during which Tennessee had a 25-3-2 record. Beattie's career rushing total, 1,888 yards, lasted 37 years as the school record. Later, he was credited as being the first NFL player to rush for 1,000 yards in one season (1934), and his 8.44 yards per attempt set another record that stood until 2006 (Michael Vick). ... Tennessee was an inaugural member of the Southeastern Conference. ... The loss to Duke snapped a 28-game unbeaten streak. ... The back-to-back losses were the first since 1924.

1934
8-2

Sept. 29	Centre	Knoxville	W	32-0
Oct. 5	North Carolina	Chapel Hill	W	19-7
Oct. 13	Ole Miss	Knoxville	W	27-0
Oct. 20	Alabama	Birmingham	L	13-6
Oct. 27	Duke	Knoxville	W	14-6
Nov. 3	Fordham	New York	L	13-12
Nov. 10	Mississippi State	Knoxville	W	14-0
Nov. 17	Vanderbilt	Nashville	W	13-6
Nov. 29	Kentucky	Knoxville	W	19-0
Dec. 8	LSU	Knoxville	W	19-13
Coach: Robert R. Neyland				175-58

Captain: Ralph Hatley
All-SEC (first team): Murray Warmath

The home victory against Ole Miss was win No. 200 for the program. ... Neyland finished his first stint leading the Volunteers with a 76-7-5 record.

1935
4-5

Sept. 28	Southwestern	Knoxville	W	20-0
Oct. 5	North Carolina	Knoxville	L	38-13
Oct. 12	Auburn	Birmingham	W	13-6
Oct. 19	Alabama	Knoxville	L	25-0
Oct. 26	Centre	Knoxville	W	25-14
Nov. 2	Duke	Durham	L	19-6
Nov. 9	Ole Miss	Memphis	W	14-13
Nov. 16	Vanderbilt	Knoxville	L	13-7
Nov. 28	Kentucky	Lexington	L	27-0
Coach: W.H. Britton				98-155

Captain: Toby Palmer

Robert R. Neyland was called to active duty in the Panama Canal Zone, leaving W.H. Britton, an end coach and scout since 1926, to take his place for one season.

Rober R. Neyland scouts Ole Miss in 1938. The Volunteers
enjoyed their first major runs at national championships
during Neyland's second stint at the helm, going 43-7-3
until he was recalled to the military for a second time during World War II.

1936
6-2-2

Sept. 26	Chattanooga	Knoxville	W	13-0
Oct. 3	North Carolina	Chapel Hill	L	14-6
Oct. 10	Auburn	Knoxville	L	6-0
Oct. 17	Alabama	Birmingham	T	0-0
Oct. 24	Duke	Knoxville	W	15-13
Oct. 31	Georgia	Athens	W	46-0
Nov. 7	Maryville	Knoxville	W	34-0
Nov. 14	Vanderbilt	Nashville	W	26-13
Nov. 26	Kentucky	Knoxville	W	7-6
Dec. 5	Ole Miss	Memphis	T	0-0
Coach: Robert R. Neyland				147-52

Captain: DeWitt Weaver
Ranking (AP): First poll NR; Postseason No. 17
All-SEC (first team): Phil Dickens

Major Robert R. Neyland returned from active duty in the army and pieced together the basis for three undefeated teams in the years to follow. Tennessee went 43-7-3 during his second stint as head coach. ... Duke was No. 2 coming into the Tennessee game.

The active service that called Major Neyland away from UT was a stint working in the Panama Canal Zone.

1937
6-3-1

Date	Opponent	Location		Score
Sept. 25	Wake Forest	Knoxville	W	32-0
Oct. 2	Virginia Tech	Knoxville	W	27-0
Oct. 9	Duke	Durham	T	0-0
Oct. 16	Alabama	Knoxville	L	14-7
Oct. 23	Sewanee	Knoxville	W	32-0
Oct. 30	Georgia	Knoxville	W	32-0
Nov. 6	Auburn	Birmingham	L	20-7
Nov. 13	Vanderbilt	Knoxville	L	13-7
Nov. 25	Kentucky	Lexington	W	13-0
Dec. 4	Ole Miss	Memphis	W	32-0
Coach: Robert R. Neyland				189-47

Captain: Joe Black Hayes

The season saw the emergence of halfback
George Cafego, whom coach Robert Neyland
called a "practice bum. On the practice field he
couldn't do anything right, but for two hours on
a Saturday afternoon he did everything an All-
American is supposed to do." ... The Vols were
briefly No. 7 after defeating Georgia, but fell out
of the rankings.

**George Cafego was one of the premier athletes
of his day. In addition to running and passing the
ball, he punted and returned kicks for the Vols.**

1938

11-0, National champions (non-consensus),
SEC champions

Sept. 24	Sewanee	Knoxville	W	26-3
Oct. 1	Clemson	Knoxville	W	20-7
Oct. 8	Auburn	Knoxville	W	7-0
Oct. 15	Alabama	Birmingham	W	13-0
Oct. 22	The Citadel	Knoxville	W	44-0
Oct. 29	LSU	Knoxville	W	14-6
Nov. 5	Chattanooga	Knoxville	W	45-0
Nov. 12	Vanderbilt	Nashville	W	14-0
Nov. 24	Kentucky	Knoxville	W	46-0
Dec. 3	Ole Miss	Memphis	W	47-0
Jan. 2	Oklahoma	Orange Bowl	W	17-0
Coach: Robert R. Neyland				293-16

Captain: Bowden Wyatt
Ranking (AP): First poll No. 8; Postseason No. 2
All-American: Bowden Wyatt, George Cafego, Bob Suffridge
All-SEC (first team): George Cafego, Bob Suffridge, Bowden Wyatt

Although a number of services including Dunkel, Litkenhous, Boand, Houlgate, and Poling had the Volunteers No. 1, Tennessee was not the consensus national champion, with Association Press voters opting for Texas Christian. .... The win against Oklahoma came after Tennessee's first modern bowl invitation. ... A touchdown by Clemson in the second game was the most any opponent scored on the defense, led by end Bowden Wyatt. ... Aided by two wins in 1937, the Vols began one of the most impressive streaks in college football history. Not only did Tennessee win 23 consecutive games, but 15 straight shutouts.

1939

10-1, SEC champions

Sept. 29	NC State	Raleigh	W	13-0
Oct. 7	Sewanee	Knoxville	W	40-0
Oct. 14	Chattanooga	Chattanooga	W	28-0
Oct. 21	Alabama	Knoxville	W	21-0
Oct. 28	Mercer	Knoxville	W	17-0
Nov. 4	LSU	Baton Rouge	W	20-0
Nov. 11	The Citadel	Knoxville	W	34-0
Nov. 18	Vanderbilt	Knoxville	W	13-0
Nov. 30	Kentucky	Lexington	W	19-0
Dec. 9	Auburn	Knoxville	W	7-0
Jan. 1	Southern Cal	Rose Bowl	L	14-0
Coach: Robert R. Neyland				212-14

Captain: Sam Bartholomew
Ranking (AP): First poll No. 5; Postseason No. 2.
All-American: George Cafego, Ed Molinski, Bob
Suffridge, Abe Shires
All-SEC (first team): George Cafego, Bob Foxx, Ed
Molinski, James Rike, Abe Shires

The 1939 Volunteers were the last team in NCAA history to finish a regular season without allowing a single point. However, Texas A&M was the consensus national champion. ... The Rose Bowl loss snapped a 23-game winning streak. ... George "Bad News" Cafego finished his career with 2,139 yards in total offense. He averaged 6.1 yards every time he carried the ball. ... Johnny Butler's sideline-to-sideline 56-yard run keyed the win against Alabama. ... The defense allowed just 1,023 yards, 103.3 per game and 2.2 per play.

1940

10-1, National champions (non-consensus),
SEC champions

Sept. 28	Mercer	Knoxville	W	49-0
Oct. 5	Duke	Knoxville	W	13-0
Oct. 12	Chattanooga	Knoxville	W	53-0
Oct. 19	Alabama	Birmingham	W	27-12
Oct. 26	Florida	Knoxville	W	14-0
Nov. 2	LSU	Knoxville	W	28-0
Nov. 9	Southwestern	Memphis	W	41-0
Nov. 16	Virginia	Knoxville	W	41-14
Nov. 23	Kentucky	Knoxville	W	33-0
Nov. 30	Vanderbilt	Nashville	W	20-0
Jan. 1	Boston College	Sugar Bowl	L	19-13
Coach: Robert R. Neyland				332-45

Captain: Norbert Ackermann
Ranking (AP): First poll No. 5; Postseason No. 4.
Major Award: Bob Suffridge, Knute Rockne
Memorial Trophy (outstanding lineman).
All-American: Bob Suffridge, Bob Foxx, Ed
Molinski.
All-SEC (first team): Bob Foxx, Abe Shires, Bob
Suffridge.

Guard Ed "Big Mo" Molinski and the rest of the
seniors finished their careers without losing a regular-season game (30-0). ... Bob Suffridge became
UT's only three-time All-American. ... Tennessee
received national title consideration from Dunkel
and Williamson services, but Minnesota was considered the consensus national champion. ...
Alabama snapped the regular-season scoreless
streak of 71 quarters, which began against LSU
in 1938, and included 17 shutouts. ... Boston
College coach Frank Leahy used a play he noticed
while watching film of Tennessee to beat the Vols
in the Sugar Bowl. Boston College backup running
back Louis Montgomery wasn't allowed to play in
the game because he was black.

George Cafego was a two-time All-American and a Heisman Trophy finalist in the final years before World War II. After serving in the war and playing in the NFL, he served as an assistant at Tennessee for 30 years.

1941

8-2

Sept. 20	Furman	Knoxville	W	32-6
Oct. 4	Duke	Durham	L	19-0
Oct. 11	Dayton	Knoxville	W	26-0
Oct. 18	Alabama	Knoxville	L	9-2
Oct. 25	Cincinnati	Knoxville	W	21-6
Nov. 1	LSU	Baton Rouge	W	13-6
Nov. 8	Howard	Knoxville	W	28-6
Nov. 15	Boston College	Boston	W	14-7
Nov. 22	Kentucky	Lexington	W	20-7
Nov. 29	Vanderbilt	Knoxville	W	26-7
Coach: John Barnhill				182-73

Captain: Ray Graves
Ranking (AP): First poll NR; Postseason No. 18
All-SEC (first team): Don Edmiston

With Robert R. Neyland called back into military service, John Barnhill took over the program and compiled a 32-5-2 record. ... Wins over No. 18 Boston College and No. 12 Vanderbilt vaulted Tennessee into the final rankings.

John Barnhill later coached at Arkansas for four seasons before becoming the school's athletic director, a position he held until 1971.

1942
9-1-1

Sept. 26	South Carolina	Columbia	T	0-0
Oct. 3	Fordham	Knoxville	W	40-14
Oct. 10	Dayton	Knoxville	W	34-6
Oct. 17	Alabama	Birmingham	L	8-0
Oct. 24	Furman	Knoxville	W	52-7
Oct. 31	LSU	Knoxville	W	26-0
Nov. 7	Cincinnati	Knoxville	W	34-12
Nov. 14	Ole Miss	Memphis	W	14-0
Nov. 21	Kentucky	Knoxville	W	26-0
Nov. 28	Vanderbilt	Nashville	W	19-7
Jan. 1	Tulsa	Sugar Bowl	W	14-7

Coach: John Barnhill 259-61

Captain: Al Hust
Ranking (AP): First poll No. 16; Postseason No. 7
All-SEC (first team): Al Hust

Tennessee accumulated 208 rushing yards while allowing minus-39 by Tulsa in the Sugar Bowl. Bill Gold and Clyde "Ig" Fuson scored touchdowns and Denver Crawford blocked a punt for a safety. Coming in, Tulsa was undefeated and averaged 42 points per game, while No. 1 Boston College was snubbed by Sugar Bowl officials in favor of UT after it lost to Holy Cross, 55-12.

1944
7-1-1

Sept. 30	Kentucky	Knoxville	W	26-13
Oct. 7	Ole Miss	Memphis	W	20-7
Oct. 14	Florida	Knoxville	W	40-0
Oct. 21	Alabama	Knoxville	T	0-0
Oct. 28	Clemson	Knoxville	W	26-7
Nov. 4	LSU	Baton Rouge	W	13-0
Nov. 18	Temple	Knoxville	W	27-14
Nov. 25	Kentucky	Lexington	W	21-7
Jan. 1	Southern Cal	Rose Bowl	L	25-0

Coach: John Barnhill 173-73

Captain: Bob Dobelstein
Ranking (AP): First poll No. 16; Postseason No. 12
All-American: Bob Dobelstein
All-SEC (first team): Bob Dobelstein, Buster Stephens

Tennessee did not field a team in 1943 due to World War II. ... LSU was Tennessee's first official night game. ... John Barnhill was named SEC Coach of the Year. ... With Tennessee lacking depth at key positions due to a small roster during World War II, the Rose Bowl was a mismatch. The Trojans scored in the opening moments when Jim Callanan returned a blocked punt by John Ferraro. Despite having the flu and a stomach disorder, Jim Hardy threw two touchdown passes and ran in another score.

1945
8-1

Sept. 29	Wake Forest	Knoxville	W	7-6
Oct. 6	William & Mary	Knoxville	W	48-13
Oct. 13	Chattanooga	Knoxville	W	30-0
Oct. 20	Alabama	Birmingham	L	25-7
Oct. 27	Villanova	Knoxville	W	33-2
Nov. 3	North Carolina	Knoxville	W	20-6
Nov. 10	Ole Miss	Memphis	W	34-0
Nov. 24	Kentucky	Lexington	W	14-0
Dec. 1	Vanderbilt	Knoxville	W	45-0

Coach: John Barnhill — 238-52

Captain: Billy Bevis
Ranking (AP): First poll No. 18; Postseason No.14
All-SEC (first team): Bob Dobelstein

Four players did not return from World War II, Bill Nowling (32), Rudy Klarer (49), Willis Tucker (61), and Clyde "Ig" Fuson (62). Their numbers were later retired. ... The defense shut out the final three opponents, and yielded eight points over the final five games.

1946

9-2, SEC champions

Sept. 28	Georgia Tech	Knoxville	W	13-9
Oct. 5	Duke	Durham	W	12-7
Oct. 12	Chattanooga	Knoxville	W	47-7
Oct. 19	Alabama	Knoxville	W	12-0
Oct. 26	Wake Forest	Knoxville	L	19-6
Nov. 2	North Carolina	Knoxville	W	20-14
Nov. 9	Ole Miss	Memphis	W	18-14
Nov. 16	Boston College	Boston	W	33-13
Nov. 23	Kentucky	Knoxville	W	7-0
Nov. 30	Vanderbilt	Nashville	W	7-6
Jan. 1	Rice	Orange Bowl	L	8-0
Coach: Robert R. Neyland				175-97

Captain: Walter Slater
Ranking (AP): First poll No. 8 (tied); Postseason No. 7
All-American: Dick Huffman.
All-SEC (first team): Dick Huffman

When General Robert R. Neyland retired from military service and returned to Tennessee in 1946, John Barnhill (32-5-2), who had been filling in as head coach, accepted the head coaching position at Arkansas, where he also served as athletics director. ... Neyland went 54-17-4 during his third and final stint as UT's head coach. ... Rice blocked two punts in the first quarter of the Orange Bowl, one resulting in a safety.

Tackle Dick Huffman carried his All-American success to the pro ranks, making a Pro Bowl while playing for the Los Angeles Rams. He later player seven years in the CFL and is enshrined in the Canadian Football Hall of Fame.

1947
5-5

Sept. 27	Georgia Tech	Atlanta	L	27-0
Oct. 4	Duke	Knoxville	L	19-7
Oct. 11	Chattanooga	Knoxville	W	26-7
Oct. 18	Alabama	Birmingham	L	10-0
Oct. 25	Tennessee Tech	Knoxville	W	49-0
Nov. 1	North Carolina	Chapel Hill	L	20-6
Nov. 8	Ole Miss	Memphis	L	43-13
Nov. 15	Boston College	Knoxville	W	38-13
Nov. 22	Kentucky	Lexington	W	13-6
Nov. 29	Vanderbilt	Knoxville	W	12-7

Coach: Robert R. Neyland   164-159

Captain: Denver Crawford

Former UT standout Ralph Hatley was hired as Memphis State's football coach. He was there until 1957, and had a 47-36-5 record.

1948
4-4-2

Sept. 25	Mississippi State	Knoxville	L	21-6
Oct. 2	Duke	Durham	T	7-7
Oct. 9	Chattanooga	Knoxville	W	26-0
Oct. 16	Alabama	Knoxville	W	21-6
Oct. 23	Tennessee Tech	Knoxville	W	41-0
Oct. 30	North Carolina	Knoxville	L	14-7
Nov. 6	Georgia Tech	Atlanta	W	13-6
Nov. 13	Ole Miss	Memphis	L	16-13
Nov. 20	Kentucky	Knoxville	T	0-0
Nov. 27	Vanderbilt	Nashville	L	28-6

Coach: Robert R. Neyland   140-98

Captain: Jim Powell
Ranking (AP): First poll 20; Postseason NR.
All-SEC (first team): Norman Meseroll

The homecoming win against Alabama was No. 300 for the program.

One of the few Tennessee players to have his number retired, Doug Atkins is seen here hitting the books. Originally recruited to UT to play on the basketball team, General Robert Neyland recruited Atkins for the football squad after seeing his combination of size and agility.

1949

7-2-1

Sept. 24	Mississippi State	Knoxville	W	10-0
Oct. 1	Duke	Knoxville	L	21-7
Oct. 8	Chattanooga	Knoxville	W	39-7
Oct. 15	Alabama	Birmingham	T	7-7
Oct. 22	Tennessee Tech	Knoxville	W	36-6
Oct. 29	North Carolina	Chapel Hill	W	35-6
Nov. 5	Georgia Tech	Knoxville	L	30-13
Nov. 12	Ole Miss	Memphis	W	35-7
Nov. 19	Kentucky	Lexington	W	6-0
Nov. 26	Vanderbilt	Knoxville	W	26-20
Coach Robert R. Neyland				214-104

Captains: Ralph Chancey, Hal Littleford
Ranking (AP): First poll NR; Postseason No. 17
All-SEC (first team): Bud Sherrod

Lindsey Nelson formed the Vol Radio Network.

1950

11-1, National champions (non-consensus)

Sept. 23	Southern Miss	Knoxville	W	56-0
Sept. 30	Mississippi State	Starkville	L	7-0
Oct. 7	Duke	Durham	W	28-7
Oct. 14	Chattanooga	Knoxville	W	41-0
Oct. 21	Alabama	Knoxville	W	14-9
Oct. 28	Washington & Lee	Knoxville	W	27-20
Nov. 4	North Carolina	Knoxville	W	16-0
Nov. 11	Tennessee Tech	Knoxville	W	48-14
Nov. 18	Ole Miss	Knoxville	W	35-0
Nov. 25	Kentucky	Knoxville	W	7-0
Dec. 2	Vanderbilt	Nashville	W	43-0
Jan. 1	Texas	Cotton Bowl	W	20-14
Coach: Robert R. Neyland				335-71

Captain: Jack Stroud
Ranking (AP): Preseason No. 4; Postseason No. 4
All-American: Ted Daffer, Bud Sherrod
All-SEC (first team): Ted Daffer, Hank Lauricella, Bud Sherrod

Leaders: Passing: Hank Lauricella (23 of 72, 364 yards); Rushing: Andy Kozar (126 carries, 648 yards); Receiving: Bert Rechichar (9 catches, 205 yards).

Although Dunkel and other services had Tennessee at No. 1, both the Associated Press and coaches' polls named Oklahoma their national champions. However, at 4-1 in conference play the Volunteers did not win the SEC title, which went to Kentucky (5-1, the lone loss to UT). ... The Associated Press held its first preseason poll. ... The 6-foot-8 Doug Atkins arrived in Knoxville on a basketball scholarship, but played end as a sopho-more before becoming an All-American defensive tackle. ... Hank Lauricella's 75-yard touchdown run keyed the Cotton Bowl victory. ... On the ground, UT tallied 3,068 yards, 306.8 per game, and 40 touchdowns.

1951

10-1, NCAA champions, SEC champions

Sept. 29	Mississippi State	Knoxville	W	14-0
Oct. 6	Duke	Knoxville	W	26-0
Oct. 13	Chattanooga	Knoxville	W	42-13
Oct. 20	Alabama	Birmingham	W	27-13
Oct. 27	Tennessee Tech	Knoxville	W	68-0
Nov. 3	North Carolina	Chapel Hill	W	27-0
Nov. 10	Washington & Lee	Knoxville	W	60-14
Nov. 17	Ole Miss	Oxford	W	46-21
Nov. 24	Kentucky	Lexington	W	28-0
Dec. 1	Vanderbilt	Knoxville	W	35-27
Jan. 1	Maryland	Sugar Bowl	L	28-13

Coach: Robert R. Neyland   386-116

Captain: Bert Rechichar
Ranking (AP): Preseason No. 1; Postseason No. 1
All-American: Hank Lauricella, Ted Daffer, Bill Pearman
All-SEC (first team): Doug Atkins, Ted Daffer, Hank Lauricella, John Michels, Bill Pearman, Bert Rechichar

Leaders: Passing: Hank Lauricella (24 of 51, 352 yards); Rushing: Hank Lauricella (111 carries, 881 yards); Receiving: John Davis (8 catches, 160 yards).

Tennessee was No. 1 in both the Associated Press and coaches' final polls, which were both held at the conclusion of the regular season. ... The Alabama game was the first televised game for both schools. ... Hank Lauricella (5-foot-10, 169 pounds, nicknamed "Mr. Everything") ran for 13 touchdowns and passed for 16 during his career as a single-wing tailback. He averaged 7.9 yards per rushing attempt during his senior season, when he finished second in Heisman Trophy voting. ... John Michels won the Jacobs Trophy as the Southeastern Conference's best blocker.

1952
8-2-1

Sept. 27	Mississippi State	Memphis	W	14-7
Oct. 4	Duke	Durham	L	7-0
Oct. 11	Chattanooga	Knoxville	W	26-6
Oct. 18	Alabama	Knoxville	W	20-0
Oct. 25	Wofford	Knoxville	W	50-0
Nov. 1	North Carolina	Knoxville	W	41-14
Nov. 8	LSU	Baton Rouge	W	22-3
Nov. 15	Florida	Knoxville	W	26-12
Nov. 22	Kentucky	Knoxville	T	14-14
Nov. 29	Vanderbilt	Nashville	W	46-0
Jan. 1	Texas	Cotton Bowl	L	16-0

Coach: Robert R. Neyland   259-79

Captain: Jim Haslam
Ranking (AP): Preseason No.6; Postseason No. 8
All-American: John Michels, Doug Atkins.
All-SEC (first team): Doug Atkins, Mack Franklin, Francis Holohan, Andy Kozar, John Michels
Leaders: Passing:Pat Shires (15 of 38, 252 yards); Rushing: Andy Kozar (122 carries, 660 yards); Receiving: John Davis (14 catches, 297 yards).

Due to poor health, Robert R. Neyland (173-31-12) retired from coaching and became Tennessee's director of athletics, a position he held until his death in 1962. Opponents failed to score in 112 of his 216 games as head coach. ... UT went 29-4-1 during defensive end Doug Atkins' career. He went on to play professionally for 17 years with Cleveland, Chicago, and New Orleans. ... Guard John Michels won the Jacobs Trophy as the best blocker in the Southeastern Conference. ... Texas had an advantage of 269 rushing yards to minus-14 in the Cotton Bowl.

1953

6-4-1

Sept. 26	Mississippi State	Knoxville	L	26-0
Oct. 3	Duke	Knoxville	L	21-7
Oct. 10	Chattanooga	Knoxville	W	40-7
Oct. 17	Alabama	Birmingham	T	0-0
Oct. 24	Louisville	Knoxville	W	59-6
Oct. 31	North Carolina	Chapel Hill	W	20-6
Nov. 7	LSU	Knoxville	W	32-14
Nov. 14	Florida	Gainesville	W	9-7
Nov. 21	Kentucky	Lexington	L	27-21
Nov. 28	Vanderbilt	Knoxville	W	33-6
Dec. 5	Houston	Houston	L	33-19
Coach Harvey Robinson				240-153

Captain: Mack Franklin
Ranking (AP): Preseason No. 17 tied; Postseason NR
All-SEC (first team): Bob Fisher
Leaders: Passing: Jimmy Wade (25 of 63, 451 yards); Rushing: Jimmy Wade (158 carries, 675 yards); Receiving: Jerry Hyde (8 catches, 173 yards).

Harvey Robinson had been a tailback for Robert Neyland, whom he replaced as coach, and had been on his staff since 1946. After two years and a .500 record, he went to Florida as an assistant coach, but returned in 1960 on Bowden Wyatt's staff. ... The first coonhound mascot, Blue Smokey, was selected at halftime against Mississippi State.

1954
4-6

Sept. 25	Mississippi State	Memphis	W	19-7
Oct. 2	Duke	Durham	L	7-6
Oct. 9	Chattanooga	Knoxville	W	20-14
Oct. 16	Alabama	Knoxville	L	27-0
Oct. 23	Dayton	Knoxville	W	14-7
Oct. 30	North Carolina	Knoxville	W	26-20
Nov. 6	Georgia Tech	Atlanta	L	28-7
Nov. 13	Florida	Knoxville	L	14-0
Nov. 20	Kentucky	Knoxville	L	14-13
Nov. 27	Vanderbilt	Nashville	L	26-0
Coach: Harvey Robinson				105-164

Captain: Darris McCord
All-American: Darris McCord
All-SEC (first team): Darris McCord, Tom Tracy
Leaders: Passing: Johnny Majors (8 of 24, 107 yards); Rushing: Tom Tracy (116 carries, 794 yards); Receiving: Hugh Garner (5 catches, 57 yards).

Tennessee went 1-5 in SEC play. ... Robert R. Neyland called dismissing Coach Harvey Robinson "the hardest thing I've ever had to do."

Johnny Majors starred for the 1956 Volunteers, and later
returned to coach Tennessee to three SEC championships. During his playing days, Majors finished second in
the Heisman Trophy voting to Notre Dame's Paul Hornung.

1955
6-3-1

Sept. 24	Mississippi State	Knoxville	L	13-7
Oct. 1	Duke	Knoxville	L	21-0
Oct. 8	Chattanooga	Knoxville	W	13-0
Oct. 15	Alabama	Birmingham	W	20-0
Oct. 22	Dayton	Knoxville	W	53-7
Oct. 29	North Carolina	Chapel Hill	W	48-7
Nov. 5	Georgia Tech	Knoxville	T	7-7
Nov. 12	Florida	Gainesville	W	20-0
Nov. 19	Kentucky	Lexington	L	23-0
Nov. 26	Vanderbilt	Knoxville	W	20-14

Coach: Bowden Wyatt — 188-92

Captain: Jim Beutel
All-SEC (first team): Johnny Majors
Leaders: Passing: Johnny Majors (36 of 65, 476 yards); Rushing: Johnny Majors (183 carries, 657 yards); Receiving: Buddy Cruze (12 catches, 232 yards).

Former Tennessee player Bowden Wyatt returned as head coach after winning championships at Wyoming and Arkansas. ... Johnny Majors played every down against Georgia. He was named SEC player of the year.

1956
10-1, SEC champions

Sept. 29	Auburn	Birmingham	W	35-7
Oct. 6	Duke	Durham	W	33-20
Oct. 13	Chattanooga	Knoxville	W	42-20
Oct. 20	Alabama	Knoxville	W	24-0
Oct. 27	Maryland	Knoxville	W	34-7
Nov. 3	North Carolina	Knoxville	W	20-0
Nov. 10	Georgia Tech	Atlanta	W	6-0
Nov. 17	Ole Miss	Knoxville	W	27-7
Nov. 24	Kentucky	Knoxville	W	20-7
Dec. 1	Vanderbilt	Nashville	W	27-7
Jan. 1	Baylor	Sugar Bowl	L	13-7

Coach: Bowden Wyatt — 275-88

Captain: John Gordy
Ranking (AP): Preseason No. 12; Postseason No. 2
All-American: Johnny Majors, Kyle (Buddy) Cruze
All-SEC (first team): Buddy Cruze, John Gordy,
Johnny Majors
Leaders: Passing: Johnny Majors (36 of 59, 552
yards); Rushing: Tommy Bronson (105 carries,
562 yards); Receiving: Buddy Cruze (20 catches,
357 yards).

Despite weighing only 168 pounds, halfback Johnny
Majors was named MVP of the Southeastern
Conference for the second consecutive year. He finished second to Notre Dame's Paul Hornung in
Heisman Trophy voting, but was named UPI's Back
of the Year. His career statistics were 1,622 rushing yards, 1,135 passing, 16 touchdowns, 83
punts for a 39.1 average, 36 punt returns for 438
yards, 15 kickoff returns for 344 yards, and two
interceptions. ... Baylor took advantage of four interceptions and a fumble recovery in the Sugar Bowl.
Tennessee entered the game No. 2, while Baylor
was unranked. The game was marred by an ugly
fight, during which backup fullback Larry Hickman
kicked defenseless UT guard Bruce Burnham in the
face, sending him to the hospital. Hickman, who was
ejected, later apologized to the entire Tennessee
team and visited Burnham in the hospital.

1957

8-3

Sept. 28	Auburn	Knoxville	L	7-0
Oct. 5	Mississippi State	Knoxville	W	14-9
Oct. 12	Chattanooga	Knoxville	W	28-13
Oct. 19	Alabama	Birmingham	W	14-0
Oct. 26	Maryland	College Park	W	16-0
Nov. 2	North Carolina	Chapel Hill	W	35-0
Nov. 9	Georgia Tech	Knoxville	W	21-6
Nov. 16	Ole Miss	Memphis	L	14-7
Nov. 23	Kentucky	Lexington	L	20-6
Nov. 30	Vanderbilt	Knoxville	W	20-6
Dec. 28	Texas A&M	Gator Bowl	W	3-0
Coach: Bowden Wyatt				164-75

Captains: Bill Anderson, Bill Johnson
Ranking (AP): Preseason 5; Postseason No. 13.
All-American: Bill Johnson
All-SEC (first team): Bobby Gordon, Bill Johnson
Leaders: Passing: Bobby Gordon (20 of 40, 260 yards); Rushing: Bobby Gordon (167 carries, 526 yards); Receiving: Tommy Potts (10 catches, 123 yards).

Tennessee defeated Paul W. "Bear" Bryant's last Texas A&M team in the Gator Bowl on a 17-yard field goal by Sammy Burklow with 5:30 remaining. It was the first field goal of his career. The game also featured a famous collision between Heisman Trophy winner John David Crow and UT tailback Bobby Gordon.

1958

4-6

Sept. 27	Auburn	Birmingham	L	13-0
Oct. 4	Mississippi State	Memphis	W	13-8
Oct. 11	Georgia Tech	Atlanta	L	21-7
Oct. 18	Alabama	Knoxville	W	14-7
Oct. 25	Florida State	Knoxville	L	10-0
Nov. 1	North Carolina	Knoxville	L	21-7
Nov. 8	Chattanooga	Knoxville	L	14-6
Nov. 15	Ole Miss	Knoxville	W	18-16
Nov. 22	Kentucky	Knoxville	L	6-2
Nov. 29	Vanderbilt	Nashville	W	10-6
Coach: Bowden Wyatt				77-122

Captain: Bobby Urbano
Leaders: Passing: Bill Majors (27 of 25, 215 yards); Rushing: Bill Majors (148 carries, 294 yards); Receiving: Murray Armstrong (14 catches, 195 yards).

The 1958 season was the first to feature the two-point conversion. University of Michigan athletics director Fritz Crisler said of the decision, "It's a progressive step which will make football more interesting for the spectators," adding that the rule "will add drama to what has been the dullest, most stupid play in the game."

1959
5-4-1

Sept. 26	Auburn	Knoxville	W	3-0
Oct. 3	Mississippi State	Knoxville	W	22-6
Oct. 10	Georgia Tech	Knoxville	L	14-7
Oct. 17	Alabama	Birmingham	T	7-7
Oct. 24	Chattanooga	Knoxville	W	23-0
Oct. 31	North Carolina	Chapel Hill	W	29-7
Nov. 7	LSU	Knoxville	W	14-13
Nov. 14	Ole Miss	Memphis	L	37-7
Nov. 21	Kentucky	Lexington	L	20-0
Nov. 28	Vanderbilt	Knoxville	L	14-0

Coach: Bowden Wyatt   112-118

Captain: Joe Schaffer
All-SEC (first team): Joe Schaffer
Leaders: Passing: Gen Etter (22 of 36, 298 yards); Rushing: Glenn Glass (75 carries, 261 yards); Receiving: Cotton Letner (8 catches, 92 yards).

Tennessee pulled off two big upsets, against No. 3 Auburn and No. 1 LSU, both in Knoxville.

1960
6-2-2

Sept. 24	Auburn	Birmingham	W	10-3
Oct. 1	Mississippi State	Memphis	T	0-0
Oct. 8	Tampa	Knoxville	W	62-7
Oct. 15	Alabama	Knoxville	W	20-7
Oct. 22	Chattanooga	Knoxville	W	35-0
Oct. 29	North Carolina	Knoxville	W	27-14
Nov. 5	Georgia Tech	Atlanta	L	14-7
Nov. 12	Ole Miss	Knoxville	L	24-3
Nov. 19	Kentucky	Knoxville	T	10-10
Nov. 26	Vanderbilt	Nashville	W	35-0

Coach: Bowden Wyatt   209-79

Captain: Mike LaSorsa
Ranking (AP): Preseason No. 18; Postseason NR
Leaders: Passing: Glenn Glass (11 of 26, 167
yards); Rushing: Glenn Glass (90 carries, 478
yards); Receiving: Ken Waddell (8 catches, 60
yards).

1961
6-4

Sept. 30	Auburn	Knoxville	L	24-21
Oct. 7	Mississippi State	Knoxville	W	17-3
Oct. 14	Tulsa	Knoxville	W	52-6
Oct. 21	Alabama	Birmingham	L	34-3
Oct. 28	Chattanooga	Knoxville	W	20-7
Nov. 4	North Carolina	Chapel Hill	L	22-21
Nov. 11	Georgia Tech	Knoxville	W	10-6
Nov. 18	Ole Miss	Memphis	L	24-10
Nov. 25	Kentucky	Lexington	W	26-16
Dec. 2	Vanderbilt	Knoxville	W	41-7
Coach: Bowden Wyatt				221-149

Captain: Mike Lucci
All-SEC (first team): Mike Lucci
Leaders: Passing: Mallon Faircloth (31 of 75,
509 yards); Rushing: Mallon Faircloth (123 carries, 475 yards); Receiving: Hubert McClain (11
catches, 149 yards).

**Before coming to UT, Mike Lucci had played one
season at Pittsburgh.**

1962 was a sad year for Volunteers fans, as they had to say goodbye to an icon. General Robert Neyland's influence is felt every time fans head to a home game at the stadium that bears his name, and a scholarship fund continues to give awards at the university in his name.

1962

4-6

Sept. 29	Auburn	Birmingham	L	22-21
Oct. 6	Mississippi State	Memphis	L	7-6
Oct. 13	Georgia Tech	Atlanta	L	17-0
Oct. 20	Alabama	Knoxville	L	27-7
Oct. 27	Chattanooga	Knoxville	W	48-14
Nov. 3	Wake Forest	Knoxville	W	23-0
Nov. 10	Tulane	Knoxville	W	28-16
Nov. 17	Ole Miss	Knoxville	L	19-6
Nov. 24	Kentucky	Knoxville	L	12-10
Dec. 1	Vanderbilt	Nashville	W	30-0
Coach: Bowden Wyatt				179-134

Captain: Pat Augustine
Leaders: Passing: Bobby Morton (20 of 40, 305 yards); Rushing: George Canale (79 carries, 455 yards); Receiving: John Bill Hudson (15 catches, 259 yards).

General Robert R. Neyland died March 28 in New Orleans. The football stadium was renamed in his honor the day of the Alabama game. ... Broadcaster George Mooney essentially created the Volunteer Navy by traveling down the Tennessee River to get to Neyland Stadium. With a new upper deck on the west side, capacity increased to 52,227. ... Steve DeLong was named SEC defensive lineman of the year for the first of three times. ... The Tulane victory was No. 400 in program history.

1963

5-5

Sept. 21	Richmond	Knoxville	W	34-6
Sept. 28	Auburn	Knoxville	L	23-19
Oct. 5	Mississippi State	Knoxville	L	7-0
Oct. 12	Georgia Tech	Knoxville	L	23-7
Oct. 19	Alabama	Birmingham	L	35-0
Oct. 26	Chattanooga	Knoxville	W	49-7
Nov. 9	Tulane	New Orleans	W	26-0
Nov. 16	Ole Miss	Memphis	L	20-0
Nov. 23	Kentucky	Lexington	W	19-0
Nov. 30	Vanderbilt	Knoxville	W	14-0
Coach: Jim McDonald				168-121

Captain: Buddy Fisher
All-American: Steve DeLong
All-SEC (first team): Steve DeLong
Leaders: Passing: Mallon Faircloth (31 of 75, 509 yards); Rushing: Mallon Faircloth (137 carries, 652 yards); Receiving: Buddy Fisher (12 catches, 242 yards).

Jim McDonald, a former Ohio State standout, was an assistant coach under Bowden Wyatt before bring promoted. After one season he became an assistant athletics director.

13

The number of points the Volunteers allowed in their five wins during the 1963 season.

1964
4-5-1

Sept. 19	Chattanooga	Knoxville	W	10-6
Sept. 26	Auburn	Birmingham	L	3-0
Oct. 3	Mississippi State	Memphis	W	14-13
Oct. 10	Boston College	Knoxville	W	16-14
Oct. 17	Alabama	Knoxville	L	19-8
Oct. 24	LSU	Baton Rouge	T	3-3
Nov. 7	Georgia Tech	Atlanta	W	22-14
Nov. 14	Ole Miss	Knoxville	L	30-0
Nov. 21	Kentucky	Knoxville	L	12-7
Nov. 28	Vanderbilt	Nashville	L	7-0
Coach: Doug Dickey				80-121

Captain: Steve DeLong
Major Award: Steve DeLong, Outland Trophy (outstanding interior lineman)
All-American: Steve DeLong
All-SEC (first team): Steve DeLong
Leaders: Passing: Art Galiffa (29 of 59, 338 yards); Rushing: Stan Mitchell (94 carries, 325 yards); Receiving: Hal Wantland (21 catches, 284 yards).

Doug Dickey was hired away from Arkansas with the objective of rebuilding the program. He put the "T" on the football helmets, and the checkerboard pattern first appeared in the end zones against Boston College.

Steve DeLong was not only successful at UT, he also played professionally for the San Diego Chargers. His son, Keith, also played for the Vols.

1965

8-1-2

Sept. 18	Army	Knoxville	W	21-0
Sept. 25	Auburn	Knoxville	T	13-13
Oct. 9	South Carolina	Knoxville	W	24-3
Oct. 16	Alabama	Birmingham	T	7-7
Oct. 23	Houston	Knoxville	W	17-8
Nov. 6	Georgia Tech	Knoxville	W	21-7
Nov. 13	Ole Miss	Memphis	L	14-13
Nov. 20	Kentucky	Lexington	W	19-3
Nov. 27	Vanderbilt	Knoxville	W	21-3
Dec. 4	UCLA	Memphis	W	37-34
Dec. 18	Tulsa	Bluebonnet Bowl	W	27-6
Coach: Doug Dickey				220-98

Captain: Hal Wantland
Ranking (AP): Preseason NR; Postseason No. 7
All-American: Frank Emanuel
All-SEC (first team): Frank Emanuel, Bobby Frazier
Leaders: Passing: Dewey Warren (44 of 79, 588 yards); Rushing: Walter Chadwick (101 carries, 470 yards); Receiving: Johnny Mills (23 catches, 328 yards).

Linebacker Frank Emanuel's career came to a close. In addition to being heavily involved in his community, he went on to become president of the NFL and University of Tennessee alumni associations. Against Kentucky, he picked up a guard's movement that tipped off the plays and made 26 tackles. ... Although it had been nine years since Tennessee had an eight-win season, the Volunteers enjoyed the first of five straight. ... Against Army, the team ran through the marching band's "T" formation for the first time.

Richmond Flowers was one of the most unique athletes
to attend Tennessee. A world-class hurdler and renowned
speedster, he was an All-American on the gridiron and
came within one-tenth of a second of three world records
on the track.

1966

8-3

Sept. 24	Auburn	Birmingham	W	28-0
Oct. 1	Rice	Knoxville	W	23-3
Oct. 8	Georgia Tech	Atlanta	L	6-3
Oct. 15	Alabama	Knoxville	L	11-10
Oct. 22	South Carolina	Knoxville	W	29-17
Oct. 29	Army	Memphis	W	38-7
Nov. 5	Chattanooga	Knoxville	W	28-10
Nov. 12	Ole Miss	Knoxville	L	14-7
Nov. 19	Kentucky	Knoxville	W	28-19
Nov. 26	Vanderbilt	Nashville	W	28-0
Dec. 31	Syracuse	Gator Bowl	W	18-12
Coach: Doug Dickey				240-99

Captains: Austin Denney, Paul Naumoff
Ranking (AP): Preseason No. 10; Postseason NR
All-American: Paul Naumoff, Austin Denney, Ron Widby, Bob Johnson
All-SEC (first team): Austin Denney, Bob Johnson, Johnny Mills, Paul Naumoff
Leaders: Passing: Dewey Warren (136 of 229, 1,716 yards); Rushing: Charlie Fulton (109 yards, 463 carries); Receiving: Johnny Mills (48 catches, 725 yards).

The College Football Hall of Fame lists center Bob Johnson's accomplishments as: in high school, team captain, honor student, Eagle Scout; in college, team captain, unanimous All-America, National Football Foundation Scholar Athlete, winner of the Jacobs Trophy as Southeastern Conference's best blocker; in pro football, first draft choice of the Cincinnati Bengals, team captain 11 years. Johnson played 1965-67, while brothers Tom (1970-72), and Paul (1973-75) also played center for the Volunteers. ... UT defeated Syracuse, with Larry Csonka and Floyd Little, in the Gator Bowl.

1967

9-2, National champions (non-consensus),
SEC champions

Sept. 16	UCLA	Los Angeles	L	20-16
Sept. 30	Auburn	Knoxville	W	27-13
Oct. 14	Georgia Tech	Knoxville	W	24-13
Oct. 21	Alabama	Birmingham	W	24-13
Oct. 28	LSU	Knoxville	W	17-14
Nov. 4	Tampa	Tampa	W	38-0
Nov. 11	Tulane	Knoxville	W	35-14
Nov. 18	Ole Miss	Memphis	W	20-7
Nov. 25	Kentucky	Lexington	W	17-7
Dec. 2	Vanderbilt	Knoxville	W	41-14
Jan. 1	Oklahoma	Orange Bowl	L	26-24
Coach: Doug Dickey				283-141

Captain: Bob Johnson
Ranking (AP): Preseason No. 9; Postseason No. 2
All-American: Bob Johnson, Albert Dorsey, Richmond Flowers
All-SEC (first team): John Boynton, Albert Dorsey, Bob Johnson, Charles Rosenfelder
Leaders: Passing: Dewey Warren (78 of 132, 1,053 yards); Rushing: Walter Chadwick (144 carries, 645 yards); Receiving: Richmond Flowers (41 catches, 585 yards).

Litkenhous had Tennessee No. 1 at the end of the regular season. Southern California was the consensus national champion. ... Center Bob Johnson won the Jacobs Trophy as the SEC's best blocker and finished sixth in voting for the Heisman Trophy. His No. 54 was the first retired jersey in Cincinnati Bengals history. ... UT defeated Alabama for the first time since 1960, and Ole Miss for the first time since 1958. ... The win against Vanderbilt was the last game played on grass at Neyland Stadium until 1994. ... Oklahoma scored the game-winning points on an interception return for a touchdown.

1968

8-2-1

Sept. 14	Georgia	Knoxville	T	17-17
Sept. 28	Memphis State	Knoxville	W	24-17
Oct. 5	Rice	Houston	W	52-0
Oct. 12	Georgia Tech	Atlanta	W	24-7
Oct. 19	Alabama	Knoxville	W	10-9
Nov. 2	UCLA	Knoxville	W	42-18
Nov. 9	Auburn	Birmingham	L	28-14
Nov. 16	Ole Miss	Knoxville	W	31-0
Nov. 23	Kentucky	Knoxville	W	24-7
Nov. 30	Vanderbilt	Nashville	W	10-7
Jan. 1	Texas	Cotton Bowl	L	36-13
Coach: Doug Dickey				261-146

Captain: Dick Williams
Ranking (AP): Preseason No. 9; Postseason No. 13
All-American: Charles Rosenfelder, Steve Kiner, Jim Weatherford
All-SEC (first team): Ken DeLong, Chip Kell, Steve Kiner, Richard Pickens, Charles Rosenfelder, Jim Weatherford
Leaders: Passing: Bubba Wyche (134 of 237, 1,539 yards); Rushing: Richard Pickens (133 carries, 736 yards); Receiving: Ken DeLong (34 catches, 393 yards).

Tennessee played its first game on Tartan Turf at Neyland Stadium against Georgia. The game also featured UT's first black player, Lester McClain. ... Led by linebacker Steve Kiner, the Volunteers set a school record by holding opponents to an average of 93 rushing yards a game. ... Memphis was known as Memphis State from 1912-1993. ... With the 6,307-seat upper-deck addition on the east side, capacity was increased to 64,429. ... Texas jumped out to a 28-0 lead and tallied 513 yards of total offense in the Cotton Bowl.

1969

9-2, SEC champions

Sept. 20	Tenn.-Chattanooga	Knoxville	W	31-0
Sept. 27	Auburn	Knoxville	W	45-19
Oct. 4	Memphis State	Memphis	W	55-16
Oct. 11	Georgia Tech	Knoxville	W	26-8
Oct. 18	Alabama	Birmingham	W	41-14
Nov. 1	Georgia	Athens	W	17-3
Nov. 8	South Carolina	Knoxville	W	29-14
Nov. 15	Ole Miss	Jackson	L	38-0
Nov. 22	Kentucky	Lexington	W	31-26
Nov. 29	Vanderbilt	Knoxville	W	40-27
Dec. 27	Florida	Gator Bowl	L	14-13
Coach: Doug Dickey				328-179

Captain: Bill Young
Ranking (AP): Preseason No. 15; Postseason No. 15
All-American: Steve Kiner, Chip Kell, Jack Reynolds
All-SEC (first team): Ken DeLong, Chip Kell, Steve Kiner, Jack Reynolds, Curt Watson, Frank Yanossy
Leaders: Passing: Bobby Scott (92 of 191, 1,352 yards); Rushing: Curt Watson (146 carries, 807 yards); Receiving: Gary Kreis (38 catches, 609 yards).

Doug Dickey (46-15-4), a former Florida quarter-back, returned to his alma mater as head coach. ... Linebacker Steve Kiner had five sacks, 16 tackles, four hurries, an interception, and a forced fumble against Alabama. "I'll remember that day for the rest of my life," he said. ... A blocked punt returned for a touchdown keyed Florida's win in the Gator Bowl, when Tennessee couldn't score inside the 10-yard line.

Conrad Graham and Tim Priest try to coax a wayward dog off the field during the 1970 Sugar Bowl. The brief delay did not slow down the Volunteers, who rolled to a 34-13 win over Air Force.

1970
11-1

Sept. 19	SMU	Knoxville	W	28-3
Sept. 26	Auburn	Birmingham	L	36-23
Oct. 3	Army	Knoxville	W	48-3
Oct. 10	Georgia Tech	Atlanta	W	17-6
Oct. 17	Alabama	Knoxville	W	24-0
Oct. 24	Florida	Knoxville	W	38-7
Oct. 31	Wake Forest	Memphis	W	41-7
Nov. 7	South Carolina	Columbia	W	20-18
Nov. 21	Kentucky	Knoxville	W	45-0
Nov. 28	Vanderbilt	Nashville	W	24-6
Dec. 5	UCLA	Knoxville	W	28-17
Jan. 1	Air Force	Sugar Bowl	W	34-13
Coach: Bill Battle				370-116

Captain: Tim Priest
Ranking (AP): Preseason NR; Postseason No. 4
All-American: Chip Kell, Jackie Walker
All-SEC (first team): Mike Bevans, Chip Kell, Bobby Majors, Tim Priest, Jackie Walker, Curt Watson
Leaders: Passing: Bobby Scott (118 of 252, 1,697 yards); Rushing: Curt Watson (190 carries, 791 yards); Receiving: Joe Thompson (37 catches, 502 yards).

Tennessee scored 24points in the first quarter of the Sugar Bowl. Don McLeary scored two touchdowns while Air Force was held to minus-12 rushing yards. ... Guard Chip Kell won his second consecutive Jacobs Memorial Award as the top blocker in the Southeastern Conference. ... At age 28, Bill Battle was the youngest coach in the nation. ... Tim Priest finished his career with 18 interceptions.

1971
10-2

Sept. 18	UC-Santa Barbara	Knoxville	W	48-6
Sept. 25	Auburn	Knoxville	L	10-9
Oct. 2	Florida	Gainesville	W	20-13
Oct. 9	Georgia Tech	Knoxville	W	10-6
Oct. 16	Alabama	Birmingham	L	32-15
Oct. 23	Mississippi State	Memphis	W	10-7
Oct. 30	Tulsa	Knoxville	W	38-3
Nov. 6	South Carolina	Knoxville	W	35-6
Nov. 20	Kentucky	Lexington	W	21-7
Nov. 27	Vanderbilt	Knoxville	W	19-7
Dec. 4	Penn State	Knoxville	W	31-11
Dec. 20	Arkansas	Liberty Bowl	W	14-13
Coach: Bill Battle				270-121

Captain: Jackie Walker
Ranking (AP): Preseason No. 8; Postseason No. 9
All-American: Bobby Majors, Jackie Walker
All-SEC (first team): George Hunt, Ray Nettles, Bobby Majors, Jackie Walker, Curt Watson
Leaders: Passing: Jim Maxwell (46 of 102, 544 yards); Rushing: Curt Watson (193 carries, 766 yards); Receiving: Joe Thompson (15 catches, 247 yards).

Tennessee played Arkansas for the first time since 1907. Curt Watson's 17-yard touchdown run set up the game-winning extra point. ... The defense set NCAA records for most interception yards returned (782), highest average per interception return (31.1), and most touchdowns by interception returns (7). Cornerback Conrad Graham led the unit with five picks for 148 yards.

1972
10-2

Sept. 9	Georgia Tech	Atlanta	W	34-3
Sept. 16	Penn State	Knoxville	W	28-21
Sept. 23	Wake Forest	Knoxville	W	45-6
Sept. 30	Auburn	Birmingham	L	10-6
Oct. 7	Memphis State	Memphis	W	38-7
Oct. 21	Alabama	Knoxville	L	17-10
Oct. 28	Hawaii	Knoxville	W	34-2
Nov. 4	Georgia	Athens	W	14-0
Nov. 18	Ole Miss	Knoxville	W	17-0
Nov. 25	Kentucky	Knoxville	W	17-7
Dec. 2	Vanderbilt	Nashville	W	30-10
Dec. 30	LSU	Bluebonnet Bowl	W	24-17
Coach: Bill Battle				297-100

Through the Years

Captain: Jamie Rotella
Ranking (AP): Preseason No. 15; Postseason No. 8
All-American: Conrad Graham, Ricky Townsend, Jamie Rotella
All-SEC (first team): Bill Emendorfer, Conrad Graham, Jamie Rotella, Ricky Townsend, John Wagster
Leaders: Passing: Condredge Holloway (73 of 120, 807 yards); Rushing: Haskel Stanback (183 carries, 890 yards); Receiving: Emmon Love (20 catches, 280 yards).

The victory against Penn State was the first night game played at Neyland Stadium. ... Although not the official fight song, "Rocky Top" was played at a game for the first time. ... Another 6,221 seats were added in the southwest corner, bumping capacity to 70,650. ... Because of his creative play, quarterback Condredge Holloway became known as "The Artful Dodger." He completed 11 of 19 passes for 94 yards and ran for 74 yards on 19 carries against LSU in the Bluebonnet Bowl.

1973
8-4

Sept. 15	Duke	Knoxville	W	21-17
Sept. 22	Army	West Point	W	37-18
Sept. 29	Auburn	Knoxville	W	21-0
Oct. 6	Kansas	Memphis	W	28-27
Oct. 13	Georgia Tech	Knoxville	W	20-14
Oct. 20	Alabama	Birmingham	L	42-21
Oct. 27	Texas Christian	Knoxville	W	39-7
Nov. 3	Georgia	Knoxville	L	35-31
Nov. 17	Ole Miss	Jackson	L	28-18
Nov. 24	Kentucky	Lexington	W	16-14
Dec. 1	Vanderbilt	Knoxville	W	20-17
Dec. 29	Texas Tech	Gator Bowl	L	28-19
Coach: Bill Battle				291-247

Captain: Eddie Brown
Ranking (AP): Preseason No. 9; Postseason No. 19
All-American: Eddie Brown, Ricky Townsend
All-SEC (first team): Eddie Brown, Condredge Holloway
Leaders: Passing: Condredge Holloway (89 of 154, 1,149 yards); Rushing: Haskel Stanback (165 carries, 682 yards); Receiving: Stanley Morgan (22 catches, 511 yards).

The Red Raiders scored a touchdown in each quarter and accumulated 276 rushing yards on 55 carries in the Gator Bowl. ... At Pitt, former UT standout Johnny Majors began to turn the Panthers around, going 6-4-1 with a trip to the Fiesta Bowl. He was named national coach of the year. ... Tennessee was No. 14 in the final coaches' poll.

Ronnie McCarthey was able to snag Texas Tech's Larry Issac on this play during the 1973 Gator Bowl, but the Volunteers struggled to slow the Red Raiders' rushing assault. Tech rushed for 276 yards in a game that capped off an uninspiring 8-4 season.

Walter White of Maryland failed to haul in this pass in the waning moments of the 1974 Liberty Bowl. Ernie Ward intercepted the pass with one second left on the clock to seal the Volunteers' 7-3 win.

1974

7-3-2

Sept. 7	UCLA	Knoxville	T	17-17
Sept. 21	Kansas	Knoxville	W	17-3
Sept. 28	Auburn	Auburn	L	21-0
Oct. 5	Tulsa	Knoxville	W	17-10
Oct. 12	LSU	Baton Rouge	L	20-10
Oct. 19	Alabama	Knoxville	L	28-6
Oct. 26	Clemson	Knoxville	W	29-28
Nov. 9	Memphis State	Knoxville	W	34-6
Nov. 16	Ole Miss	Memphis	W	29-17
Nov. 23	Kentucky	Knoxville	W	24-7
Nov. 30	Vanderbilt	Nashville	T	21-21
Dec. 16	Maryland	Liberty Bowl	W	7-3
Coach: Bill Battle				211-181

Captains: Condredge Holloway, Jim Watts
Ranking (AP): Preseason No. 16; Postseason No. 20
All-SEC (first team): Neil Clabo, Mickey Marvin, Stanley Morgan
Leaders: Passing: Condredge Holloway (76 of 133, 1,146 yards); Rushing: Stanley Morgan (128 carries, 723 yards); Receiving: Larry Seivers (25 catches, 347 yards).
Subbing for injured quarterback Condredge Holloway, sophomore Randy Wallace threw an 11-yard touchdown pass to Larry Seivers with 2:44 remaining in the Liberty Bowl. Mike Gayles gained 106 yards on 17 carries, while the defense led by Reggie White and Ron McCartney only yielded a field goal. ... Tennessee was No. 15 in the final coaches' poll.

1975
7-5

Sept. 13	Maryland	Knoxville	W	26-8
Sept. 20	UCLA	Los Angeles	L	34-28
Sept. 27	Auburn	Knoxville	W	21-17
Oct. 11	LSU	Knoxville	W	24-10
Oct. 18	Alabama	Birmingham	L	30-7
Oct. 25	North Texas State	Knoxville	L	21-14
Nov. 1	Colorado State	Knoxville	W	28-7
Nov. 8	Utah	Knoxville	W	40-7
Nov. 15	Ole Miss	Memphis	L	23-6
Nov. 22	Kentucky	Lexington	W	17-13
Nov. 29	Vanderbilt	Knoxville	L	17-14
Dec. 6	Hawaii	Honolulu	W	28-6
Coach: Bill Battle				253-193

Captain: Ron McCartney
Ranking (AP): Preseason No. 18; Postseason NR
All-American: Larry Seivers
All-SEC (first team): Mickey Marvin, Mike Mauck, Ron McCartney, Larry Seivers, Andy Spiva
Leaders: Passing: Randy Wallace (72 of 145, 1,318 yards); Rushing: Stanley Morgan (133 carries, 809 yards); Receiving: Larry Seivers (41 catches, 840 yards).

The victory at Kentucky was No. 500 in program history. ... Future head coach Lane Monte Kiffin was born May 9.

1976
6-5

Sept. 11	Duke	Knoxville	L	21-18
Sept. 18	Texas Christian	Knoxville	W	31-0
Sept. 25	Auburn	Birmingham	L	38-28
Oct. 2	Clemson	Knoxville	W	21-19
Oct. 9	Georgia Tech	Atlanta	W	42-7
Oct. 16	Alabama	Knoxville	L	20-13
Oct. 23	Florida	Knoxville	L	20-18
Nov. 6	Memphis State	Memphis	W	21-14
Nov. 13	Ole Miss	Knoxville	W	32-6
Nov. 20	Kentucky	Knoxville	L	7-0
Nov. 27	Vanderbilt	Nashville	W	13-10
Coach: Bill Battle				237-162

Captains: Larry Seivers, Andy Spiva
All-American: Larry Seivers
All-SEC (first team): Craig Colquitt, Mickey Marvin, Stanley Morgan, Larry Seivers, Andy Spiva
Leaders: Passing: Randy Wallace (68 of 130, 1,046 yards); Rushing: (Bobby Emmons 75 carries, 462 yards); Receiving: Larry Seivers (51 catches, 737 yards).

Bill Battle's last season left him with in a 59-22-2 record at Tennessee.

Bill Battle's age when he became the Tennessee coach. He was the youngest coach in college football at the time, and guided the Vols to three top-10 finishes.

1977

4-7

Sept. 10	California	Knoxville	L	27-17
Sept. 17	Boston College	Knoxville	W	24-18
Sept. 24	Auburn	Knoxville	L	14-12
Oct. 1	Oregon State	Knoxville	W	41-10
Oct. 8	Georgia Tech	Knoxville	L	24-8
Oct. 15	Alabama	Birmingham	L	24-10
Oct. 22	Florida	Gainesville	L	27-17
Nov. 5	Memphis State	Knoxville	W	27-14
Nov. 12	Ole Miss	Memphis	L	43-14
Nov. 19	Kentucky	Lexington	L	21-17
Nov. 26	Vanderbilt	Knoxville	W	42-7

Coach: Johnny Majors   229-229

Captains: Pert Jenkins, Greg Jones, Brent Watson
All-SEC (first team): Craig Colquitt, Robert Shaw
Leaders: Passing: Jimmy Streater (59 of 105, 742 yards); Rushing: Kelsey Finch (154 carries, 770 yards); Receiving: Reggie Harper (30 catches, 331 yards).

A former All-America tailback, Johnny Majors returned to his alma mater after guiding Pittsburgh to the 1976 national championship. The rallying cry was "Follow me to Tennessee." ... Kelsey Finch tied an NCAA record with a 99-yard touchdown run against Florida.

When Johnny Majors lost out on the Heisman Trophy to Notre Dame's Paul Hornung, he became a footnote in college football lore. Hornung's win is to date the only Heisman Trophy awarded to a player on a losing team.

1978
5-5-1

Sept. 16	UCLA	Knoxville	L	13-0
Sept. 23	Oregon State	Knoxville	T	13-13
Sept. 30	Auburn	Birmingham	L	29-10
Oct. 7	Army	Knoxville	W	31-13
Oct. 21	Alabama	Knoxville	L	30-17
Oct. 28	Mississippi State	Memphis	L	34-21
Nov. 4	Duke	Knoxville	W	34-0
Nov. 11	Notre Dame	South Bend	L	31-14
Nov. 18	Ole Miss	Knoxville	W	41-17
Nov. 25	Kentucky	Knoxville	W	29-14
Dec. 2	Vanderbilt	Nashville	W	41-15
Coach: Johnny Majors				251-209

Captains: Robert Shaw, Dennis Wolfe
All-SEC (first team): Roland James, Robert Shaw
Leaders: Passing: Jimmy Streater (101 of 198, 1,418 yards); Rushing: Jimmy Streater (146 carries, 593 yards); Receiving: Reggie Harper (31 catches, 356 yards).

1979
7-5

Sept. 15	Boston College	Boston	W	28-16
Sept. 22	Utah	Knoxville	W	51-18
Sept. 29	Auburn	Knoxville	W	35-17
Oct. 6	Mississippi State	Memphis	L	28-9
Oct. 13	Georgia Tech	Knoxville	W	31-0
Oct. 20	Alabama	Birmingham	L	27-17
Nov. 3	Rutgers	Knoxville	L	13-7
Nov. 10	Notre Dame	Knoxville	W	40-18
Nov. 17	Ole Miss	Jackson	L	44-20
Nov. 24	Kentucky	Lexington	W	20-17
Dec. 1	Vanderbilt	Knoxville	W	31-10
Dec. 31	Purdue	Bluebonnet Bowl	L	27-22
Coach: Johnny Majors				311-235

Through the Years

Johnny Majors spent much of 1976 deflecting media
questions about returning to Tennessee while leading the
Pitt Panthers to a national championship. Majors coached
at UT from 1977-1992 before giving way to Phillip Fulmer.
He coached four more years at Pitt before retiring.

Captains: Roland James, Craig Puki, Jimmy Streater
All-American: Roland James
All-SEC (first team): Reggie Harper, Roland James, Craig Puki, Jimmy Streater.
Leaders: Passing: Jimmy Streater (80 of 161, 1,256 yards); Rushing: Hubert Simpson (157 carries, 792 yards); Receiving: Anthony Hancock (34 catches, 687 yards).

Tennessee was trailing 21-0 in the third quarter, but saw its comeback in the bluebonnet Bowl fall short when Purdue quarterback Mark Herrmann threw a game-winning 17-yard touchdown pass to Charley Young with 1:30 remaining. Quarterback Jimmy Streater had 270 yards passing and rushing, but also had three interceptions.

1980
5-6

Sept. 6	Georgia	Knoxville	L	16-15
Sept. 13	Southern California	Knoxville	L	20-17
Sept. 20	Washington State	Knoxville	W	35-23
Sept. 27	Auburn	Auburn	W	42-0
Oct. 11	Georgia Tech	Atlanta	W	23-10
Oct. 18	Alabama	Knoxville	L	27-0
Oct. 25	Pittsburgh	Knoxville	L	30-6
Nov. 1	Virginia	Knoxville	L	16-13
Nov. 15	Ole Miss	Memphis	L	20-9
Nov. 22	Kentucky	Knoxville	W	45-14
Nov. 29	Vanderbilt	Nashville	W	51-13
Coach: Johnny Majors				256-189

Captain: Jim Noonan
All-SEC (first team): Tim Irwin, Jim Noonan, Lee North
Leaders: Passing: Steve Alatorre (58 of 119, 747 yards); Rushing: James Berry (131 carries, 543 yards); Receiving: Anthony Hancock (33 catches, 580 yards).

Neyland Stadium was expanded again, and 95,288 were onhand for the season-opening loss to Georgia, which went on to win the national championship.

1981

8-4

Sept. 5	Georgia	Athens	L	44-0
Sept. 12	Southern California	Los Angeles	L	43-7
Sept. 19	Colorado State	Knoxville	W	42-0
Sept. 26	Auburn	Knoxville	W	10-7
Oct. 10	Georgia Tech	Knoxville	W	10-7
Oct. 17	Alabama	Birmingham	L	38-19
Oct. 24	Memphis State	Memphis	W	28-9
Nov. 7	Wichita State	Knoxville	W	24-21
Nov. 14	Ole Miss	Knoxville	W	28-20
Nov. 21	Kentucky	Lexington	L	21-10
Nov. 28	Vanderbilt	Knoxville	W	38-34
Dec. 13	Wisconsin	Garden State Bowl	W	28-21
Coach: Johnny Majors				244-265

Captains: James Berry, Lemont Holt Jeffers, Lee North
All-SEC (first team): Lee North
Leaders: Passing: Steve Alatorre (58 of 119, 747 yards); Rushing: James Stewart (190 carries, 939 yards); Receiving: Anthony Hancock (32 catches, 437 yards).

Steve Alatorre completed 24 of 42 passes for a career-high 315 yards and one touchdown in the Garden State Bowl. Wide receiver Anthony Hancock made 11 catches for 196 yards, including a 43-yard touchdown.

16

The number of years former Heisman Trophy runner-up Johnny Majors coached at Tennessee.

Lemont Holt Jeffers pressures USC's John Mazur during the Volunteers' 1981 game in Los Angeles. This two-point conversion was unsuccessful, but the Trojans won big, 43-7.

1982

6-5-1

Sept. 4	Duke	Knoxville	L	25-24
Sept. 11	Iowa State	Knoxville	W	23-21
Sept. 25	Auburn	Auburn	L	24-14
Oct. 2	Washington State	Knoxville	W	10-3
Oct. 9	LSU	Baton Rouge	T	24-24
Oct. 16	Alabama	Knoxville	W	35-28
Oct. 23	Georgia Tech	Atlanta	L	31-21
Nov. 6	Memphis State	Knoxville	W	29-3
Nov. 13	Ole Miss	Jackson	W	30-17
Nov. 20	Kentucky	Knoxville	W	28-7
Nov. 27	Vanderbilt	Nashville	L	28-21
Dec. 31	Iowa	Peach Bowl	L	28-22

Coach: Johnny Majors   281-239

Captain: Mike L. Cofer
All-American: Willie Gault, Jimmy Colquitt
All-SEC (first team): Willie Gault, Fuad Reveiz
Leaders: Passing: Alan Cockrell (174 of 294, 2,021 yards); Rushing: Chuck Coleman (113 carries, 600 yards); Receiving: Willie Gault (50 catches, 668 yards).

With the World's Fair in the background, Tennessee defeated Alabama for the first time since 1970. Crimson Tide coach Paul W. "Bear" Bryant died January 26, 1983. ... Jimmy Colquitt averaged 46.9 yards per punt, and finished with a career average of 43.9. ... Quarterback Alan Cockrell, and running backs Chuck Coleman and Doug Furnas led a fierce comeback against Iowa in the Peach Bowl, but UT was stopped at the Iowa 7 in the final moments.

Fuad Reveiz made eight field goals 50 yards or longer during the 1982 season.

1983
9-3

Sept. 3	Pittsburgh	Knoxville	L	13-3
Sept. 10	New Mexico	Knoxville	W	31-6
Sept. 24	Auburn	Knoxville	L	37-14
Oct. 1	The Citadel	Memphis	W	45-6
Oct. 8	LSU	Knoxville	W	20-6
Oct. 15	Alabama	Birmingham	W	41-34
Oct. 22	Georgia Tech	Knoxville	W	37-3
Oct. 29	Rutgers East	Rutherford	W	7-0
Nov. 12	Ole Miss	Knoxville	L	13-10
Nov. 19	Kentucky	Lexington	W	10-0
Nov. 26	Vanderbilt	Knoxville	W	34-24
Dec. 17	Maryland	Florida Citrus Bowl	W	30-23
Coach: Johnny Majors				282-165

Through the Years

Captain: Reggie White
All-American: Reggie White, Jimmy Colquitt
All-SEC (first team): Johnnie Jones, Bill Mayo, Glenn Streno, Reggie White
Leaders: Passing: Alan Cockrell (128 of 243, 1,683 yards); Rushing: Johnnie Jones (191 carries, 1,116 yards); Receiving: Clyde Duncan (33 catches, 640 yards).

Defensive tackle Reggie White finished his career with Tennessee records for sacks in a game (four), season (15), and career (32). He also accumulated 201 unassisted tackles, 92 assists, and four fumble recoveries. ... A 66-yard carry by Johnnie Jones keyed the win against Alabama, and he also had 154 rushing yards on 29 carries in the Florida Citrus Bowl. Alvin Toles recovered a fumble and intercepted a pass, both leading to scores.

1984

7-4-1

Sept. 1	Washington State	Knoxville	W	34-27
Sept. 15	Utah	Knoxville	W	27-21
Sept. 22	Army	Knoxville	T	24-24
Sept. 29	Auburn	Auburn	L	29-10
Oct. 13	Florida	Knoxville	L	43-30
Oct. 20	Alabama	Knoxville	W	28-27
Oct. 27	Georgia Tech	Atlanta	W	24-21
Nov. 10	Memphis State	Knoxville	W	41-9
Nov. 17	Ole Miss	Jackson	W	41-17
Nov. 24	Kentucky	Knoxville	L	17-12
Dec. 1	Vanderbilt	Nashville	W	29-13
Dec. 22	Maryland	Sun Bowl	L	28-27
Coach: Johnny Majors				327-276

Captains: Johnnie Jones, Carl Zander
All-American: Bill Mayo
All-SEC (first team): Johnnie Jones, Bill Mayo, Tony Robinson
Leaders: Passing: Tony Robinson (156 of 253, 1,963 yards); Rushing: Johnnie Jones (229 carries, 1,290 yards); Receiving: Tim McGee (54 catches, 809 yards).

Tennessee blew a 21-point lead in the Sun Bowl, and Maryland secured the victory with a last-minute fumble forced by defensive back Keeta Covington from quarterback Tony Robinson. ... After 30 years as an assistant coach, former Tennessee halfback George Cafego retired. ... UT rallied from a 27-13 deficit to beat Alabama.

1985

9-1-2, SEC champions

Sept. 14	UCLA	Knoxville	T	26-26
Sept. 28	Auburn	Knoxville	W	38-20
Oct. 5	Wake Forest	Knoxville	W	31-29
Oct. 12	Florida	Gainesville	L	17-10
Oct. 19	Alabama	Birmingham	W	16-14
Oct. 26	Georgia Tech	Knoxville	T	6-6
Nov. 2	Rutgers	Knoxville	W	40-0
Nov. 9	Memphis State	Memphis	W	17-7
Nov. 16	Ole Miss	Knoxville	W	34-14
Nov. 23	Kentucky	Lexington	W	42-0
Nov. 30	Vanderbilt	Knoxville	W	30-0
Jan. 1	Miami (Fla.)	Sugar Bowl	W	35-7
Coach: Johnny Majors				325-140

Through the Years

**Captains: Tim McGee, Tommy Sims, Chris White
Ranking (AP): Preseason NR; Postseason No. 4
All-American: Tim McGee, Chris White
All-SEC (first team): Dale Jones, Tim McGee,
Carlos Reveiz, Chris White, Bruce Wilkerson
Leaders: Passing: Tony Robinson (91 of 143,
1,246 yards); Rushing: Keith Davis (141 carries,
684 yards); Receiving: Tim McGee (50 catches,
947 yards).**

**Tennessee defeated No. 1 Auburn en route to
the SEC championship. ... After starting quarterback Tony Robinson sustained a knee injury against
Alabama and was lost for the season, Daryl Dickey
(former coach Doug Dickey's son) stepped in and
didn't have a loss the rest of the season. ... UT
scored 35 unanswered points against Miami in the
Sugar Bowl. The Vols created six turnovers, seven
sacks, and five tackles for a loss, among them Tim
McGee's fumble recovery in the end zone.**

Keith Davis searches for daylight in the 1986 Liberty Bowl
win over Minnesota. Davis failed to reach the end zone,
but Jeff Francis threw for three touchdowns in Tennessee's 21-14 win.

TENNESSEE FOOTBALL

1986
7-5

Sept. 6	New Mexico	Knoxville	W	35-21
Sept. 13	Mississippi State	Knoxville	L	27-23
Sept. 27	Auburn	Auburn	L	34-8
Oct. 4	Texas-El Paso	Knoxville	W	26-16
Oct. 11	Army	Knoxville	L	25-21
Oct. 18	Alabama	Knoxville	L	56-28
Oct. 25	Georgia Tech	Atlanta	L	14-13
Nov. 8	Memphis State	Knoxville	W	33-3
Nov. 15	Ole Miss	Jackson	W	22-10
Nov. 22	Kentucky	Knoxville	W	28-9
Nov. 29	Vanderbilt	Nashville	W	35-20
Dec. 29	Minnesota	Liberty Bowl	W	21-14
Coach: Johnny Majors				293-249

Captains: Joey Clinkscales, Dale Jones, Bruce Wilkerson
Ranking (AP): Preseason No. 10; Postseason NR
All-SEC (first team): Dale Jones, Bruce Wilkerson
Leaders: Passing: Jeff Francis (150 of 233, 1,946 yards); Rushing: William Howard (177 carries, 787 yards); Receiving: Joey Clinkscales (37 catches, 511 yards).

Jeff Francis threw three touchdown passes against Minnesota in the Liberty Bowl, two to wide receiver Joey Clinkscales, the other to fullback William Howard.

All three captains from the 1986 Volunteers went on to be drafted into the NFL. They were joined on Draft Day by kicker Carlos Reveiz.

1987

10-2-1

Aug. 30	Iowa	East Rutherford	W	23-22
Sept. 5	Colorado State	Knoxville	W	49-3
Sept. 12	Mississippi State	Starkville	W	38-10
Sept. 26	Auburn	Knoxville	T	20-20
Oct. 3	California	Knoxville	W	38-12
Oct. 17	Alabama	Birmingham	L	41-22
Oct. 24	Georgia Tech	Knoxville	W	29-15
Oct. 31	Boston College	Boston	L	20-18
Nov. 7	Louisville	Knoxville	W	41-10
Nov. 14	Ole Miss	Knoxville	W	55-13
Nov. 21	Kentucky	Lexington	W	24-22
Nov. 28	Vanderbilt	Knoxville	W	38-36
Jan. 2	Indiana	Peach Bowl	W	27-22
Coach: Johnny Majors				422-246

Captains: Harry Galbreath, Kelly Ziegler
Ranking (AP): Preseason No. 17; Postseason No. 14
All-American: Harry Galbreath
All-SEC (first team): Harry Galbreath, Mark Hovanic, Terry McDaniel
Leaders: Passing: Jeff Francis (191 of 314, 2,237 yards); Rushing: Reggie Cobb (237 carries, 1,197 yards); Receiving: Thomas Woods (26 catches, 335 yards).

Tennessee took a 21-3 lead early in the second quarter of the Peach Bowl, but needed a 9-yard touchdown pass from Jeff Francis to Reggie Cobb to win. Charles Kimbrough sealed the victory with an interception. ... The season opener against Iowa was the Kickoff Classic.

1988

5-6

Sept. 3	Georgia	Athens	L	28-17
Sept. 10	Duke	Knoxville	L	31-26
Sept. 17	LSU	Knoxville	L	34-9
Sept. 24	Auburn	Auburn	L	38-6
Oct. 1	Washington State	Knoxville	L	52-24
Oct. 15	Alabama	Knoxville	L	28-20
Oct. 22	Memphis State	Memphis	W	38-25
Nov. 5	Boston College	Knoxville	W	10-7
Nov. 12	Ole Miss	Oxford	W	20-12
Nov. 19	Kentucky	Knoxville	W	28-24
Nov. 26	Vanderbilt	Nashville	W	14-7

Coach Johnny Majors   212-286

Captains: Keith DeLong, Nate Middlebrooks
Ranking (AP): Preseason No. 17; Postseason NR
All-American: Keith DeLong
All-SEC (first team): Keith DeLong, Eric Still
Leaders: Passing: Jeff Francis (191 of 314, 2,237 yards); Rushing: Reggie Cobb (118 carries, 547 yards); Receiving: Thomas Woods (58 catches, 689 yards).

The last season of artificial turf at Neyland Stadium was unkind to the Volunteers, though their five-game winning streak to close the season jump-started what became a 10-game winning streak.

1989

11-1, SEC champions

Sept. 2	Colorado State	Knoxville	W	17-14
Sept. 9	UCLA	Pasadena	W	24-6
Sept. 16	Duke	Knoxville	W	28-6
Sept. 30	Auburn	Knoxville	W	21-14
Oct. 7	Georgia	Knoxville	W	17-14
Oct. 21	Alabama	Birmingham	L	47-30
Oct. 28	LSU	Baton Rouge	W	45-39
Nov. 11	Akron	Knoxville	W	52-9
Nov. 18	Ole Miss	Knoxville	W	33-21
Nov. 25	Kentucky	Lexington	W	31-10
Dec. 2	Vanderbilt	Knoxville	W	17-10
Jan. 1	Arkansas	Cotton Bowl	W	31-27

Coach: Johnny Majors 346-217

Captain: Eric Still
Ranking (AP): Preseason NR; Postseason No. 5
All-American: Eric Still
All-SEC (first team): Antone Davis, Kent Elmore, Marion Hobby, Eric Still, Chuck Webb
Leaders: Passing: Andy Kelly (92 of 156, 1,299 yards); Rushing: Chuck Webb (209 carries, 1,236 yards); Receiving: Thomas Woods (34 catches, 511 yards).

Coming off a 5-6 season, Tennessee was the most improved team in the country. ... Tifway 419 hybrid-Bermuda grass was installed and the checkerboard end zones returned to Neyland Stadium. ... The Cotton Bowl victory was No. 600 in program history. ... Chuck Webb gained 250 rushing yards on 26 carries and scored twice against Arkansas. Webb's 294 rushing yards against Ole Miss set a school record.

1990

9-2-2, SEC champions

Aug. 26	Colorado	Anaheim	T	31-31
Sept. 1	Pacific	Knoxville	W	55-7
Sept. 8	Mississippi State	Starkville	W	40-7
Sept. 15	Texas-El Paso	Knoxville	W	56-0
Sept. 29	Auburn	Auburn	T	26-26
Oct. 13	Florida	Knoxville	W	45-3
Oct. 20	Alabama	Knoxville	L	9-6
Nov. 3	Temple	Knoxville	W	41-20
Nov. 10	Notre Dame	Knoxville	L	34-29
Nov. 17	Ole Miss	Memphis	W	22-13
Nov. 24	Kentucky	Knoxville	W	42-28
Dec. 1	Vanderbilt	Nashville	W	49-20
Jan. 1	Virginia	Sugar Bowl	W	23-22
Coach: Johnny Majors				465-220

Through the Years

Captain: Tony Thompson
Ranking (AP): Preseason No. 8; Postseason No. 8
All-American: Antone Davis, Dale Carter
All-SEC (first team): Dale Carter, Joey Chapman,
Antone Davis, Charles McRae, Carl Pickens,
Tony Thompson
Leaders: Passing: Andy Kelly (179 of 304,
2,241 yards); Rushing: Tony Thompson (219 car-
ries, 1,261 yards); Receiving: Carl Pickens (53
catches, 917 yards).

Although Virginia lost three of its last four games,
the Sugar Bowl still invited the Cavaliers to face
Tennessee, and the two teams were very similar
on paper. After trailing for 59:29, Tennessee won
on Tony Thompson's 1-yard touchdown to complete a 20-point fourth quarter. The key play was
Greg Amsler gaining 6 yards on fourth-and-1 at
the Virginia 23. Thompson finished with 151 rushing yards. Dale Carter had two interceptions in
the game. ... The Colorado game was the Pigskin
Classic. ... Carter led the NCAA in kickoff returns
by averaging 29.8 yards. ... Tennessee football
celebrated its 100-year anniversary.

Tony Thompson leaps into the end zone for the game – winning touchdown in the 1991 Sugar Bowl against Virginia. The win capped a 20-point fourth quarter and gave the Volunteers a 9-2-2 finish to cap off an SEC championship season.

1991
9-3

Sept. 5	Louisville	Louisville	W	28-11
Sept. 14	UCLA	Knoxville	W	30-16
Sept. 21	Mississippi State	Knoxville	W	26-24
Sept. 28	Auburn	Knoxville	W	30-21
Oct. 12	Florida	Gainesville	L	35-18
Oct. 19	Alabama	Birmingham	L	24-19
Nov. 2	Memphis State	Knoxville	W	52-24
Nov. 9	Notre Dame	South Bend	W	35-34
Nov. 16	Ole Miss	Knoxville	W	36-25
Nov. 23	Kentucky	Lexington	W	16-7
Nov. 30	Vanderbilt	Knoxville	W	45-0
Jan. 1	Penn State	Fiesta Bowl	L	42-17
Coach: Johnny Majors				352-263

Captain: Earnest Fields, John Fisher
Ranking (AP): Preseason No. 11; Postseason No. 14
All-American: Dale Carter, Carl Pickens
All-SEC (first team): Dale Carter, Darryl Hardy, Jeremy Lincoln, Chris Mims, Tom Myslinski, Carl Pickens, Chuck Smith
Leaders: Passing: Andy Kelly (228 of 361, 2,759 yards); Rushing: James Stewart (190 carries, 939 yards); Receiving: Carl Pickens (49 catches, 877 yards).

Tennessee came back from a 31-7 deficit in the second quarter to win at Notre Dame, 35-34, when the Fighting Irish missed a 27-yard field goal as time expired. Sparking the rally was a blocked field goal the Vols returned 85 yards for a touchdown. ... Despite UT's yardage advantage of 441-226, Penn State scored 35 unanswered points in the Fiesta Bowl.

1992
9-3

Date	Opponent	Location		Score
Sept. 5	SW Louisiana	Knoxville	W	38-3
Sept. 12	Georgia	Athens	W	34-31
Sept. 19	Florida	Knoxville	W	31-14
Sept. 26	Cincinnati	Knoxville	W	40-0
Oct. 3	LSU	Baton Rouge	W	20-0
Oct. 10	Arkansas	Knoxville	L	25-24
Oct. 17	Alabama	Knoxville	L	17-10
Oct. 31	South Carolina	Columbia	L	24-23
Nov. 14	Memphis State	Memphis	W	26-21
Nov. 21	Kentucky	Knoxville	W	34-13
Nov. 28	Vanderbilt	Nashville	W	29-25
Jan. 1	Boston College	Hall of Fame Bowl	W	38-23
Coach: Johnny Majors				347-196

Captains: Todd Kelly, J.J. McCleskey
Ranking (AP): Preseason No. 21; Postseason No. 12
All-SEC (first team): Todd Kelly, Mike Stowell
Leaders: Passing: Heath Shuler (130 of 224, 1,712 yards); Rushing: Charlie Garner (154 carries, 928 yards); Receiving: Cory Fleming (40 catches, 490 yards).

The first three games of 1992 were credited to the coaching record of Phillip Fulmer, the other eight regular-season games to Johnny Majors (116-62-8). Fulmer was officially named head coach Nov. 29. ... Quarterback Heath Shuler completed 18 of 23 passes for 245yards and touchdown passes to Cory Fleming and Mose Phillips in the Hall of Fame Bowl.

The first three games of the 1992 season were credited as the first of 152 wins for Phillip Fulmer at Tennessee. The 1992 team overcame a three-game losing streak to go on to a bowl win on the right arm of future congressman Heath Shuler.

1993

10-2

Sept. 4	Louisiana Tech	Knoxville	W	50-0
Sept. 11	Georgia	Knoxville	W	38-6
Sept. 18	Florida	Gainesville	L	41-34
Sept. 25	LSU	Knoxville	W	42-20
Oct. 2	Duke	Knoxville	W	52-19
Oct. 9	Arkansas	Little Rock	W	28-14
Oct. 16	Alabama-x	Birmingham	T	17-17
Oct. 30	South Carolina	Knoxville	W	55-3
Nov. 6	Louisville	Knoxville	W	45-10
Nov. 20	Kentucky	Lexington	W	48-0
Nov. 27	Vanderbilt	Knoxville	W	62-14
Jan. 1	Penn State	Florida Citrus Bowl	L	31-13
Coach: Phillip Fulmer				484-175

Captains: Craig Faulkner, Cory Fleming, Horace
Morris, James Wilson
Ranking (AP): Preseason No. 10; Postseason
No. 12
All-American: John Becksvoort
All-SEC (first team): John Becksvoort, Cory
Fleming, Heath Shuler, Jeff Smith
Leaders: Passing: Heath Shuler (184 of 285,
2,353 yards); Rushing: Charlie Garner (159 car-
ries, 1,161 yards); Receiving: Craig Faulkner (40
catches, 680 yards).

Cory Fleming had 101 yards on seven receptions and one touchdown, but Penn State scored
21 unanswered points in the Florida Citrus
Bowl. ... The Alabama game was later forfeited to Tennessee due to NCAA sanctions. ...
Quarterback Heath Shuler finished second in
Heisman Trophy voting.

1994

8-4

Sept. 3	UCLA	Pasadena	L	25-23
Sept. 10	Georgia	Athens	W	41-23
Sept. 17	Florida	Knoxville	L	31-0
Sept. 24	Mississippi State	Starkville	L	24-21
Oct. 1	Washington State	Knoxville	W	10-9
Oct. 8	Arkansas	Knoxville	W	38-21
Oct. 15	Alabama	Knoxville	L	17-13
Oct. 29	South Carolina	Columbia	W	31-22
Nov. 12	Memphis	Knoxville	W	24-13
Nov. 19	Kentucky	Knoxville	W	52-0
Nov. 26	Vanderbilt	Nashville	W	65-0
Dec. 30	Virginia Tech	Gator Bowl	W	45-23

Coach: Phillip Fulmer   363-208

Through the Years

Captains: Kevin Mays, Ben Talley
Ranking (AP): Preseason No. 13; Postseason No. 22
All-SEC (first team): Kevin Mays
Leaders: Passing: Peyton Manning (89 of 144, 1,141 yards); Rushing: James Stewart (170 carries, 1,028 yards); Receiving: Joey Kent (36 catches, 470 yards).

James Stewart scored three touchdowns and passed for another in the Gator Bowl, and Tennessee scored on five of seven first half possessions. ... Starting quarterback Jerry Colquitt was injured during the opening minutes of the season. After a 1-3 start, Peyton Manning was inserted at quarterback and started every subsequent game until he graduated.

1995
11-1

Sept. 2	East Carolina	Knoxville	W	27-7
Sept. 9	Georgia	Knoxville	W	30-27
Sept. 16	Florida	Gainesville	L	62-37
Sept. 23	Mississippi State	Knoxville	W	52-14
Sept. 30	Oklahoma State	Knoxville	W	31-0
Oct. 7	Arkansas	Fayetteville	W	49-31
Oct. 14	Alabama	Birmingham	W	41-14
Oct. 28	South Carolina	Knoxville	W	56-21
Nov. 4	Southern Miss	Knoxville	W	42-0
Nov. 18	Kentucky	Lexington	W	34-31
Nov. 25	Vanderbilt	Knoxville	W	12-7
Jan. 1	Ohio State	Florida Citrus Bowl	W	20-14

Coach: Phillip Fulmer   431-228

Captains: Scott Galyon, Jason Layman, Bubba Miller
Ranking (AP): Preseason no. 8; Postseason No. 3
All-SEC (first team): Jeff Hall, DeRon Jenkins, Joey Kent, Jason Layman, Peyton Manning, Bubba Miller, Jeff Smith
Leaders: Passing: Peyton Manning (244 of 380, 2,954 yards); Rushing: Jay Graham (272 carries, 1,438 yards); Receiving: Joey Kent (69 catches, 1,055 yards).

Jeff Hall made two fourth-quarter field goals to lift Tennessee past Ohio State and Heisman Trophy winner Eddie George in the Florida Citrus Bowl. Running back Jay Graham had 154 rushing yards, including a 69-yard touchdown. Quarterback Peyton Manning completed 20 of 35 passes for 182 yards, and Joey Kent had seven catches for 109 yards, with a 47-yard touchdown reception.

1996
10-2

Aug. 31	UNLV	Knoxville	W	62-3
Sept. 7	UCLA	Knoxville	W	35-20
Sept. 21	Florida	Knoxville	L	35-29
Oct. 3	Ole Miss	Memphis	W	41-3
Oct. 12	Georgia	Athens	W	29-17
Oct. 26	Alabama	Knoxville	W	20-13
Nov. 2	South Carolina	Columbia	W	31-14
Nov. 9	Memphis	Memphis	L	21-17
Nov. 16	Arkansas	Knoxville	W	55-14
Nov. 23	Kentucky	Knoxville	W	56-10
Nov. 30	Vanderbilt	Nashville	W	14-7
Jan. 1	Northwestern	Florida Citrus Bowl	W	48-28
Coach: Phillip Fulmer				437-185

**Captains: Raymond Austin, Jay Graham
Ranking (AP): Preseason No. 2; Postseason No. 9
All-SEC (first team): Terry Fair, Jeff Hall, Joey
Kent, Leonard Little
Leaders: Passing: Peyton Manning (243 of 380,
3,287 yards); Rushing: Jay Graham (179 carries,
797 yards); Receiving: Joey Kent (68 catches,
1,080 yards).**

Peyton Manning completed 27 of 39 passes
for 408 yards against Northwestern. Jeff Kent
caught five passes for 122 yards and two touchdowns, and Peerless Price had six catches for
110 yards, including a 43-yard touchdown.
Linebacker Tyrone Hines' 30-yard interception
return for a touchdown keyed a 20-point run. ...
The NCAA switched to an overtime format so that
games could not end in a tie.

Through the Years

Peyton Manning rushes toward the end zone in a 1995 game against Georgia. In 1997, Manning nearly swept the college football awards, falling short only in the race for the Heisman Trophy. He left the school as its most prolific passer, and is on pace for a Hall of Fame career in the NFL.

1997

11-2, SEC champions

Aug. 30	Texas Tech	Knoxville	W	52-17
Sept. 6	UCLA	Pasadena	W	30-24
Sept. 20	Florida	Gainesville	L	33-20
Oct. 4	Ole Miss	Knoxville	W	31-17
Oct. 11	Georgia	Knoxville	W	38-13
Oct. 18	Alabama	Birmingham	W	38-21
Nov. 1	South Carolina	Knoxville	W	22-7
Nov. 8	Southern Miss	Knoxville	W	44-20
Nov. 15	Arkansas	Little Rock	W	30-22
Nov. 22	Kentucky	Lexington	W	59-31
Nov. 29	Vanderbilt	Knoxville	W	17-10
Dec. 6	Auburn	SEC Championship	W	30-29
Jan. 2	Nebraska	Orange Bowl	L	42-17
Coach Phillip Fulmer				428-286

Captains: Leonard Little, Peyton Manning
Ranking (AP): Preseason No. 5; Postseason No. 7
Major Awards: Peyton Manning, Maxwell Award (outstanding player), Davey O'Brien Award (best quarterback), and Johnny Unitas Golden Arm Award (best senior quarterback)
All-American: Leonard Little, Peyton Manning
All-SEC (first team): Jonathan Brown, Terry Fair, Leonard Little, Peyton Manning, Marcus Nash, Trey Teague, Al Wilson
Leaders: Passing: Peyton Manning (387 of 477, 3,819 yards); Rushing: Jamal Lewis (232 carries, 1,364 yards); Receiving: Marcus Nash (76 catches, 1,170 yards).

Heisman Trophy runner-up Peyton Manning finished his career with 33 school, seven SEC, and two NCAA passing records. He threw 89 touchdown passes, had more than 11,000 career yards, and just 33 interceptions in 1,381 attempts. He was 39-6 as a starter, with four of the losses to Florida. ... Manning threw for 508 yards against Kentucky. ... Nebraska had a 14-3 lead and scored 21 points in the third quarter to put the Orange Bowl away en route to the national championship.

1998

13-0, National champions, SEC champions

Sept. 5	Syracuse	Syracuse	W	34-33
Sept. 19	Florida	Knoxville	W OT	20-17
Sept. 26	Houston	Knoxville	W	42-7
Oct. 3	Auburn	Auburn	W	17-9
Oct. 10	Georgia	Athens	W	22-3
Oct. 24	Alabama	Knoxville	W	35-18
Oct. 31	South Carolina	Columbia	W	49-14
Nov. 7	UAB	Knoxville	W	37-13
Nov. 14	Arkansas	Knoxville	W	28-24
Nov. 21	Kentucky	Knoxville	W	59-21
Nov. 28	Vanderbilt	Nashville	W	41-0
Dec. 5	Mississippi State	SEC Championship	W	24-14
Jan. 4	Florida State	Fiesta Bowl	W	23-16
Coach: Phillip Fulmer				431-189

Captains: Shawn Bryson, Jeff Hall, Mercedes Hamilton, Al Wilson
Ranking (AP): Preseason No. 10; Postseason No. 1
All-American: Al Wilson
All-SEC (first team): Cosey Coleman, Jeff Hall, Raynoch Thompson, Darwin Walker, Al Wilson
Leaders: Passing: Tee Martin (153 of 267, 2,164 yards); Rushing: Travis Henry (176 carries, 970 yards); Receiving: Peerless Price (61 catches, 920 yards).

Tennessee reached the national title game in the first year of the Bowl Championship Series. The Volunteers took the lead off an interception return for a touchdown by Dwayne Goodrich, and essentially put the game away on Tee Martin's 79-yard touchdown pass to Peerless Price. Martin completed 11 of 18 passes for 278 yards, and Price had four catches for 199 yards. ... The Vols finished off an impressive going 45-5. ... Kicker Jeff Hall keyed season-opening wins against Syracuse and Florida, and Tennessee had a game-winning drive following an Arkansas turnover late in the fourth quarter to preserve the undefeated season.

1999
9-3

Sept. 4	Wyoming	Knoxville	W	42-17
Sept. 18	Florida	Gainesville	L	23-21
Sept. 25	Memphis	Knoxville	W	17-16
Oct. 2	Auburn	Knoxville	W	24-0
Oct. 9	Georgia	Knoxville	W	37-20
Oct. 23	Alabama	Tuscaloosa	W	21-7
Oct. 30	South Carolina	Knoxville	W	30-7
Nov. 6	Notre Dame	Knoxville	W	38-14
Nov. 13	Arkansas	Fayetteville	L	28-24
Nov. 20	Kentucky	Lexington	W	56-21
Nov. 27	Vanderbilt	Knoxville	W	38-10
Jan. 2	Nebraska	Fiesta Bowl	L	31-21

Coach: Phillip Fulmer   369-194

Captains: Chad Clifton, Dwayne Goodrich, Tee Martin, Billy Ratliff, Spencer Riley, Darwin Walker
Ranking (AP): Preseason No. 2; Postseason No. 9
All-American: Cosey Coleman, Deon Grant, Raynoch Thompson
All-SEC (first team): Cosey Coleman, Shaun Ellis, Dwayne Goodrich, Deon Grant, Tee Martin, Raynoch Thompson, Darwin Walker
Leaders: Passing: Tee Martin (165 of 305, 2,317 yards); Rushing: Jamal Lewis (182 carries, 816 yards); Receiving: Cedrick Wilson (57 catches, 827 yards).

Tennessee returned to the site of its national championship the previous year, but Nebraska cranked out 321 rushing yards while yielding just 44. ... The awarding of the Beer Barrel trophy in the Kentucky series was discontinued. ... Tennessee played in Tuscaloosa for the first time since 1930 (Alabama had been playing most of its marquee games at Legion Field in Birmingham).

Travis Stephens leaps over a pair of Louisiana-Monroe tacklers in 2000. The next year, he set a Tennessee record for rushing yards in a season when he carried for 1,464 yards.

2000
8-4

Date	Opponent	Location	Result	Score
Sept. 2	Southern Miss	Knoxville	W	19-16
Sept. 16	Florida	Knoxville	L	27-23
Sept. 23	Louisiana-Monroe	Knoxville	W	70-3
Sept. 30	LSU	Baton Rouge	L OT	38-31
Oct. 7	Georgia	Athens	L	21-10
Oct. 21	Alabama	Knoxville	W	20-10
Oct. 28	South Carolina	Columbia	W	17-14
Nov. 4	Memphis	Memphis	W	19-17
Nov. 11	Arkansas	Knoxville	W	63-20
Nov. 18	Kentucky	Knoxville	W	59-20
Nov. 25	Vanderbilt	Nashville	W	28-26
Jan. 1	Kansas State	Cotton Bowl	L	35-21
Coach: Phillip Fulmer				380-247

Captains: David Leaverton, Eric Westmoreland, Cedrick Wilson
Ranking (AP): Preseason No. 12; Postseason NR
Major Award: John Henderson, Outland Trophy
All-American: John Henderson
All-SEC (first team): John Henderson, Travis Henry, Will Overstreet, Alex Walls, Eric Westmoreland
Leaders: Passing: Casey Clausen (121 of 194, 1,473 yards); Rushing: Travis Henry (253 carries, 1,314 yards); Receiving: Cedrick Wilson (62 catches, 681 yards).

Kansas State scored on its first two possessions of the third quarter and held Tennessee scoreless until the final minutes of the Cotton Bowl. Running back Travis Henry had 180 rushing yards on 17 carries, including an 81-yard touchdown, and Jabari Smith intercepted a pass tipped by Chavis Smith and returned it 78 yards for a score. ... The win against Southern Miss was victory No. 700 for the program. ... Tennessee was ranked 25th in the final coaches' poll.

2001

11-2

Sept. 1	Syracuse	Knoxville	W	33-9
Sept. 8	Arkansas	Fayetteville	W	13-3
Sept. 29	LSU	Knoxville	W	26-18
Oct. 6	Georgia	Knoxville	L	26-24
Oct. 20	Alabama	Tuscaloosa	W	35-24
Oct. 27	South Carolina	Knoxville	W	17-10
Nov. 3	Notre Dame	South Bend	W	28-18
Nov. 10	Memphis	Knoxville	W	49-28
Nov. 17	Kentucky	Lexington	W	38-35
Nov. 24	Vanderbilt	Knoxville	W	38-0
Dec. 1	Florida	Gainesville	W	34-32
Dec. 8	LSU	SEC Championship	L	31-20
Jan. 1	Michigan	Florida Citrus Bowl	W	45-17
Coach: Phillip Fulmer				400-251

Captains: Will Bartholomew, John Henderson, Andre Lott, Will Overstreet, Fred Weary
Ranking (AP): Preseason No. 8; Postseason No. 4
All-American: John Henderson, Travis Stephens
All-SEC (first team): John Henderson, Andre Lott, Will Overstreet, Travis Stephens, Fred Weary
Leaders—Passing: Casey Clausen (227 of 354, 2,969 yards); Rushing: Travis Stephens (291 carries, 1,464 yards); Receiving: Kelley Washington (64 catches, 1,010 yards).

Tennessee headed to the SEC Championship game undefeated and only needing a victory to play for the national title, but lost to LSU. ... UT played Michigan for the first time. Quarterback Casey Clausen threw for a career-high 306 yards, completing 24 of 36 passes, and three touchdowns. Donte Stallworth caught eight passes for 119 yards and had 190 all-purpose yards, Kelley Washington had two scores, and Jason Witten had six catches for a career-high 125 yards. John Henderson, who caused one fumble and recovered another on the same play, was the Florida Citrus Bowl's defensive MVP.

Kelley Washington hauled in this touchdown pass from Casey Clausen in the 2001 SEC Championship game, but the Tigers went on to win. Tennessee finished on a high note, however, beating up on Michigan in the Florida Citrus Bowl.

2002
8-5

Aug. 31	Wyoming	Nashville	W	47-7
Sept. 7	Middle Tenn. State	Knoxville	W	26-3
Sept. 21	Florida	Knoxville	L	30-13
Sept. 28	Rutgers	Knoxville	W	35-14
Oct. 5	Arkansas	Knoxville	W 6OT	41-38
Oct. 12	Georgia	Athens	L	18-13
Oct. 26	Alabama	Knoxville	L	34-14
Nov. 2	South Carolina	Columbia	W	18-10
Nov. 9	Miami (Fla.)	Knoxville	L	26-3
Nov. 16	Mississippi State	Starkville	W	35-17
Nov. 23	Vanderbilt	Nashville	W	24-0
Nov. 30	Kentucky	Knoxville	W	24-0
Dec. 31	Maryland	Peach Bowl	L	30-3

Coach: Phillip Fulmer   296-227

Captains: Omari Hand, Eddie Moore, Will Ofenheusle
Ranking (AP): Preseason No. 5; Postseason NR
All-SEC (first team): Rashad Baker, Julian Battle, Will Ofenheusle, Jason Witten
Leaders: Passing: Casey Clausen (194 of 310, 2,297 yards); Rushing: Cedric Houston (153 carries, 779 yards); Receiving: Jason Witten (39 catches, 493 yards).

Maryland's defense shut down Tennessee in the Peach Bowl with six sacks and allowed just four of 13 third-down conversions, and 45 rushing yards on 27 carries. The Volunteers actually outgained the Terrapins 287-274. ... Coach Phillip Fulmer enjoyed career victory No. 100 in his 123rd game, the 18-10 win at South Carolina.

Through the Years

2003
10-3

Aug. 30	Fresno State	Knoxville	W		24-6
Sept. 6	Marshall	Knoxville	W		34-24
Sept. 20	Florida	Gainesville	W		24-10
Sept. 27	South Carolina	Knoxville	W	OT	23-20
Oct. 4	Auburn	Auburn	L		28-21
Oct. 11	Georgia	Knoxville	L		41-14
Oct. 25	Alabama	Tuscaloosa	W	OT	51-43
Nov. 1	Duke	Knoxville	W		23-6
Nov. 8	Miami (Fla.)	Miami	W		10-6
Nov. 15	Mississippi State	Knoxville	W		59-21
Nov. 22	Vanderbilt	Knoxville	W		48-0
Nov. 29	Kentucky	Lexington	W		20-7
Jan. 2	Clemson	Peach Bowl	L		27-14
Coach: Phillip Fulmer					365-239

Through the Years

Captains: Casey Clausen, Kevin Burnett, Michael Munoz, Rashad Baker, Scott Wells, Constantin Ritzmann
Ranking (AP): Preseason No. 12; Postseason No. 15
All-American: Dustin Colquitt
All-SEC (first team): Dustin Colquitt, Scott Wells
Leaders: Passing: Casey Clausen (233 of 412, 2,968 yards); Rushing: Cedric Houston (149 carries, 744 yards); Receiving: James Banks (42 catches, 621 yards).

In his final game, Casey Clausen completed 31 of 55 passes for 384 yards and two touchdowns, but Tennessee lost for the second straight year at the Peach Bowl. The Volunteers made 10 penalties, including two for pass interference, two for unsportsmanlike conduct, and two for roughing the quarterback. Leading rusher Cedric Houston fumbled on his first carry, and Tennessee had just 38 rushing yards on 26 carries. ... Tennessee snapped No. 6 Miami's 26-game home winning streak, which dated back to Penn State on Sept. 18, 1999. UT won with just 170 yards of offense, 81 passing and 89 rushing. "It was probably the prettiest, ugliest win I've ever had," said coach Phillip Fulmer, who posed for pictures with his family in the Orange Bowl.

2004
10-3

Date	Opponent	Location		Score
Sept. 5	UNLV	Knoxville	W	42-17
Sept. 18	Florida	Knoxville	W	30-28
Sept. 25	Louisiana Tech	Knoxville	W	42-17
Oct. 2	Auburn	Knoxville	L	34-10
Oct. 9	Georgia	Athens	W	19-14
Oct. 16	Ole Miss	Oxford	W	21-17
Oct. 23	Alabama	Knoxville	W	17-13
Oct. 30	South Carolina	Columbia	W	43-29
Nov. 6	Notre Dame	Knoxville	L	17-13
Nov. 20	Vanderbilt	Nashville	W	38-33
Nov. 27	Kentucky	Knoxville	W	37-31
Dec. 4	Auburn	SEC Championship	L	38-28
Jan. 1	Texas A&M	Cotton Bowl	W	38-7

Coach: Phillip Fulmer   378-295

Captains: Michael Munoz, Parys Haralson, Jason Respert, Tony Brown, Kevin Burnett, Jason Allen
Ranking (AP): Preseason No. 14; Postseason No. 13
All-American: Kevin Burnett, Jesse Mahelona, Michael Munoz.
All-SEC (first team): Jason Allen, Kevin Burnett, Jesse Mahelona, Michael Munoz
Leaders: Passing: Erik Ainge (109 of 198, 1,452 yards); Rushing: Gerald Riggs Jr. (193 carries, 1,107 yards); Receiving: Tony Brown (31 catches, 388 yards).

Tennessee enjoyed the most lopsided victory in the school's 45-game bowl history. Against Texas A&M, the Volunteers came within 5:13 of their first bowl shutout since the last time they played the Aggies, in the 1957 Gator Bowl. Third-string quarterback Rick Clausen was 18-of-27 for 222 yards with three touchdowns, no interceptions, and no sacks. Gerald Riggs Jr. followed his career-high 182 yards in the SEC Championship Game with 102 yards and a touchdown on 18 carries. He and Cedric Houston became the first UT teammates to have 1,000 yards in the same season. ... Against Florida, 108,768 fans packed into Neyland Stadium. ... Tennessee enjoyed its ninth win in 10 years against Alabama.

Kevin Burnett celebrates with fans after the Volunteers' 19-14 win over Georgia. The win helped to propel UT to the SEC Championship Game, though they fell short in their bid for a BCS bowl.

2005
5-6

Sept. 3	UAB	Knoxville	W	17-10
Sept. 17	Florida	Gainesville	L	16-7
Sept. 26	LSU	Baton Rouge	W OT	30-27
Oct. 1	Ole Miss	Knoxville	W	27-10
Oct. 8	Georgia	Knoxville	L	27-14
Oct. 22	Alabama	Tuscaloosa	L	6-3
Oct. 29	South Carolina	Knoxville	L	16-15
Nov. 5	Notre Dame	South Bend	L	41-21
Nov. 12	Memphis	Knoxville	W	20-16
Nov. 19	Vanderbilt	Knoxville	L	28-24
Nov. 26	Kentucky	Lexington	W	27-8
Coach: Phillip Fulmer				205-205

Captains: Jason Allen, Rick Clausen, Cody Douglas, Parys Haralson, Jesse Mahelona, Rob Smith
Ranking (AP): Preseason No. 3; Postseason NR
All-SEC (first team): Aaron Sears
Leaders: Passing: Rick Clausen (120 of 209, 1,441 yards); Rushing: Adrian Foster (183 carries, 879 yards); Receiving: Robert Meachem (29 catches, 383 yards).

Tennessee was not bowl eligible for the first time since 1988. ... Vanderbilt won in Neyland Stadium for the first time since 1975, and snapped the Volunteers' 22-game winning streak, the second-longest between major teams in Division I-A (Notre Dame vs. Navy, 42). "Before you start building back anything, you have to hit rock bottom. This is rock bottom," Coach Phillip Fulmer said. Arian Foster had 223 rushing yards on 40 carries and scored two touchdowns in the loss. ... The Volunteers haven't lost to both Vanderbilt and Kentucky in the same season since 1964.

2006

9-4

Sept. 2	California	Knoxville	W	35-18
Sept. 9	Air Force	Knoxville	W	31-30
Sept. 16	Florida	Knoxville	L	21-20
Sept. 23	Marshall	Knoxville	W	33-7
Sept. 30	Memphis	Memphis	W	41-7
Oct. 7	Georgia	Athens	W	51-33
Oct. 21	Alabama	Knoxville	W	16-13
Oct. 28	South Carolina	Columbia	W	31-24
Nov. 4	LSU	Knoxville	L	28-24
Nov. 11	Arkansas	Fayetteville	L	31-14
Nov. 18	Vanderbilt	Nashville	W	39-10
Nov. 25	Kentucky	Knoxville	W	17-12
Jan. 1	Penn State	Outback Bowl	L	20-10

Coach Phillip Fulmer   362-254

Captains: Justin Harrell, Turk McBride, Marvin Mitchell, Jayson Swain, Aaron Sears
Ranking (AP): Preseason No. 23; Postseason 25
All-American: Robert Meachem, Aaron Sears
All-SEC (first team): Britton Colquitt, Turk McBride, Robert Meachem, Aaron Sears, James Wilhoit
Leaders: Passing: Erik Ainge (233 of 348, 2,989 yards); Rushing: LaMarcus Coker (108 carries, 696 yards); Receiving: Robert Meachem (71 catches, 1,298 yards).

With Joe Paterno watching from the press box while recovering from a broken leg, Tony Hunt ran for 158 yards and Tony Davis returned a fumble 88 yards for a touchdown to lead Penn State in the rainy Outback Bowl. Erik Ainge completed 25 of 37 passes for 267 yards, but also had his first interception since the Alabama game. ... Ainge was 11-for-18, for 295 yards and four touchdowns in the opener against No. 9 Cal. Robert Meachem had five receptions for 182 yards and two touchdowns. Tennessee had been 0-6 against top 10 teams in Neyland Stadium since 2000.

2007
10-4

Sept. 1	California	Berkeley	L	45-31
Sept. 8	Southern Miss	Knoxville	W	39-19
Sept. 15	Florida	Gainesville	L	59-20
Sept. 22	Arkansas State	Knoxville	W	48-27
Oct. 6	Georgia	Knoxville	W	35-14
Oct. 13	Mississippi State	Starkville	W	33-21
Oct. 20	Alabama	Tuscaloosa	L	41-7
Oct. 27	South Carolina	Knoxville	W OT	27-24
Nov. 3	Louisiana-Lafayette	Knoxville	W	59-7
Nov. 10	Arkansas	Knoxville	W	34-13
Nov. 17	Vanderbilt	Knoxville	W	25-24
Nov. 24	Kentucky	Lexington	W 4OT	52-50
Dec. 1	LSU	Atlanta	L	21-14
Jan. 1	Wisconsin	Outback Bowl	W	21-17

Coach Phillip Fulmer   445-382

Captains: Game captains
Ranking (AP): Preseason No. 15; Postseason No. 12
All-American: Daniel Lincoln.
All-SEC (first team): Jonathan Hefney, Jerod Mao, Anthony Parker
Leaders: Passing: Erik Ainge (325 of 519, 3,522 yards); Rushing: Arian Foster (245 carries, 1,193 yards); Receiving: Lucas Taylor (73 catches, 1,000 yards).

Erik Ainge had seven touchdowns against Kentucky, breaking the Tennessee record for most touchdowns in a game. The previous record was five, done seven times and most recently by Casey Clausen against Mississippi State in 2003. The win also secured a spot in the SEC Championship Game against LSU. ... A month after having an interception returned for the winning score for LSU, Ainge completed 25 of 43 passes without a turnover in the Outback Bowl. ... No. 12 Cal got revenge for the previous year's opening loss by scoring the most points against Tennessee in 12 years (eclipsed two weeks later by Florida). Despite a broken pinkie, Ainge attempted 47 passes, completing 32 for 270 yards and three touchdowns.

Through the Years

2008

5-7

Sept. 1	UCLA	Pasadena	L OT	27-24
Sept. 13	UAB	Knoxville	W	35-3
Sept. 20	Florida	Knoxville	L	30-6
Sept. 27	Auburn	Auburn	L	14-12
Oct. 4	Northern Illinois	Knoxville	W	13-9
Oct. 11	Georgia	Athens	L	26-14
Oct. 18	Mississippi State	Knoxville	W	34-3
Oct. 25	Alabama	Knoxville	L	29-9
Nov. 1	South Carolina	Columbia	L	27-6
Nov. 8	Wyoming	Knoxville	L	13-7
Nov. 22	Vanderbilt	Nashville	W	20-10
Nov. 29	Kentucky	Knoxville	W	28-10
Coach Phillip Fulmer				208-201

Captains: Robert Ayers, Ramon Foster, Lucas Taylor, Ellix Wilson, Montario Hardesty, Eric Berry
Ranking (AP): Preseason No. 18; Postseason NR
All-American: Eric Berry
All-SEC (first team): Robert Ayers, Eric Berry
Leaders: Passing: Jonathan Compton (86 of 167, 889 yards); Rushing: Arian Foster (131 carries, 570 yards); Receiving: Lucas Taylor (26 catches, 332 yards).

Coach Phillip Fulmer announced Nov. 3 that he had agreed to step down effective the end of the season. Five days later, Tennessee lost to the lowest scoring team in major college football, Wyoming. Following the victory at Vanderbilt, Fulmer compared it to a "three-week long funeral," but the Volunteers sent him off with a victory against Kentucky. Fulmer (152-52) left as the second-winningest coach in Tennessee history behind Gen. Robert R. Neyland. ... Sophomore safety Eric Berry led the nation with seven interceptions. His 265 return yards set both Tennessee and Southeastern Conference records (244 yards by Florida's Joe Brodsky, 1956), leaving him just 14 short of Terrell Buckley's NCAA record of 501 interception return yards (1989-91, Florida State).

BOWL GAMES

Overall Record: 25-22

Date	Bowl	Opp	W/L	Score
Jan. 2, 1939	Orange	Oklahoma	W	17-0
Jan. 1, 1940	Rose	Southern CA	L	14-0
Jan. 1, 1941	Sugar	Boston College	L	19-13
Jan. 1, 1943	Sugar	Tulsa	W	14-7
Jan. 1, 1945	Rose	Southern CA	L	25-0
Jan. 1, 1947	Orange	Rice	L	8-0
Jan. 1, 1951	Cotton	Texas	W	20-14
Jan. 1, 1952	Sugar	Maryland	L	28-13
Jan. 1, 1953	Cotton	Texas	L	16-0
Jan. 1, 1957	Sugar	Baylor	L	13-7
Dec. 28, 1957	Gator	Texas A&M	W	3-0
Dec. 18, 1965	Bluebonnet	Tulsa	W	27-6
Dec. 31, 1966	Gator	Syracuse	W	18-12
Jan. 1, 1968	Orange	Oklahoma	L	26-24
Jan. 1, 1969	Cotton	Texas	L	36-13
Dec. 27, 1969	Gator	Florida	L	14-13
Jan. 1, 1971	Sugar	Air Force	W	34-13
Dec. 20, 1971	Liberty	Arkansas	W	14-13
Dec. 30, 1972	Bluebonnet	LSU	W	24-17
Dec. 29, 1973	Gator	Texas Tech	L	28-19
Dec. 16, 1974	Liberty	Maryland	W	7-3
Dec. 31, 1979	Bluebonnet	Purdue	L	27-22
Dec. 13, 1981	Garden State	Wisconsin	W	28-21
Dec. 31, 1982	Peach	Iowa	L	28-22
Dec. 17, 1983	Florida Citrus	Maryland	W	30-23
Dec. 22, 1984	Sun	Maryland	L	28-27
Jan. 1, 1986	Sugar	Miami (Fla.)	W	35-7
Dec. 29, 1986	Liberty	Minnesota	W	21-14
Jan. 2, 1988	Peach	Indiana	W	27-22
Jan. 1, 1990	Cotton	Arkansas	W	31-27
Jan. 1, 1991	Sugar	Virginia	W	23-22

Jan. 1, 1992	Fiesta	Penn State	L	42-17
Jan. 1, 1993	Hall of Fame	Boston College	W	38-23
Jan. 1, 1994	Florida Citrus	Penn State	L	31-13
Dec. 30, 1994	Gator	Virginia Tech	W	45-23
Jan. 1, 1996	Florida Citrus	Ohio State	W	20-14
Jan. 1, 1997	Florida Citrus	Northwestern	W	48-28
Jan. 2, 1998	Orange	Nebraska	L	42-17
Jan. 4, 1999	Fiesta	Florida State	W	23-16
Jan. 2, 2000	Fiesta	Nebraska	L	31-21
Jan. 1, 2001	Cotton	Kansas State	L	35-21
Jan. 1, 2002	Florida Citrus	Michigan	W	45-17
Dec. 31, 2002	Peach	Maryland	L	30-3
Jan. 2, 2004	Peach	Clemson	L	27-14
Jan. 1, 2005	Cotton	Texas A&M	W	38-7
Jan. 1, 2007	Outback	Penn State	L	20-10
Jan. 1, 2008	Outback	Wisconsin	W	21-17

3

Teams that have won more bowl games than Tennessee's 25. Only Alabama, USC, and Penn State have won more bowl games than the Volunteers.

OPPONENTS
All-time records vs. opponents

OPPONENT	FIRST	LAST	W-L-T
Air Force	1970	2006	2-0-0
Akron	1989		1-0-0
Alabama	1901	2008	38-46-7
UAB	1998	2008	3-0-0
American University	1905	1906	2-0-1
Arkansas	1907	2007	13-3-0
Arkansas State	2007		1-0-0
Army	1923	1986	5-2-1
Asheville Athletes	1893		1-0-0
Athens	1913		1-0-0
Auburn	1900	2008	21-26-3
Baylor	1956		0-1-0
Boston College	1940	1992	8-2-0
Bristol A.C.	1897	1897	1-0-0
California	1977	2007	2-2-0
California-Santa Barbara	1971		1-0-0
Camp Benning	1922		1-0-0
Carson-Newman	1903	1931	12-0-0
Central University	1896		1-0-0
Centre	1905	1935	10-3-2
Chattanooga A.C.	1892	1896	2-0-0
Cincinnati	1904	1992	4-1-0
The Citadel	1938	1983	3-0-0
Clemson	1901	2003	11-6-2
Colorado	1990		0-0-1
Colorado State	1975	1989	4-0-0
Cumberland (Ky.)	1896	1897	2-0-0
Cumberland (Tenn.)	1915		1-0-0
Dartmouth	1921		0-1-0
Davidson	1913		1-0-0
Dayton	1941	1955	4-0-0
Duke	1893	2003	14-13-2

East Carolina	1995		1-0-0
Emory & Henry	1920	1925	5-0-0
Florida	1916	2008	19-19-0
Florida State	1958	1998	1-1-0
Fordham	1934	1942	1-1-0
Fresno State	2003		1-0-0
Furman	1941	1942	2-0-0
George Washington	1933		1-0-0
Georgetown (Ky.)	1900	1923	3-0-0
Georgia	1899	2008	20-16-2
Georgia Tech	1902	1987	24-17-2
Hawaii	1972	1975	2-0-0
Houston	1953	1998	2-1-0
Howard	1910	1941	2-0-0
Indiana	1987		1-0-0
Iowa	1982	1987	1-1-0
Iowa State	1982		1-0-0
Kansas	1973	1974	2-0-0
Kansas State	2000		0-1-0
Kentucky	1893	2008	72-23-9
King	1897	1914	7-0-0
Louisiana-Lafeyette	1992	2007	2-0-0
Louisiana-Monroe	2000	2000	1-0-0
LSU	1925	2007	20-7-3
Louisiana Tech	1993	2004	2-0-0
Louisville	1914	1993	5-0-0
Marshall	2003	2006	2-0-0
Maryland	1951	2002	5-3-0
Maryville	1892	1936	25-1-1
Memphis	1968	2006	20-1-0
Mercer	1912	1940	2-1-0
Miami (Fla.)	1985	2003	2-1-0
Michigan	2001		1-0-0
Middle Tennessee	2002		1-0-0
Minnesota	1986		1-0-0
Ole Miss	1902	2005	43-18-1

Mississippi State	1907	2008	28-15-1
Mooney School	1910	1911	2-0-0
Nashville	1901	1904	2-1-1
Nebraska	1997	1999	0-2-0
UNLV	1996	2004	2-0-0
New Mexico	1983	1986	2-0-0
New York University	1931		1-0-0
North Carolina	1893	1961	20-10-1
North Carolina State	1911	1939	1-1-0
North Texas State	1975		0-1-0
Northern Illinois	2008		1-0-0
Northwestern	1996		1-0-0
Notre Dame	1978	2005	4-4-0
Ohio State	1995		1-0-0
Oklahoma	1938	1967	1-1-0
Oklahoma State	1995		1-0-0
Oregon State	1977	1978	1-0-1
Pacific		1990	1-0-0
Penn State	1971	2006	2-3-0
Pittsburgh	1980	1983	0-2-0
Purdue		1979	0-1-0
Rhodes	1911	1940	3-0-0
Rice	1946	1968	2-1-0
Richmond	1963		1-0-0
Rutgers	1979	2002	3-1-0
Sewanee	1891	1939	12-10-0
South Carolina	1903	2008	21-4-2
Southern California	1939	1981	0-4-0
Southern Methodist	1970		1-0-0
Southern Miss	1950	2007	5-0-0
Syracuse	1966	2001	3-0-0
Tampa	1960	1967	2-0-0
Temple	1944	1990	2-0-0

Tennessee-Chattanooga	1899	1969	37-2-2
Tennessee Medical School	1911	1912	1-0-1
Tennessee Military Institute	1907		1-0-0
Tennessee School for Deaf	1905		1-0-0
Tennessee Tech	1947	1951	5-0-0
Texas	1950	1968	1-2-0
Texas A&M	1957	2004	2-0-0
Texas Christian	1973	1976	2-0-0
UTEP	1986	1990	2-0-0
Texas Tech	1973	1997	1-1-0
Transylvania	1899	1927	4-1-0
Tulane	1923	1967	4-1-0
Tulsa	1942	1974	5-0-0
Tusculum	1915	1919	3-0-0
UCLA	1965	2008	7-5-2
Utah	1975	1984	3-0-0
Vanderbilt	1892	2008	70-27-5
Villanova	1945		1-0-0
Virginia	1927	1990	3-1-0
Virginia Military	1923		0-1-0
Virginia Tech	1896	1994	5-2-0
Wake Forest	1892	1985	6-3-0
Washington & Lee	1899	1951	5-0-0
Washington State	1980	1994	4-1-0
Wichita State	1981		1-0-0
William & Mary	1945		1-0-0
Wisconsin	1981	2007	2-0-0
Wofford	1952	1952	1-0-0
Wyoming	1999	2008	2-1-0

Through the Years

THE GREATEST PLAYERS

The Honors

Tennessee's roster of greats reads like a who's who of college football legends. The names are familiar to fans of college football, and for the fans of the Vols' rivals, they still bring a shiver of dread. Here are some of the stars who have shone brightest during their tenures in Knoxville.

Heisman Winners: None.

National Honors: Bob Suffridge, 1940 Knute Rockne Memorial Trophy (outstanding lineman); Steve DeLong, 1964 Outland Trophy (outstanding interior lineman); Peyton Manning, 1997 Maxwell Award (outstanding player), Davey O'Brien Award (quarterback), Johnny Unitas Golden Arm Award (senior quarterback), 1997 Draddy Trophy (academic Heisman); John Henderson, 2000 Outland Trophy; Michael Munoz, 2004 Draddy Trophy.

Retired Jerseys: 16 Peyton Manning; 32 Bill Nowling; 49 Rudy Klarer; 61 Willis Tucker; 62 Clyde Fuson, 91 Doug Atkins, 92 Reggie White.

College Football Hall of Fame

Doug Atkins, 1950-52, tackle, inducted 1985; George Cafego, 1937-39, halfback, 1969; Steve DeLong, 1962-64, middle guard, 1993; Doug Dickey, 1964-69, coach, 2003; Bobby Dodd, 1928-30; quarterback, 1959; Nathan Dougherty, 1906-09, guard, 1967; Frank Emanuel, 1963-165, linebacker, 2004; Beattie Feathers, 1931-33, halfback, 1955; Herman Hickman, 1929-31, guard, 1959; Bob Johnson, 1965-67, center, 1989; Steve Kiner, 1967-69, linebacker, 1999; Hank Lauricella, 1949-51, halfback, 1981; Johnny Majors, 1954-56, halfback, 1987; Gene McEver, 1928-29, 1931, halfback, 1954; John Michels, 1950-52, guard, 1996; Ed

Molinski, 1938-40, guard, 1990; Bob Neyland, 1926-52, coach, 1956; Joe Steffy, 1944, guard, 1956; Bob Suffridge, 1938-40, guard, 1961; Reggie White, 1980-83, defensive tackle, 2002; Bowden Wyatt, 1936-38, end (coach 1955-62), 1972.

First-Team All-Americans

Gene McEver, HB, 1929; Bobby Dodd, QB, 1930; Herman Hickman, G, 1931; Beattie Feathers, HB, 1933; Bowden Wyatt, E, 1938; Bob Suffridge, G, 1938-40; George Cafego, HB, 1938-39; Ed Molinski, G, 1939-40; Abe Shires, T, 1939; Bob Foxx, HB, 1940; Bob Dobelstein, G, 1944; Dick Huffman, T, 1946; Ted Daffer, G, 1950-51; Bud Sherrod, E, 1950; Hank Lauricella, HB, 1951; Bill Pearman, T, 1951; Doug Atkins, T, 1952; John Michels, G, 1952; Darris McCord, T, 1954; Johnny Majors, HB, 1956; Kyle (Buddy) Cruze, E, 1956; Buddy Johnson, G, 1957; Steve DeLong, G, 1963-64; Frank Emanuel, LB, 1965; Paul Naumoff, LB, 1966; Austin Denney, E, 1966; Ron Widby, P, 1966; Bob Johnson, C, 1966-67; Albert Dorsey, DB, 1967; Richmond Flowers, WB, 1967; Charlie Rosenfelder, G, 1968; Steve Kiner, LB, 1968-69; Jim Weatherford, DB, 1968; Chip Kell, G, 1969-70; Jack Reynolds, LB, 1969; Jackie Walker, LB, 1970-71; Bobby Majors, DB, 1971; Jamie Rotella, LB, 1972; Conrad Graham, DB, 1972; Ricky Townsend, K, 1972-73; Eddie Brown, DB, 1973; Larry Seivers, E, 1975-76; Roland James, DB, 1979; Willie Gault, WR, 1982; Reggie White, DT, 1983; Jimmy Colquitt, P, 1983; Bill Mayo, G, 1984; Tim McGee, G, 1984; Chris White, S, 1985; Harry Galbreath, G, 1987; Keith Delong, LB, 1988; Eric Still, G, 1989; Antone Davis, T, 1990; Dale Carter, DB, 1991; Carl Pickens, WR, 1991; John Becksvoort, K, 1993; Leonard Little, LB, 1997; Peyton Manning, QB, 1997; Al Wilson, LB, 1998; Cosey Coleman, OL, 1999; Deon

Grant, DB, 1999; Raynoch Thompson, LB, 1999; John Henderson, DT, 2000-01; Travis Stephens, RB, 2001; Dustin Colquitt, P, 2003; Michael Munoz, OL, 2004; Kevin Burnett, LB, 2004; Jesse Mahelona, DT, 2004; Aaron Sears, T, 2006; Robert Meachem, WR, 2006; Daniel Lincoln, K, 2007; Eric Berry, SS, 2008.

First-Team Academic All-Americans (CoSIDA):

Charles Rader, T, 1956; Bill Johnson, G, 1957; Mack Gentry, DT, 1965; Bob Johnson, C, 1967; Tim Priest, DB, 1970; Timothy Irwin, T, 1980; Mike Terry, DL, 1982; Peyton Manning, QB, 1997; William Overstreet, DL, 2001; James Wilhoit, K, 2006.

All-Centennial Team

(Selected by fan vote and a panel of school officials)
Offense — G Harry Galbreath, 1984-87; G Eric Still, 1988-89; T Tim Irwin, 1978-80; T Bruce Wilkerson, 1983-86; C Bob Johnson, 1965-67; WR Stanley Morgan, 1973-76; WR Larry Seivers, 1974-76; WR Willie Gault, 1979-82; QB Condredge Holloway, 1972-74; B Hank Lauricella, 1948-51; B Johnny Majors, 1954-56; RB Curt Watson, 1969-71; RB Reggie Cobb, 1987-88; K Fuad Reveiz, 1981-84.
Defense — DE Doug Atkins, 1950-52; DE Dale Jones, 1983-86; DT Reggie White, 1980-83; DT Marion Hobby, 1986-89; G Steve DeLong, 1962-64; LB Steve Kiner, 1967-69; LB Jack Reynolds, 1967-69; LB Keith DeLong, 1985-88; DB Bobby Majors, 1969-71; DB Eddie Brown, 1971-73; DB Roland James, 1976-79; DB Bill Bates, 1979-82; P Craig Colquitt 1975-77.

Tennesee Players in the College Football Hall of Fame

NATHAN DOUGHERTY
Guard, 1906–1909
Inducted 1967

A 6'2", 185-pound guard, Dougherty was nicknamed "the Big One." He played fullback part time and scored a touchdown in UT's 15–0 win over Georgia in 1907. He also returned a kickoff for a touchdown in 1908. He was a two-year All-Southern player and team captain in 1909. Later, as chairman of Tennessee's Athletic Council, Dougherty was responsible for bringing Bob Neyland to Knoxville as head coach.

GENE MCEVER
Halfback, 1928–1929, 1931
Inducted 1954

McEver was the personification of power football in his day. Stocky, strong, and fast, he was nicknamed "the Wild Bull." McEver was a unanimous All-American halfback for three years: 1928, 1929, and 1931. (Knee surgery kept him sidelined for 1930.) In 1929, he led all of college football in scoring with 130 points. His 98-yard kickoff return against Alabama in 1928 helped thrust the Vols into the nation's consciousness.

BEATTIE FEATHERS
Halfback, 1931–1933
Inducted 1955

A halfback on Neyland's great teams of the early 1930s, William Beattie Feathers seemed to fly through opposing defenses. He was a threat to score from anywhere on the field. In Tennessee's 7–3 win over

The Greatest Players

Alabama in 1932, he averaged 48 yards on 21 punts and ran for the game's only touchdown. He was the SEC MVP and All-America in 1933. As a halfback with the Chicago Bears in 1934, Feathers set an NFL single-season record with 8.4 yards per carry, a mark that still stands.

BOBBY DODD
Quarterback, 1928–1930
Inducted 1959 (player), 1993 (coach)

As the quarterback of Tennessee's famous Hack, Mack, and Dodd backfield of 1928–1930, Bobby Dodd guided the Vols to a 27-1-2 record and made All-America in 1930. Like his coach, Bob Neyland, Dodd has a stadium named after him—at Georgia Tech, where he was head coach for 22 years (1945–1966) and won 71 percent of his games. Dodd is one of only three men enshrined in the College Football Hall of Fame as both a player and a coach.

HERMAN HICKMAN
Guard, 1929–1931
Inducted 1959

Up through his playing days at Tennessee (1929–1931), Herman Hickman ranked with Yale's Pudge Heffelfinger as the greatest guards ever to play the game. Hickman's legendary speed, power, and agility made him the most famous lineman in Southern football. He could outrun almost all of his teammates. He was a human road grader on offense, and on defense he left opposing blockers and ball carriers together in heaps on the ground. After playing professionally for three years, Hickman later went on to coach at both Army and Yale.

BOB SUFFRIDGE
Guard, 1938–1940
Inducted 1961

Bob Suffridge is the only three-time consensus All-American in Tennessee history. With Suffridge at guard, the Vols plowed through three straight regular-season slates without a loss. Not particularly big for a guard (6'1", 185 pounds) even in his day, Suffridge boasted a charge that has been compared to the thrust of a jet engine. According to Neyland: "Suff had the quickest and most powerful defensive charge of any lineman I've ever seen. He never made a bad play." He was arguably the best ever of the pulling single-wing guards.

GEORGE CAFEGO
Tailback, 1937–1939
Inducted 1969

George "Bad News" Cafego was a two-year All-America single-wing tailback for some of Neyland's greatest teams. Of Cafego, the immortal coach remarked: "In practice he couldn't do anything right. But for two hours on Saturday afternoons he did everything an All-American is supposed to do." Cafego's powerful, churning legs made him hard to bring down. He also possessed blinding speed and was a deadly accurate passer. Cafego was the SEC Player of the Year in 1938, when the Volunteers went 11–0. Later in life, Cafego spent 30 years as an assistant football coach at his alma mater.

BOWDEN WYATT
End, 1936–1938
Inducted 1972 (player), 1997 (coach)

As a senior in 1938, Bowden Wyatt was captain of the 11–0 Tennessee squad. He was an All-SEC and All-America end that year, in addition to his duties as placekicker. He went on to an illustrious head coaching career at Wyoming, Arkansas and Tennessee. Along with Amos Alonzo Stagg and fellow Vol Bobby Dodd, Wyatt ranks as one of just three men in the College Football Hall of Fame as both a player and a coach.

ED MOLINSKI
Guard, 1938–1940
Inducted 1990

Molinski teamed with Bob Suffridge to form possibly the top guard combo of all time through the halcyon days of 1938, 1939 and 1940. He was a key to the Tennessee defense that made shutouts a regular occurrence, including the unscored-upon unit of 1939. Molinski was All-SEC and All-America in 1939 and 1940.

HANK LAURICELLA
Tailback, 1949–1951
Inducted 1981

Lauricella, a New Orleans native, was an All-SEC selection in 1950 and an All-American in 1951, when he finished as runner-up in the Heisman voting behind Princeton's Dick Kazmaier. Lauricella was the ultimate single-wing tailback—a position made famous at UT during Robert Neyland's tenure. Lauricella's shining moment as a Vol came in the 1951 Cotton Bowl game when he weaved through the Texas defense for 75 yards to set up the first touchdown of the day in the Vols' 20–14 victory. He then proceeded to lead Tennessee to its first consensus national title the following season.

The Greatest Players

JOHN MICHELS
Guard, 1950–1952
Inducted 1996

John Michels may be overshadowed by the likes of Suffridge, Molinski, Dougherty and Hickman as UT guards, but as a blocker he took a back seat to none. He was All-SEC in 1951 and All-America in 1952. Tennessee won 27 of 32 games with Michels in the lineup. He later went on to a career as an assistant coach in the NFL. He was on the staff of the Minnesota Vikings for 27 years, including four Super Bowl campaigns.

DOUG ATKINS
End, 1950–1952
Inducted 1985

If Doug Atkins isn't the scariest defensive end ever to play organized football, he is certainly in the top three. He was All-SEC in 1951, All-America in 1952 and the first-round draft pick of the Chicago Bears in 1953. Atkins was voted the SEC Player of the Quarter Century (1950–1974) by the Football Writers Association. He is the only UT Vol in both the College and Pro Football halls of fame.

JOHNNY MAJORS
Tailback, 1954–1956
Inducted 1987

Johnny Majors finished second in the Heisman voting after leading Tennessee to a 10–1 record in 1956. (Paul Hornung of 2–8 Notre Dame won it.) Through his career, Majors led the Vols in passing, rushing, scoring, punting, punt returns, and kickoff returns. He was a two-time SEC Player of the Year, in 1955 and 1956. After his playing career, Majors held head coaching jobs at Iowa State, Pittsburgh, and UT, winning a national title in 1976 at Pitt.

BOB JOHNSON
Center, 1965–1967
Inducted 1989

Bob Johnson was a two-time All-America center for Tennessee in 1966 and 1967, captaining coach Doug Dickey's 1967 squad that won a share of the national championship. A member of the SEC All-Quarter Century team, Johnson also was an Academic All-American and recipient of the National Football Foundation Post-Graduate Scholarship in 1967. He was the first overall NFL Draft choice in 1968, taken by the expansion Cincinnati Bengals.

FRANK EMANUEL
Linebacker, 1963–1965
Inducted 2004

Emanuel played a key role in helping to revive the Tennessee football program in the early 1960s. A consensus First Team All-American, Emanuel led the Vols to an 8–1–2 record and a Bluebonnet Bowl victory in 1965—their first bowl appearance in eight years. Emanuel was the first draft choice of the Miami Dolphins and was featured on the cover of *Sports Illustrated* as an example of the bidding war for players between the NFL and the AFL.

STEVE DELONG
Middle Guard, 1962–1964
Inducted 1993

Steve DeLong was a two-time All-American in 1963 and 1964, and team captain in 1964. Tennessee's football fortunes were on a down cycle in DeLong's senior year, but that didn't deter the Norfolk, Virginia, native from dominating games at his middle guard position. He took home the Outland Trophy as the nation's best interior lineman and was a first-round draft pick in 1965.

STEVE KINER
Linebacker, 1967–1969
Inducted 1999

Bear Bryant once compared Steve Kiner to former 'Bama great Lee Roy Jordan. Kiner was one of the finest linebackers the SEC ever produced. The conference's Sophomore of the Year in 1967, Kiner was an All-American in 1968 and 1969. He possessed more speed than most running backs and was the toughest linebacker in the game during his day.

REGGIE WHITE
Defensive Tackle, 1980–1983
Inducted 2002

It might require a knowledge of history to recognize the names of some of Tennessee's Hall of Famers, almost everybody knows Reggie White, the Vols' latest inductee. The "Minister of Defense" holds school records for sacks in a single season with 15 in 1983 and in a career with 32. He holds the NFL record for career sacks with 192.5. In 1983, White was the SEC Player of the Year and an All-American.

1,112
Tackles by Reggie White during his 17-year professional career

Iowa's Chuck Long was on the receiving end of this Reggie White sack, but he's in common company. The "Minister of Defense" had 32 sacks during his career at Tennessee.

Other Tennessee Greats

CONDREDGE HOLLOWAY
Quarterback, 1972–1974

Condredge Holloway threw for more than 3,000 yards as a quarterback at Tennessee, and he may be even better remembered as a dazzling open-field runner. But his greatest legacy is the one he left as the first black quarterback in the history of the Southeastern Conference. Holloway also was a gifted baseball player, and turned down a lucrative offer from the Montreal Expos to remain at UT. After graduation, Holloway enjoyed a long and successful career in the Canadian Football League.

PEYTON MANNING
Quarterback, 1994–1997

Peyton Manning's return home from the Downtown Athletic Club without the 1997 Heisman Trophy was tough for fans to swallow. He had just led the Vols to an 11–2 record and the SEC title. He finished his career having rewritten the school passing record book and extensively edited the SEC records. He left Knoxville in possession of conference marks for career wins as a starter, completions, completion percentage, passing yards, and total offense, among others. He held NCAA records for lowest interception percentage for a season and career, and he ranked third in NCAA history in passing yards and total offense. He won the 1997 Davey O'Brien and Johnny Unitas Awards, was the SEC Player of the Year, and was a unanimous All-American.

One of the greatest athletes to suit up for Tennessee, Condredge Holloway only came to UT after his mother refused to sign his contract to join baseball's Montreal Expos. Holloway eventually made his way to Canada as a quarterback, and was a 1998 inductee to the Canadian Football Hall of Fame.

PEERLESS PRICE
Wide Receiver, 1995–1998

Price was the ultimate deep threat for the Vols during the 1998 title run, and he always came through in the clutch. Against Alabama, Price had a 100-yard kickoff return to break open the game. In the SEC Championship Game win over Mississippi State, Price reeled in an over-the-shoulder 41-yard TD pass. He was also the MVP of the 23–16 win over Florida State in the 1998 title game with four receptions for 199 yards and a touchdown.

AL WILSON
Linebacker, 1995–1998

Wilson is the standard by which all modern-era UT linebackers are measured. Tough, mean, and aggressive between the lines, Wilson was the unquestioned leader of the 1998 national championship team. In the 20–17 overtime win over Florida, Wilson had 13 tackles and three forced fumbles, and he played most of the rest of the season with a shoulder that would regularly pop out of place.

TEE MARTIN
Quarterback, 1996–1999

Martin entrenched himself in UT history by leading the Vols to a perfect 13–0 record and the 1998 national championship. He finished his career 13–0 as a starter in games played at Neyland Stadium. Martin's big arm and mobility were key on two of Tennessee's signature plays during his tenure: the bootleg and deep passes to receivers Peerless Price and Cedrick Wilson. Like Peyton Manning, Martin has a wax figurine of his likeness in the Vols' Hall of Fame room and a street named after him near the stadium.

DEON GRANT
Free Safety, 1996–1999

Grant will be remembered as one of the greatest athletes to grace the UT secondary, playing "center field" at free safety, enabling the Vols to play what amounted to an eight-man front. Grant's TD-saving fourth quarter interception against Florida, of which he said, "The angels lifted me," will forever be remembered as a keystone play of the 1998 national championship season. Grant went on to win the SEC's Defensive Player of the Year award in 1999 with nine interceptions.

JAMAL LEWIS
Running Back, 1997–1999

"Give the Ball to Jamal" was a familiar refrain among Vols' fans during this powerful running back's tenure. Lewis' rare blend of power and speed enabled him to rush for a UT freshman-record 1,364 yards during the 1997 season and lead the Vols to the SEC Championship and an Orange Bowl appearance. Lewis was key early in the 1998 national title run before he sustained a season-ending knee injury the fourth game of the season against Auburn.

TRAVIS HENRY
Tailback, 1997–2000

Known to Tennessee fans as "the Cheese," Henry quickly became a fan favorite with his powerful bursts into scrimmage and pile-moving ways. It was Henry who put the Vols on his shoulders in the final minutes of Tennessee's miraculous 28–24 come-from-behind win over Arkansas, powering his way through the Razorbacks and into the end zone. Henry finished his career as the school's all-time leading rusher with 3,078 yards on 556 carries and a career 5.5 yards-per-carry rushing average.

The Greatest Players

JOHN HENDERSON
Defensive Tackle, 1999–2001

John Henderson won the 2000 Outland Trophy and was a finalist for the 2001 award despite fighting through injuries like a trooper. In 2000, his second year as a starter, the Nashville native recorded 71 tackles and 12 sacks, forced four fumbles, and recovered three. He added another 39 stops and 4.5 sacks during his injury-shortened 2001 campaign. Big John was a two-year All-American, plugging the middle for the vaunted Vol defense.

CASEY CLAUSEN
Quarterback, 2000–2003

The school's second all-time leading passer, Clausen slew the mighty Florida Gators at the Swamp in consecutive road trips, giving UT its first wins in Gainesville since Phillip Fulmer was a player in 1971. What Clausen—a.k.a. "the Iceman"—lacked in athleticism, he made up for with poise, toughness, and competitive fire. In his first start as a true freshman, Clausen beat Alabama on the road with a 17-of-24, two-TD passing performance that included one play where he continued to fight for yardage in a pileup despite his helmet having been torn off.

34

Wins in Casey Clausen's career at Tennessee. He only lost in 10 starts over four seasons.

Part of one of the most famous college football quarter-backing families, Casey Clausen paved the way for his younger brothers and is the second-most-prolific passer in UT history. Clausen started all but three games during his Tennessee career, and finished 14-1 on the road.

NFL Draft Picks

1936: Roy Rose, end, 4, 36, New York Giants

1937: Phil Dickens, back, 6, 52, Chicago Cardinals

1938: None

1939: Babe Wood, back, 8, 86, Chicago Bears; Bowden Wyatt, end, 11, 91, Chicago Cardinals

1940: George Cafego, back, 1, 1, Chicago Cardinals; Jim Rike, center, 4, 46, Detroit; Boyd Clay, tackle, 11, 95, Cleveland; Sam Bartholomew, back, 11, 118, Washington; Len Coffman, back, 14, 14, Brooklyn

1941: Marshall "Abe" Shares, tackle, 2, 14, Cleveland; Bob Foxx, back, 3, 17, Chicago Cardinals; Bob Suffridge, guard, 6, 42, Pittsburgh; Ed Cifers, end, 6, 50, Washington

1942: Johnny Butler, back, 7, 51, Pittsburgh; Ray Graves, center, 9, 73, Philadelphia; Ike Peel, back, 15, 132, Cleveland; Don Edmiston, tackle, 17, 160, Chicago Bears

1943: Al Hust, end, 3, 29, Chicago Cardinals

1944: Bob Cifers, back, 2, 14, Detroit; Jim Gaffney, back, 15, 149, Washington; Jim Myers, guard, 15, 151, Pittsburgh; Bud Hubbell, end, 15, 152, Cleveland

One of the captains on Tennessee's historic 1939 team, Samuel Bartholomew was one of five Volunteers taken in the 1940 NFL Draft. He played both ways on the 1941 Philadelphia Eagles before his pro career was ended by World War II.

Walter Slater is seen here discussing strategy with Robert Neyland in preparation for the Orange Bowl against Rice. Slater captained the 1946 Volunteers and was later taken in the NFL Draft by the Philadelphia Eagles.

1945: Bob Dobelstein, guard, 4, 28, Chicago Cardinals; Casey Stephenson, back, 7, 65, Green Bay; Dick Huffman, tackle, 9, 81, Cleveland; Art Brandau, center, 10, 89, Pittsburgh; Roy Cross, end, 10, 90, Brooklyn; Billy Bevis, back, 12, 119, New York Giants; Jim Chadwell, tackle, 23, 240, New York Giants; Russ Morrow, center, 24, 247, Detroit

1946: Walter Slater, back, 3, 37, Philadelphia; Jim Vugrin, guard, 26, 241, Chicago Cardinals; Bob Long, back, 28, 268, Philadelphia

1947: Max Partin, back, 9, 73, Los Angeles Rams; Denver Crawford, tackle, 15, 130, Green Bay; Billy Gold, back, 16, 139, Washington; Bill Hillman, back, 27, 246, Detroit. AAFC: Bud Hubbell, end, 9, 65, Miami; Walter Slater, back, 13, 102, San Francisco

1948: Jim Powell, end, 30, 285, Chicago Cardinals

1949: Al Russas, end, 13, 122, Detroit; Bob Lund, back, 14, 141, Philadelphia. AAFC: Al Russas, end, 10, 75, Buffalo; Bob Lind, back, 11, 84, San Francisco

1950: Norm Messeroll, tackle, 15, 185, New York Bulldogs

1951: Jack Stroud, tackle, 5, 61, New York Giants; J.W. Sherrill, back, 10, 120, Chicago Bears; Jimmy Hill, back, 15, 178, Detroit; Bud Sherrod, end, 17, 206, New York Giants; Bill Pearman, guard, 26, 309, Pittsburgh; John Gruble, end, 30, 356, Pittsburgh

The Greatest Players

1952: Bert Rechichar, back, 1, 10, Cleveland; Gordon Polofsky, back, 5, 61, Los Angeles Rams; Herky Payne, back, 9, 102, Pittsburgh; Andy Kozar, back, 12, 140, Chicago Bears; Vince Kaseta, end, 16, 182, New York Yankees; Hank Lauricella, back, 17, 202, Detroit; Ted Daffer, guard, 21, 248, Chicago Bears; Charlie Stokes, tackle, 26, 303, Green Bay

1953: Doug Atkins, tackle, 1, 11, Cleveland; Frank Holohan, tackle, 10, 114, Pittsburgh; Jim Haslam, tackle, 24, 283, Green Bay; Ed Morgan, back, 24, 284, San Francisco; John Michels, guard, 25, 297, Philadelphia; Pat Shires, back, 29, 339, Washington; Andy Myers, guard, 30, 358, Cleveland

1954: Bill Barbish, back, 8, 95, Cleveland; Bob Fisher, tackle, 10, 115, Pittsburgh

1955: Darris McCord, tackle, 3, 36, Detroit; Ed Nickla, guard, 14, 167, Chicago Bears; Pat Oleksiak, back, 18, 216, Detroit; Jimmy Wade, back, 20, 238, Philadelphia; Lamar Leachman, center, 30, 360, Cleveland

1956: Tom Tracy, back, 5, 50, Detroit; Buddy Cruze, end, 12, 143, Chicago Bears

1957: John Gordy, tackle, 2, 24, Detroit; Frank Kolinsky, tackle, 28, 329, Pittsburgh

1958: Bill Anderson, back, 3, 31, Washington; Bobby Gordon, back, 6, 63, Chicago Cardinals; Al Carter, back, 22, 257, Chicago Bears; Bobby Sandlin, back, 24, 285, Baltimore

1959: Carl Smith, back, 9, 101, Detroit; Lebron Shields, tackle, 22, 256, Detroit

1960: **AFL:** Joe Schaffer, tackle, Buffalo

1961: Mike Lucci, center, 5, 69, Cleveland; Billy Majors, back, 12, 168, Philadelphia; Charlie Baker, tackle, 20, 279, Cleveland. **AFL:** Bill Majors, halfback, 9, Buffalo; Mike Lucci, center, 20, Los Angeles Chargers; Charlie Baker, tackle, 22, Buffalo

1962: Glenn Glass, halfback, 17, 231, Chicago Bears. **AFL:** Glenn Glass, halfback, 17, 231, Chicago Bears; Glenn Glass, halfback, 2, 12, Buffalo; Mike Stratton, end, 13, 100, Buffalo

1963: None

1964: Dick Evey, tackle, 1, 14, Chicago Bears; Bob Zvolerin, tackle, 12, 158, Washington; Ed Beard, tackle, 14, 183, San Francisco. **AFL:** Dick Evey, tackle, 2, 12, Buffalo; Ed Beard, tackle, 20, 159, Oakland

1965: Steve DeLong, tackle, 1, 6, Chicago Bears; Whit Canale, fullback, 17, 227, Pittsburgh. **AFL:** Steve DeLong, tackle, 1, 8, San Diego

The Greatest Players

Though his Olympic hopes were dashed in 1968 by an injured hamstring, Richmond Flowers still played in the pro ranks. For five years he suited up for the Dallas Cowboys and New York Giants.

1966: Tom Fisher, linebacker, 3, 40, New York Giants; Frank Emanuel, linebacker, 4, 52, Philadelphia; Stan Mitchell, fullback, 8, 115, Washington; Austin Denney, end, 11, 160, Dallas; Bob Petrella, defensive back, 12, 181, Minnesota; Hal Wantland, halfback, 16, 235, Washington. **AFL:** Frank Emanuel, linebacker, 2, Miami; Bob Petrella, defensive back, 8, Miami. Redshirt: Tom Fisher, linebacker, 1, Houston; Austin Denney, end, 2, New York Jets; John Crumbacher, tackle, 4, Oakland

1967: Paul Naumoff, linebacker, 3, 60, Detroit; Ron Widby, kicker, 4, 81, New Orleans; John Mills, end, 8, 199, San Diego; Harold Stancell, defensive back, 9, 231, Philadelphia; Doug Archibald, defensive back, 16, 405, New York Jets

1968: Bob Johnson, center, 1, 2, Cincinnati; Dewey Warren, quarterback, 6, 155, Cincinnati; Walter Chadwick, running back, 6, 164, Green Bay; John Boynton, tackle, 7, 172, Miami; Elliot Gammage, tight end, 8, 209, San Diego; Joe Graham, guard, 15, 394, Philadelphia; Charley Fulton, running back, 16, 413, Boston

1969: Richmond Flowers, flanker, 2, 49, Dallas; Karl Kresmer, kicker, 5, 128, Miami; Jim Weatherford, defensive back, 15, 366, Atlanta; Chick McGeehan, flanker, 15, 375, Miami; Bill Justus, defensive back, 15, 386, Dallas

1970: Jack Reynolds, linebacker, 1, 22, Los Angeles Rams; Steve Kiner, linebacker, 3, 73, Dallas; Herman Weaver, punter, 9, 227, Detroit; Pete Athas, defensive back, 10, 257, Dallas; Ken DeLong, tight end, 15, 387, Dallas; Frank Yanossy, defensive tackle, 16, 391

1971: Lester McClain, wide receiver, 9, 220, Chicago Bears; Bobby Scott, quarterback, 14, 340, New Orleans; Chip Kell, center, 17, 429, San Diego

1972: Bobby Majors, defensive back, 3, 76, Philadelphia; George Hunt, kicker, 5, 122, Cleveland; Jackie Walker, linebacker, 6, 148, San Francisco; Curt Watson, running back, 6, 150, New Orleans; Ray Nettles, linebacker, 6, 155, Miami; Gary Theiler, tight end, 12, 308, Baltimore; Joe Balthrop, guard, 16, 397, New Orleans

1973: Jamie Rotella, linebacker, 3, 62, Baltimore; Conrad Graham, defensive back, 8, 187, Chicago Bears; Carl Johnson, linebacker, 10, 254, Dallas; Richard Earl, tackle, 11, 265, Buffalo

1974: Bill Rudder, running back, 3, 59, San Diego; Haskel Stanback, running back, 5, 114, Cincinnati; Eddie Brown, defensive back, 8, 199, Cleveland; Gary Valbuena, quarterback, 10, 260, Miami; Gene Killian, offensive lineman, 16, 413, Dallas

1975: Neil Clabo, punter, 10, 258, Minnesota; Condredge Holloway, quarterback, 12, 306, New England; Ricky Townsend, kicker, 13, 314, New York Giants; Paul Careathers, running back, 15, 389, Oakland

1976: Ron McCartney, linebacker, 2, 53, Los Angeles Rams; Tommy West, linebacker, 16, 433, Tampa Bay

1977: Stanley Morgan, wide receiver, 1, 25, New England; Larry Seivers, wide receiver, 4, 111, Seattle; Mickey Marvin, guard, 4, 112, Oakland; Andy Spiva, linebacker, 5, 135, St. Louis

1978: Craig Colquitt, punter, 3, 76, Pittsburgh; Jessie Turnbow, defensive tackle, 8, 205, Cleveland; Russ Williams, defensive back, 9, 250, Dallas; Brent Watson, tackle, 10, 261, Cleveland; Pat Ryan, quarterback, 11, 281, New York Jets

1979: Robert Shaw, center, 1, 27, Dallas; Jeff Moore, wide receiver, 3, 58, Los Angeles Rams; Kelsey Finch, running back, 12, 311, New Orleans

1980: Roland James, defensive back, 1, 14, New England; Craig Puki, linebacker, 3, 77, San Francisco

1981: Tim Irwin, 3, 74, Minnesota; Danny Spradlin, linebacker, 5, 137, Dallas; Alan Duncan, kicker, 7, 174, Philadelphia; Hubert Simpson, running back, 10, 258, Cincinnati; Brad White, defensive tackle, 12, 310, Tampa Bay

1982: Anthony Hancock, wide receiver, 1, 11, Kansas City; Brian Ingram, linebacker, 4, 111, New England; Lamont Jeffers, linebacker, 6, 153, Washington; Terry Daniels, defensive back, 10, 265, Washington

College and Pro Football Hall of Famer Reggie White had his number retired at Tennessee on October 1, 2005. Sadly, White had passed away the year before and was not around to see his alma mater honor his legacy.

1983: Willie Gault, wide receiver, 1, 18, Chicago; Darryal Wilson, wide receiver, 2, 47, New England; Mike Cofer, defensive end, 3, 67, Detroit; Mike Miller, wide receiver, 4, 104, Green Bay; Lee Jenkins, defensive back, 11, 281, New York Giants

1984: Clyde Duncan, wide receiver 1, 11, St. Louis; Mark Studaway, defensive end, 4, 85, Houston; Curt Singer, tackle, 6, 167, Washington; Randall Morris, running back, 10, 270, Seattle; Lenny Taylor, wide receiver, 12, 313, Green Bay; Glenn Streno, center, 12, 327, Detroit. Supplemental: Reggie White, defensive end, 1, 4, Philadelphia

1985: Alvin Toles, linebacker, 1, 24, New Orleans; Carl Zander, linebacker, 2, 43, Cincinnati; Johnnie Jones, running back, 5, 137, Seattle; Faud Reveiz, kicker, 7, 195, Miami; Reggie McKenzie, linebacker, 10, 275, Los Angeles Raiders; Raleigh McKenzie, guard, 11, 290, Washington; Tony Simmons, defensive end, 12, 318, San Diego

1986: Tim McGee, wide receiver, 1, 21, Cincinnati; Jeff Powell, running back, 6, 166, Chicago; Eric Swanson, wide receiver, 7, 170, St. Louis; Tommy Sims, defensive back, 7, 190, Indianapolis; David Douglas, guard, 8, 204, Cincinnati

1987: Bruce Wilkerson, tackle, 2, 52, Los Angeles Raiders; Joey Clinkscales, wide receiver, 9, 233, Pittsburgh; Dale Jones, linebacker, 10, 262, Dallas; Carlos Reveiz, kicker, 11, 302, New England

1988: Terry McDaniel, defensive back, 1, 9, Los Angeles Raiders; Anthony Miller, wide receiver, 1, 15, San Diego; John Bruhin, guard, 4, 86, Tampa Bay; William Howard, running back, 5, 113, Tampa Bay; Harry Galbreath, guard, 8, 212, Miami; Joey Howard, tackle, 9, 238, San Diego

1989: Keith DeLong, linebacker, 1, 28, San Francisco; Jeff Francis, quarterback, 6, 140, Los Angeles Raiders

1990: Reggie Cobb, running back, 2, 30, Tampa Bay; Marion Hobby, defensive end, 3, 74, Minnesota; Eric Still, guard, 4, 99, Houston; Tracy Hayworth, linebacker, 7, 174, Detroit; Kent Elmore, punter, 7, 190, Los Angeles Rams; Thomas Woods, wide receiver, 8, 205, Miami

1991: Charles McRae, tackle, 1, 7, Tampa Bay; Antone Davis, tackle, 1, 8, Green Bay; Alvin Harper, wide receiver, 1, 12, Dallas; Chuck Webb, running back, 3, 81, Green Bay; Harlan Davis, defensive back, 5, 128, Seattle; Anthony Morgan, wide receiver, 5, 134, Chicago; Greg Amsler, running back, 8, 198, Phoenix; Roland Poles, running back, 10, 254, San Diego; Vince Moore, wide receiver, 11, 279, New England

Reggie Cobb celebrates his Peach Bowl winning touchdown on January 2, 1989. After a standout career as a
Volunteer, Cobb spent seven years in the NFL.

1992: Dale Carter, defensive back, 1, 20, Kansas City; Chris Mims, defensive end, 1, 23, San Diego; Carl Pickens, wide receiver, 2, 31, Cincinnati; Chuck Smith, defensive end, 2, 51, Atlanta; Jeremy Lincoln, defensive back, 3, 80, Chicago; Tom Myslinski, offensive lineman, 4, 109, Dallas; Shazzon Bradley, nose tackle, 9, 240, Green Bay; Bernard Dafney, tackle, 9, 247, Houston; Daryl Hardy, linebacker, 10, 270, Atlanta

1993: Todd Kelly, defensive end, 1, 27, San Francisco; Dave Thomas, defensive back, 8, 203, Dallas

1994: Heath Shuler, quarterback, 1, 3, Washington; Charlie Garner, running back, 2, 42, Philadelphia; Cory Fleming, wide receiver, 3, 87, San Francisco; Shane Bonham, defensive tackle, 3, 93, Detroit; Horace Morris, linebacker, 5, 152, New York Jets

1995: James Stewart, running back, 1, 19, Jacksonville; Ronald Davis, defensive back, 2, 41, Atlanta; Aaron Hayden, running back, 4, 104, San Diego; Ben Talley, linebacker, 4, 133, New York Giants; Jerry Colquit (forfeited), quarterback, 6, 191, Carolina; Billy Williams, wide receiver, 7, 212, Arizona

1996: Jason Layman, tackle, 2, 48, Houston; DeRon Jenkins, defensive back, 2, 55, Baltimore; Shane Burton, defensive tackle, 5, 150, Miami; Nilo Silvan, wide receiver, 6, 180, Tampa Bay; Scott

Galyon, linebacker, 6, 182, New York Giants; Steve White, linebacker, 6, 194, Philadelphia; Leslie Ratliffe, tackle, 7, 213, Denver; Jeff Smith, center, 7, 241, Kansas City

1997: Joey Kent, wide receiver, 2, 46, Houston; Jay Graham, running back, 3, 64, Baltimore; Ray Austin, defensive back, 5, 145, New York Jets

1998: Peyton Manning, quarterback, 1, 1, Indianapolis; Terry Fair, defensive back, 1, 20, Detroit; Marcus Nash, wide receiver, 1, 30, Denver; Leonard Little, defensive end, 3, 65, St. Louis; Jonathan Brown, defensive end, 3, 90, Green Bay; Trey Teague, center, 7, 200, Denver; Andy McCullough, wide receiver, 7, 204, New Orleans; Corey Gaines, defensive back, 7, 231, Indianapolis

1999: Al Wilson, linebacker, 1, 31, Denver; Peerless Price, wide receiver, 2, 53, Buffalo; Shawn Bryson, running back, 3, 86, Buffalo; Steve Johnson, defensive back, 6, 170, Seattle; Jeff Hall, kicker, 6, 181, Washington; Corey Terry, defensive end, 7, 250, Indianapolis

2000: Jamal Lewis, running back, 1, 5, Baltimore; Shaun Ellis, defensive end, 1, 12, New York Jets; Raynoch Thompson, linebacker, 2, 41, Arizona; Chad Clifton, tackle, 2, 44, Green Bay; Dwayne Goodrich, defensive back, 2, 49, Dallas; Cosey Coleman, guard, 2, 51, Tampa Bay; Deon Grant, defensive back, 2, 57, Carolina; Darwin Walker, defensive tackle, 3, 71, Arizona; Tee Martin, quarterback, 5, 163, Pittsburgh

2001: Travis Henry, running back, 2, 58, Buffalo; Eric Westmoreland, linebacker, 3, 73, Jacksonville; David Leaverton, punter, 5, 142, Jacksonville; Cedrick Wilson, wide receiver, 6, 169, San Francisco; David Martin, tight end, 6, 198, Green Bay

2002: John Henderson, defensive tackle, 1, 9, Jacksonville; Donte' Stallworth, wide receiver, 1, 13, New Orleans; Albert Haynesworth, defensive tackle, 1, 15, Tennessee; Fred Weary, guard, 3, 66, Houston; Will Overstreet, defensive end, 3, 80, Atlanta; Travis Stephens, running back, 4, 119, Tampa Bay; Andre Lott, defensive back, 5, 159, Washington; Reggie Coleman, tackle, 6, 192, Washington; Teddy Gaines, defensive back, 7, 256, San Francisco; Dominique Stevenson, linebacker, 7, 260, Buffalo

2003: Eddie Moore, linebacker, 2, 49, Miami; Kelley Washington, wide receiver, 3, 65, Cincinnati; Jason Witten, tight end, 3, 69, Dallas; Julian Battle, defensive back, 3, 92, Kansas City; Aubrayo Franklin, defensive tackle, 5, 146, Baltimore; Keyon Whiteside, linebacker, 5, 162, Indianapolis; Rashad Moore, defensive tackle, 6, 183, Seattle; Demetrin Veal, defensive end, 7, 238, Atlanta

2004: Gibril Wilson, defensive back, 5, 136, New York Giants; Troy Fleming, running back, 6, 191, Tennessee; Mark Jones, wide receiver, 7, 206, Tampa Bay; Scott Wells, center, 7, 251, Green Bay

Jason Witten scores in the sixth overtime of the 2002 game against Arkansas. He has gone on to tremendous success in the professional ranks, making five straight Pro Bowls.

2005: Kevin Burnett, linebacker, 2, 42, Dallas; Dustin Colquitt, punter, 3, 99, Kansas City; Cedric Houston, running back, 6, 182, New York Jets

2006: Jason Allen, defensive back, 1, 16, Miami; Parys Haralson, defensive end, 5, 140, San Francisco; Omar Gaither, linebacker, 5, 168, Philadelphia; Jesse Mahelona, defensive tackle, 5, 169, Tennessee; Kevin Simon, linebacker, 7, 250, Washington

2007: Justin Harrell, defensive tackle, 1, 16, Green bay; Robert Meachem, wide receiver, 1, 27, New Orleans; Arron Sears, tackle, 2, 35, Tampa Bay; Turk McBride, defensive end, 2, 54, Kansas City; Jonathan Wade, cornerback, 3, 84, St. Louis; Marvin Mitchell, linebacker, 7, 220, New Orleans

2008: Jerod Mayo, linebacker, 1, 10, New England; Brad Cottam, tight end, 3, 76, Kansas City; Erik Ainge, quarterback, 5, 162, New York Jets

2009: Robert Ayers defensive end, 1, 18, Denver

140

Tackles by Jerod Mayo in 2007, the most in the SEC.

Jerod Mayo returns an interception for a touchdown in a 2007 game against Arkansas. The 2008 AP Defensive Rookie of the Year, Mayo finished his rookie pro season with 128 tackles.

Records & Leaders
Rushing

GAME

YARDS	NAME	OPPONENT	YEAR
1. 294	Chuck Webb	Mississippi	1989
2. 250	Chuck Webb	Arkansas	1990
3. 248	Tony Thompson	Mississippi State	1990
4. 248	Johnnie Jones	Vanderbilt	1983
5. 236	Tony Thompson	Vanderbilt	1990
6. 234	Johnnie Jones	Rutgers	1983
7. 232	Jamal Lewis	Georgia	1997
8. 226	Travis Stephens	Florida	2001
9. 225	Reggie Cobb	Auburn	1989
10. 223	Arian Foster	Vanderbilt	2005

SEASON

NAME	YEAR	ATT.	YARDS
1. Travis Stephens	2001	291	1,464
2. Jay Graham	1995	272	1,438
3. Jamal Lewis	1997	232	1,364
4. Travis Henry	2000	253	1,314
5. Johnnie Jones	1984	229	1,290
6. Tony Thompson	1990	219	1,261
7. Chuck Webb	1989	209	1,236
8. Reggie Cobb	1987	237	1,197
9. Arian Foster	2007	245	1,193
10. Charlie Garner	1993	159	1,161

Travis Stephens carries for a go-ahead touchdown against Georgia in 2001. His 1,464 rushing yards that season remain a school record.

CAREER

NAME	YEARS	ATT	YARDS
1. Travis Henry	1997-2000	556	3,078
2. Arian Foster	2005-08	650	2,991
3. James Stewart	1991-94	531	2,890
4. Johnnie Jones	1981-84	517	2,852
5. Jamal Lewis	1997-99	487	2,677
6. Cedric Houston	2001-04	501	2,634
7. Jay Graham	1993-96	540	2,609
8. Curt Watson	1969-71	529	2,364
9. Reggie Cobb	1987-89	445	2,360
10. Travis Stephens	1997-01	488	2,336

Passing

GAME

NAME	OPPONENT	YEAR	YARDS
1. Peyton Manning	Kentucky	1997	523
2. Peyton Manning	Florida	1996	492
3. Peyton Manning	Northwestern	1997	408
4. Peyton Manning	Southern Miss	1997	399
(tie) Andy Kelly	Notre Dame	1990	399
6. Erik Ainge	Kentucky	2007	397
7. Casey Clausen	Michigan	2001	393
8. Andy Kelly	Florida	1991	392
9. Tony Robinson	UCLA	1985	387
10. Bobby Scott	Florida	1970	385

SEASON

NAME	YEAR	YARDS
1. Peyton Manning	1997	3,819
2. Erik Ainge	2007	3,522
3. Peyton Manning	1996	3,287
4. Erik Ainge	2006	2,989
5. Casey Clausen	2001	2,969
6. Casey Clausen	2003	2,968
7. Peyton Manning	1995	2,954
8. Andy Kelly	1991	2,759
9. Heath Shuler	1993	2,353
10. Tee Martin	1999	2,317

CAREER

NAME	YEARS	ATT	COMP	YARDS	TDS
1. Peyton Manning					
	1994-97	1,381	863	11,201	89
2. Casey Clausen					
	2000-03	1,270	775	9,707	75
3. Erik Ainge					
	2000-07	1,210	783	8,700	72
4. Andy Kelly					
	1988-91	846	514	6,397	36
5. Jeff Francis					
	1985-88	768	476	5,867	31
6. Tee Martin					
	1996-99	588	326	4,592	32
7. Heath Shuler					
	1991-93	513	316	4,088	36
8. Alan Cockrell					
	1981-83	568	317	3,823	26
9. Jimmy Streater					
	1976-79	467	241	3,433	17
10. Bobby Scott					
	1968-70	498	236	3,371	32

The Greatest Players

Receiving

GAME

YARDS	NAME	OPPONENT	YEAR
1. 256	Kelley Washington	LSU	2001
2. 225	Johnny Mills	Kentucky	1966
3. 217	Willie Gault	Vanderbilt	1981
4. 201	Carl Pickens	Kentucky	1990
(tie) 201	Stanley Morgan	Texas Christian	1976
6. 199	Peerless Price	Florida State	1998
7. 197	Kelley Washington	Rutgers	2002
8. 196	Anthony Hancock	Wisconsin	1981
9. 195	Marcus Nash	Kentucky	1997
10. 190	Tim McGee	Vanderbilt	1984

SEASON

NAME	YEAR	NO.	YARDS	TD
1. Robert Meachem	2006	71	1,298	11
2. Marcus Nash	1997	76	1,170	13
3. Joey Kent	1996	68	1,080	7
4. Joey Kent	1995	69	1,055	9
5. Kelley Washington	2001	64	1,010	5
6. Lucas Taylor	2007	73	1,000	5
7. Tim McGee	1985	50	947	7
8. Peerless Price	1998	61	920	10
9. Carl Pickens	1990	53	917	6
10. Carl Pickens	1991	49	877	5

CAREER

NAME	YEARS	NO.	YARDS
1. Joey Kent	1993-96	183	2,814
2. Marcus Nash	1994-97	177	2,447
3. Peerless Price	1995-98	147	2,298
4. Robert Meachem	2004-06	125	2,140
5. Cedrick Wilson	1997-2000	159	2,137
6. Tim McGee	1982-85	123	2,042
7. Larry Seivers	1973-76	117	1,924
8. Carl Pickens	1989-91	109	1,875
9. Anthony Hancock	1978-81	106	1,826
10. Donte Stallworth	1999-2001	99	1,747

Marcus Nash won a pair of Super Bowl rings during his NFL career. In 2000, he failed to appear in a game due to a broken jaw, but still became a champion when his Baltimore Ravens won the Super Bowl.

Other Records

Points, game: 30, Gene McEver vs. South Carolina, 1929 (modern record 24)

Points, season: 130, Gene McEver, 1929 (21 touchdowns, four PATs)

Points, career: 371, Jeff Hall, 1995-98 (61 field goals, 188 PATs)

All-purpose, game: 294, Chuck Webb vs. Ole Miss, 1989

All-purpose, season: 1,721, Reggie Cobb, 1987

All-purpose, career: 4,642, Stanley Morgan, 1973-76

Interceptions, game: 3, Deon Grant vs. Auburn, 1999; Preston Warren vs. Boston College, 1988; Chris White vs. UCLA, 1985; Tim Priest vs. Alabama, 1970; Bill Young vs. Rice, 1968; Albert Dorsey vs. Alabama, 1967; J.W. Sherrill vs. Kentucky, 1949; Bob Lund vs. North Carolina, 1948

Interceptions, season: 10, Bobby Majors, 1970

Interceptions, career: 18, Tim Priest, 1968-70

Tackles, game: 28, Tom Fisher vs. Auburn (21 tackles, 7 assists), 1964

Tackles, season: 194, Andy Spiva (134 tackles, 60 assists), 1976

Tackles, career: 547, Andy Spiva (354 tackles, 193 assists), 1973-76

Sacks, game: 4, Reggie White vs. Citadel, 1983

Sacks, season: 15, Reggie White, 1983

Sacks, career: 32, Reggie White, 1980-83

The Greatest Players

THE COACHES

It has taken the leadership of great men to produce the legacy and tradition that embody Tennessee football.

J.A. Pierce	1899-1900	8-4-1
George Kelley	1901	3-3-2
H.F. Fisher	1902-03	10-7
S.D. Crawford	1904	3-5-1
J.D. DePree	1905-06	4-11-3
George Levene	1907-09	15-10-3
Andrew A. Stone	1910	3-5-1
Z.G. Clevenger	1911-15	26-15-2
John R. Bender	1916-20	18-5-4
M.B. Banks	1921-25	27-15-3
Robert R. Neyland	1926-34, 1936-40, 1946-52	173-31-12
W.H. (Bill) Britton	1935	4-5
John H. Barnhill	1941-45	32-5-2
Harvey L. Robinson	1953-54	10-10-1
Bowden Wyatt	1955-62	49-29-4
Jim McDonald	1963	5-5
Doug Dickey	1964-69	46-15-4
Bill Battle	1970-76	59-22-4
Johnny Majors	1977-92	116-62-8
Phillip Fulmer	1992-2008	152-52
Lane Kiffin	2009-	

Note: Fulmer and Majors shared the record for the 1992 season. There was no team in 1894, 1895, 1898, 1917, 1918, and 1943.

General Robert R. Neyland

The man who changed everything at Tennessee was Robert R. Neyland, who simply became known as "The General"—because, well, he was one. When he took the job in 1926, Neyland (pronounced NEE-land) was also an ROTC instructor who had graduated from West Point and served in France during World War I. Twice he was called upon to leave the football team, for a peacetime tour in Panama followed by a tour of duty as a brigadier general in the Pacific theater during World War II. Twice he came back to the Volunteers.

Dean Nathan Daugherty, the faculty chairman of athletics, called Neyland's hiring, "The best move I ever made."

As a coach, Neyland was known for organization, discipline, and teamwork. He had a fondness for tough defensive play in particular and helped put Tennessee at the forefront of college football over and over again.

"If Neyland could score a touchdown against you, he had you beat," said Herman Hickman, one of Neyland's players who went on to join the original staff of *Sports Illustrated*. "If he could score two, he had you in a rout."

Neyland's first stint with the Vols was from 1926–1934, when he held the military rank of captain, and posted an incredible record of 76-7-5.

In the midst of a 28-game unbeaten streak, Neyland secured his second Southern Conference Championship in 1932 after finishing 9-0-1. When team captain Malcolm Aitken was asked what he remembered most, he replied: "The infectious germ of being a winner."

During his second stint, Neyland dominated college

football from 1938–1940, winning three SEC championships and two national titles, through not consensus
(Texas Christian had that honor in 1938 and Minnesota
in 1940). Led by George "Bad News" Cafego, Ed
Molinski, and Bob Suffridge, the 1939 team shut out
all 10 opponents in the regular season, the last team to
do so.

After returning from the China-Burma-India
front in 1946, Neyland predicted: "It will take us five
years to put Tennessee back on top." Five years later,
the Volunteers won their first consensus national
championship.

"The general was always in complete control,"
guard John Michels said. "He never got excited. He was
highly organized and a great disciplinarian."

Neyland's final stint produced a 54–17–4 record,
adding up to a career mark of 173–31–12. In those 216
games, the opponent failed to score in 112 of them.

The Coaches

**Years since General Neyland's
1939 team held all regular
season opponents scoreless.
The feat has not been
duplicated since and
likely never will.**

7 Maxims

Coach Neyland's legendary "7 Maxims of Football" were written decades ago but are timeless bits of wisdom:

1. The team that makes the fewest mistakes will win.

2. Play for and make the breaks, and when one comes your way—SCORE.

3. If at first the game—or the breaks—go against you, don't let up...put on more steam.

4. Protect our kickers, our quarterback, our lead and our ball game.

5. Ball, oskie, cover, block, cut and slice, pursue, and gang tackle...for this is the WINNING EDGE.

6. Press the kicking game. Here is where the breaks are made.

7. Carry the fight to our opponent and keep it there for 60 minutes.

The Coaches

Phillip Fulmer

When he first arrived in Knoxville as a player, Phillip Fulmer was a guard and helped the Volunteers compile a 30-5 record from 1969–1971. When he was named head coach prior to the 1993 season, he won 10 games and quarterback Heath Shuler finished second in Heisman Trophy voting, which quarterback Peyton Manning matched a few years later.

But it was the season after Manning left for which Fulmer will always be remembered, 1998. For the first time since 1992, Tennessee survived Florida with a 20-17 overtime victory, beginning a string of narrow victories that lasted through the SEC Championship Game, a 24-14 win over Mississippi State.

"Sometimes you've just got to win ugly," Fulmer said.

In the first year of the controversial Bowl Championship Series, the final obstacle was Florida State at the Fiesta Bowl. With Vice-President Al Gore looking on, a 54-yard interception return by defensive back Dwayne Goodrich gave the Vols a lead they would never relinquish in the 23-16 victory.

Fulmer came close to another title run in 2001 when LSU pulled off a 31-20 upset in the SEC Championship Game. After that high point, Fulmer never could lead the Vols back to either an SEC championship or a top-10 national finish. In 2008, in the middle of a disappointing losing season, he announced he was accepting the school's decision for him to step down.

After Fulmer's final game, a 28-10 victory against the team he tortured the most, Kentucky, the game ball was thrust into his hands and he was hoisted to the shoulders of his players. "We've had a great run. I wasn't really ready for it to end, but it probably ended as well as it could," said Fulmer, who had a record of 152-52.

The Coaches

Phillip Fulmer hoists the National Championship trophy. The crystal football came only after Tennessee toppled Florida State 23-16, in the Fiesta Bowl.

Johnny Majors

As a player, Johnny Major's 5-foot-11, 168-pound frame caused many coaches to turn him away, thinking he couldn't withstand the rigors of the Southeastern Conference. Majors made them regret that. As a do-everything back—running, passing, blocking, and punting—he was named the Southeastern Conference's most valuable player both his junior and senior seasons.

After leading the Volunteers to an undefeated regular season in his final year, Majors finished second in Heisman Trophy voting to Notre Dame's Paul Hornung (Jim Brown of Syracuse finished fourth), the only player to win the award while playing on a losing team.

Majors' career statistics were 1,622 rushing yards, 1,135 passing, 16 touchdowns, 83 punts for a 39.1 average, 36 punt returns for 438 yards, 15 kickoff returns for 344 yards, and two interceptions.

Even though he was a gifted player, Majors accomplished even more as a coach. His first head coaching job was at Iowa State, where he revived a moribund program and led the Cyclones to their first two bowl games. He moved next to Pittsburgh, where he led the Panthers to three bowl games in four seasons, culminating in the 1976 national championship. Riding this wave of success, Majors returned to his alma mater, with the rallying cry of "Follow me to Tennessee."

Majors won three SEC Championships at Tennesseee (1985, 1989, and 1990) and led the team to 11 bowl games (posting seven wins), but he was never able to win another national chapionship. His best run came after a disappointing 5–6 season in 1988; his teams posted impressive 11–1, 9–2–2, and 9–3 marks the next three years. But in 1992, while recovering from heart surgery, Majors was forced to resign. Assistant coach Phillip Fulmer took over the team—leaving a wound that never healed.

"You mean the season of my ignominious demise?" Majors responded when asked to comment on the 1992 season by the *Chattanooga Times Free Press* in 2008. "The season when, while I was recovering from my heart surgery, a few people whom I won't name were operating on my back."

The Coaches

Actor Lee Majors knew Johnny Majors well, and could often be seen stalking the sidelines at Pitt and Tennessee. The two were not related: the actor had borrowed the coach's last name for his stage name.

Southeastern Conference

Eastern Division

Florida

Location: Gainesville, Florida
Founded: 1853
Enrollment: 51,520
Nickname: Gators
Colors: Orange and blue
Mascot: Albert and Alberta Gator
Stadium: Ben Hill Griffin Stadium at Florida Field (88,548)
Coach: Urban Meyer
National Championships (3): 1996, 2006, 2008
SEC Championships (8): 1991, 1993, 1994, 1995, 1996, 2000, 2006, 2008
First season: 1906
Heisman Winners (3): Steve Spurrier, quarterback, 1966; Danny Wuerffel, quarterback, 1996; Tim Tebow, quarterback, 2007
Retired Jerseys: None

Georgia

Location: Athens, Georgia
Founded: 1785
Enrollment: 33,405
Nickname: Bulldogs
Colors: Red and black
Mascot: Uga
Stadium: Sanford Stadium (92,746)
Coach: Mark Richt
National Championships (2): 1942, 1980
The "Other" Three: Georgia was voted No. 1 in various polls in 1927, 1946, and 1968.
SEC Championships (12): 1942, 1946, 1948, 1959, 1966, 1968, 1976, 1980, 1981, 1982, 2002, 2005
First season: 1892
Heisman Winners (2): Frank Sinkwich, halfback, 1942; Herschel Walker, running back, 1982
Retired Jerseys: 21 Frank Sinkwich; 34 Herschel Walker; 40 Theron Sapp; 62 Charley Trippi

Kentucky

Location: Lexington, Kentucky
Founded: 1865
Enrollment: 27,000
Nickname: Wildcats
Colors: Blue and white

Mascots: Wildcat and Scratch. Live mascots have included Tom, TNT, Whiskers, Hot Tamale, Colonel, and Blue.
Stadium: Commonwealth Stadium (67,606)
Coach: Rich Brooks
National Championships (0): None
SEC Championships (2): 1950, 1976
First season: 1881
Heisman Winners: None
Retired Jerseys: 2 Tim Couch; 2 Ermal Allen; 8 Clyde Johnson; 10 Vito "Babe" Parilli;11 Rick Norton; 12 Derrick Ramsey; 13 Bob Davis; 16 George Blanda; 19 Howard Schnellenberger; 20 Charlie McClendon; 21 Calvin Bird; 21 Roger Bird; 22 Mark Higgs; 24 Dicky Lyons; 27 Wallace "Wah-Wah" Jones; 32 Larry Seiple; 33 George Adams; 40 Sonny Collins; 44 John "Shipwreck" Kelly; 45 Jay Rhod-emyre; 48 Washington "Wash" Serini; 50 Jim Kovach; 50 Harry Ulinski; 51 Doug Moseley; 52 Rick Nuzum; 55 Irvin "Irv" Goode; 57 Dermontti Dawson; 59 Joe Federspiel; 65 Ray Correll; 66 Ralph Kercheval; 69 Warren Bryant; 70 Bob Gain; 70 Herschel Turner; 73 Sam Ball; 74 Dave Roller; 79 Lou Michaels; 80 Rick Kestner; 80 Tom Hutchinson; 80 Steve Meilinger; 88 Jeff Van Note; 97 Art Still; Paul "Bear" Bryant; Jerry Claiborne; Blanton Collier; Bernie Shively

South Carolina

Location: Columbia, South Carolina
Founded: 1801
Enrollment: 23,772
Nickname: Fighting Gamecocks
Colors: Garnet and black
Mascot: Cocky
Stadium: Williams-Brice Stadium (80,250)
Coach: Steve Spurrier
National Championships: None
SEC Championships: None
First season: 1892
Heisman Winners (1): George Rogers, running back, 1980
Retired Jerseys: 2 Sterling Sharpe; 37 Steve Wadiak; 38 George Rogers; 56 Mike Johnson

Tennessee

Location: Knoxville, Tennessee
Founded: 1794
Enrollment: 25,515
Nickname: Volunteers
Colors: Orange and white
Mascot: Smokey
Stadium: Neyland Stadium/Shields-Watkins Field (104,079)
Coach: Lane Kiffin
National Championships (2): 1951, 1998
The "Other" Four: The *Official NCAA Football Records Book* also recognizes Tennessee as producing national champions in 1938, 1940, 1950, and 1967.
SEC Championships (13): 1938, 1939, 1940, 1946, 1951, 1956, 1967, 1969, 1985, 1989, 1990, 1997, 1998
First season: 1891
Heisman Winners: None
Retired Jerseys: 16 Peyton Manning; 32 Bill Nowling; 49 Rudy Klarer; 61 Willis Tucker; 62 Clyde Fuson, 91 Doug Atkins, 92 Reggie White

Vanderbilt

Location: Nashville, Tennessee
Founded: 1873
Enrollment: 6,241
Nickname: Commodores
Colors: Black and gold
Mascot: A costumed Commodore, though there once was
George the basset hound, followed by Samantha.
Stadium: Dudley Field/Vanderbilt Stadium (39,773)
Coach: Bobby Johnson
National Championships: None
SEC Championships: None
First season: 1890
Heisman Winners: None
Retired Jerseys: None

Western Division

Alabama

Location: Tuscaloosa, Alabama
Founded: 1831
Enrollment: 27,052
Nickname: Crimson Tide
Colors: Crimson and white
Mascot: Big Al (the elephant)
Stadium: Bryant-Denny Stadium (92,138, but being reno-
vated to bring capacity over 101,000)
Head Coach: Nick Saban
National Championships (12): 1925, 1926, 1930, 1934,
1941, 1961, 1964, 1965, 1973, 1978, 1979, 1992
The "Other" Five: The *Official NCAA Football Records Book*
also recognizes Alabama as producing national champions
in 1945, 1962, 1966, 1975, and 1977
SEC Championships (21): 1933, 1934, 1937, 1945,
1953, 1961, 1964, 1965, 1966, 1971, 1972, 1973,
1974, 1975, 1977, 1978, 1979, 1981, 1989, 1992,
1999
First season: 1892
Heisman Trophies: None
Retired Jerseys: None

SEC

Arkansas

Location: Fayetteville, Arkansas
Founded: 1871
Enrollment: 18,648
Nickname: Razorbacks
Colors: Cardinal and white
Mascot: Tusk (a Russian boar)
Stadium: Donald W. Reynolds Razorback Stadium (72,000)
Coach: Bobby Petrino
National Championship (1): 1964
SEC Championships: None
First season: 1894
Heisman Winners: None
Retired Jerseys: 12 Clyde Scott, 12 Steve Little; 77 Brandon Burlsworth

Auburn

Location: Auburn, Alabama
Founded: 1856
Enrollment: 24,137
Nickname: Tigers
Colors: Burnt orange and navy blue
Battle cry/Mascot: War Eagle (the eagle is named Tiger; the cartoonish costumed tiger mascot is named Aubie)
Stadium: Jordan-Hare Stadium (87,451)
Head Coach: Gene Chizik
National Championships (1): 1957
SEC Championships (6): 1957, 1983, 1987, 1988, 1989, 2004
First season: 1892
Heisman Winners (2): Pat Sullivan, quarterback, 1971; Bo Jackson, running back, 1985
Retired Jerseys: 34 Bo Jackson; 7 Pat Sullivan; 88 Terry Beasley

SEC

LSU

Location: Baton Rouge, Louisiana
Founded: 1860
Enrollment: 31,234
Nickname: Tigers
Colors: Purple and gold
Mascot: Mike the Tiger
Stadium: Tiger Stadium (92,400)
Coach: Les Miles
National Championships (3): 1958, 2003, 2007
SEC Championships (9): 1935, 1936, 1958, 1961, 1970, 1986, 1988, 2001, 2003
First season: 1893
Heisman Winner (1): Billy Cannon, halfback, 1959
Retired Jersey: 20 Billy Cannon

Ole Miss

Location: Oxford, Mississippi
Founded: 1848
Enrollment: 17,325
Nickname: Rebels
Colors: Cardinal red and navy blue
Mascot: Colonel Rebel (unofficial since 2003)
Stadium: Vaught-Hemingway Stadium/Hollingsworth Field (60,580)
Coach: Houston Nutt
National Championship (1): 1960
SEC Championships (6): 1947, 1954, 1955, 1960, 1962, 1963
First season: 1893
Heisman Winners: None
Retired Jerseys: 18 Archie Manning

SEC

Mississippi State

Location: Starkville, Mississippi
Founded: 1878
Enrollment: 17,039
Nickname: Bulldogs
Colors: Maroon and white
Mascot: Bully
Stadium: Davis Wade Stadium at Scot Field (55,082)
Coach: Dan Mullen
National Championships: None
SEC Championship (1): 1941
First season: 1895
Heisman Winners: None
Retired Jerseys: None

SEC

Eric Berry set an SEC record in the 2008 game against Mississippi State, returning an interception 72 yards for a touchdown in the Vols' dominant win.

The Volunteers have won 16 conference titles, including 13 in the SEC. Players are seen here carrying away some signage after the 1997 win, the first of back-to-back conference titles. No team has won consecutive conference crowns since.

SEC Football Champions, 1933-1999

Year	Champion	SEC	Overall	Coach
1933	Alabama	5-0-1	7-1-1	Frank Thomas
1934	Tulane	8-0	10-1	Ted Cox
	Alabama	7-0	10-0	Frank Thomas
1935	LSU	5-0	9-2	Bernie Moore
1936	LSU	6-0	9-1-1	Bernie Moore
1937	Alabama	6-0	9-1	Frank Thomas
1938	Tennessee	7-0	11-0	Bob Neyland
1939	Tennessee	6-0	10-1	Bob Neyland
	Georgia Tech	6-0	8-2	Bill Alexander
	Tulane	5-0	8-1-1	"Red" Dawson
1940	Tennessee	5-0	10-1	Bob Neyland
1941	Mississippi State	4-0-1	8-1-1	Allyn McKeen
1942	Georgia	6-1	11-1	Wally Butts
1943	Georgia Tech	3-0	7-4	Bill Alexander
1944	Georgia Tech	4-0	9-2	Bill Alexander
1945	Alabama	6-0	10-0	Frank Thomas
1946	Georgia	5-0	11-0	Wally Butts
	Tennessee	5-0	9-2	Bob Neyland
1947	Ole Miss	6-1	9-2	John Vaught
1948	Georgia	6-0	9-2	Wally Butts
1949	Tulane	5-1	7-2-1	Henry Frnka
1950	Kentucky	5-1	11-1	Paul "Bear" Bryant
1951	Georgia Tech	7-0	11-0-1	Bobby Dodd
	Tennessee	5-0	10-1	Bob Neyland
1952	Georgia Tech	6-0	12-0	Bobby Dodd
1953	Alabama	4-0-3	6-3-3	Red Drew
1954	Ole Miss	5-1	9-2	John Vaught
1955	Ole Miss	5-1	10-1	John Vaught
1956	Tennessee	6-0	10-1	Bowden Wyatt
1957	Auburn	7-0	10-0	Ralph Jordan

Year	Team	Conf	Overall	Coach
1958	LSU	6-0	11-0	Paul Dietzel
1959	Georgia	7-0	10-1	Wally Butts
1960	Ole Miss	5-0-1	10-0-1	John Vaught
1961	Alabama	7-0	11-0	Paul "Bear" Bryant
	LSU	6-0	10-1	Paul Dietzel
1962	Ole Miss	6-0	10-0	John Vaught
1963	Ole Miss	5-0-1	7-1-2	John Vaught
1964	Alabama	8-0	10-1	Paul "Bear" Bryant
1965	Alabama	6-1-1	9-1-1	Paul "Bear" Bryant
1966	Alabama	6-0	11-0	Paul "Bear" Bryant
	Georgia	6-0	10-1	Vince Dooley
1967	Tennessee	6-0	9-2	Doug Dickey
1968	Georgia	5-0-1	8-1-2	Vince Dooley
1969	Tennessee	5-1	9-2	Doug Dickey
1970	LSU	5-0	9-3	Charlie McClendon
1971	Alabama	7-0	11-1	Paul "Bear" Bryant
1972	Alabama	7-1	10-2	Paul "Bear" Bryant
1973	*Alabama	8-0	11-1	Paul "Bear" Bryant
1974	Alabama	6-0	11-1	Paul "Bear" Bryant
1975	Alabama	6-0	11-1	Paul "Bear" Bryant
1976	Georgia	5-1	10-2	Vince Dooley
	Kentucky	5-1	9-3	Fran Curci
1977	Alabama	7-0	11-1	Paul "Bear" Bryant
1978	Alabama	6-0	11-1	Paul "Bear" Bryant
1979	Alabama	6-0	12-0	Paul "Bear" Bryant
1980	Georgia	6-0	12-0	Vince Dooley
1981	Georgia	6-0	10-2	Vince Dooley
	Alabama	6-0	9-2-1	Paul "Bear" Bryant
1982	Georgia	6-0	11-1	Vince Dooley
1983	Auburn	6-0	11-1	Pat Dye
1984	Vacated			
1985	Tennessee	5-1	9-1-2	Johnny Majors
1986	LSU	5-1	9-3	Bill Arnsparger
1987	Auburn	5-0-1	9-1-2	Pat Dye
1988	Auburn	6-1	10-2	Pat Dye
	LSU	6-1	8-4	Mike Archer
1989	Alabama	6-1	10-2	Bill Curry
	Tennessee	6-1	11-1	Johnny Majors
	Auburn	6-1	10-2	Pat Dye

1990	Tennessee	5-1-1	9-2-2	Johnny Majors
1991	Florida	7-0	10-2	Steve Spurrier
1992	Alabama	8-0	13-0	Gene Stallings
1993	Florida	7-1	11-2	Steve Spurrier
1994	Florida	7-1	10-2-1	Steve Spurrier
1995	Florida	8-0	12-1	Steve Spurrier
1996	Florida	8-0	12-1	Steve Spurrier
1997	Tennessee	7-1	11-2	Phillip Fulmer
1998	Tennessee	8-0	13-0	Phillip Fulmer
1999	Alabama	7-1	10-3	Mike DuBose

SEC Summary 2000

EASTERN DIVISION

School	Conference				Overall			
	W-L-T	Pct.	Pts.	Opp.	W-L-T	Pct.	Pts.	Opp.
Florida	7-1	.875	318	181	10-2	.833	448	236
Georgia	5-3	.625	213	164	7-4	.636	294	198
South Carolina	5-3	.625	173	152	7-4	.636	259	174
Tennessee	5-3	.625	251	176	8-3	.727	359	212
Vanderbilt	1-7	.125	120	223	3-8	.273	193	273
Kentucky	0-8	.000	152	300	2-9	.182	254	383

WESTERN DIVISION

School	Conference				Overall			
	W-L-T	Pct.	Pts.	Opp.	W-L-T	Pct.	Pts.	Opp.
Auburn	6-2	.750	178	144	9-3	.750	288	235
LSU	5-3	.625	196	195	7-4	.636	292	221
Ole Miss	4-4	.500	187	210	7-4	.636	314	280
Mississippi State	4-4	.500	225	199	7-4	.636	347	265
Arkansas	3-5	.375	136	221	6-5	.545	264	258
Alabama	3-5	.375	166	150	3-8	.273	228	246

SEC Championship Game:
Florida 28, Auburn 6

Bowl Games: Las Vegas (UNLV 31, Arkansas 14), Oahu (Georgia 37, Virginia 14), Music City (West Virginia 49, Ole Miss 38), Peach (LSU 28, Georgia Tech 14), Independence (Mississippi State 43, Texas A&M 41-OT), Outback (South Carolina 24, Ohio State 7), Cotton (Kansas State 35, Tennessee 21), Florida Citrus (Michigan 31, Auburn 28), Sugar (Miami, Fla. 37, Florida 20).

All-SEC

Offense: TE Derek Smith, Kentucky; TE Robert Royal, LSU; OL Kenyatta Walker, Florida; OL Terrence Metcalf, Ole Miss; OL Mike Pearson, Florida; OL Kendall Simmons, Auburn; OL Jonas Jennings, Georgia; OL Pork Chop Womack, Mississippi State; C Paul Hogan, Alabama; WR Jabar Gaffney, Florida; WR Josh Reed, LSU; QB Josh Booty, LSU; RB Rudi Johnson, Auburn; RB Travis Henry, Tennessee; PK Alex Walls, Tennessee

Defense: DL Alex Brown, Florida; DL John Henderson, Tennessee; DL Richard Seymour, Georgia; OLB Kalimba Edwards, South Carolina; OLB Eric Westmoreland, Tennessee; ILB Quinton Caver, Arkansas; ILB Jamie Winborn, Vanderbilt; DB Lito Sheppard, Florida; DB Fred Smoot, Mississippi State; DB Tim Wansley, Georgia; DB Rodney Crayton, Auburn; DB Ken Lucas, Ole Miss; P Damon Duval, Auburn

SEC Summary 2001

EASTERN DIVISION

Conference					Overall			
School	W-L-T	Pct.	Pts.	Opp.	W-L-T	Pct.	Pts.	Opp.
Tennessee	7-1	.875	225	148	10-2	.833	355	234
Florida	6-2	.750	341	122	9-2	.818	482	155
South Carolina	5-3	.625	189	160	8-3	.727	279	202
Georgia	5-3	.625	204	167	8-3	.727	315	208
Kentucky	1-7	.125	206	285	2-9	.182	259	367
Vanderbilt	0-8	.000	128	315	2-9	.182	226	402

WESTERN DIVISION

Conference					Overall			
School	W-L-T	Pct.	Pts.	Opp.	W-L-T	Pct.	Pts.	Opp.
LSU	5-3	.625	231	203	9-3	.750	371	268
Auburn	5-3	.625	152	193	7-4	.636	244	265
Alabama	4-4	.500	203	177	6-5	.545	304	219
Arkansas	4-4	.500	208	220	7-4	.636	291	269
Ole Miss	4-4	.500	262	262	7-4	.636	391	310
Mississippi State	2-6	.250	119	216	3-8	.273	196	288

SEC Championship Game:
LSU 31, Tennessee 20

Bowls: Independence (Alabama 14, Iowa State 13), Music City (Boston College 20, Georgia 16), Peach (North Carolina 16, Auburn 10), Cotton (Oklahoma 10, Arkansas 3), Outback (South Carolina 31, Ohio State 28), Florida Citrus (Tennessee 45, Michigan 17), Orange (Florida 56, Maryland 23), Sugar (LSU 47, Illinois 34).

All-SEC

Offense: TE Randy McMichael, Georgia; OL Terrence Metcalf, Ole Miss; OL Fred Weary, Tennessee; OL Mike Pearson, Florida; OL Kendall Simmons, Auburn; C Zac Zedalis, Florida; WR Jabar Gaffney, Florida; WR Josh Reed, LSU; QB Rex Grossman, Florida; RB Travis Stephens, Tennessee; RB LaBrandon Toefield, LSU; PK Damon Duval, Auburn

Defense: DL Alex Brown, Florida; DL John Henderson, Tennessee; DL Will Overstreet, Tennessee; OLB Kalimba Edwards, South Carolina; OLB Bradie James, LSU; ILB Trev Faulk, LSU; ILB Saleem Rasheed, Alabama; DB Lito Sheppard, Florida; DB Syniker Taylor, Ole Miss; DB Tim Wansley, Georgia; DB Andre Lott, Tennessee; DB Sheldon Brown, South Carolina; P Damon Duval, Auburn

SEC Summary 2002

EASTERN DIVISION

School	W-L-T	Pct.	Pts.	Opp.	W-L-T	Pct.	Pts.	Opp.
Conference				**Overall**				
Georgia	7-1	.875	226	144	12-1	.923	424	199
Florida	6-2	.750	191	160	8-4	.667	306	241
Tennessee	5-3	.625	182	147	8-4	.667	293	197
South Carolina	3-5	.375	108	156	5-7	.417	225	262
Vanderbilt	0-8	.000	121	260	2-10	.167	221	368
#Kentucky	3-5	.375	215	228	7-5	.583	385	301

WESTERN DIVISION

School	W-L-T	Pct.	Pts.	Opp.	W-L-T	Pct.	Pts.	Opp.
Conference					**Overall**			
Arkansas	5-3	.625	223	184	9-4	.692	356	248
Auburn	5-3	.625	213	150	8-4	.667	375	222
LSU	5-3	.625	179	160	8-4	.667	303	203
Ole Miss	3-5	.375	175	230	6-6	.500	324	308
Mississippi State	0-8	.000	123	265	3-9	.250	227	339
#Alabama	6-2	.750	227	99	10-3	.769	377	200

#On probation, banned from bowl games

SEC Championship Game:
Georgia 30, Arkansas 3

Bowls: Independence (Ole Miss 27, Nebraska 23), Music City (Minnesota 29, Arkansas 14), Peach (Maryland 30, Tennessee 3), Outback (Michigan 38, Florida 30), Cotton (Texas 35, LSU 20), Capital One (Auburn 13, Penn State 9), Sugar (Georgia 26, Florida State 13).

All-SEC

Offense: TE Jason Witten, Tennessee; OL Shawn Andrews, Arkansas; OL Jon Stinchcomb, Georgia; OL Antonio Hall, Kentucky; OL Stephen Peterman, LSU; OL Marico Portis, Alabama; OL Wesley Britt, Alabama; C Ben Nowland, Auburn; WR Taylor Jacobs, Florida; WR Terrence Edwards, Georgia; QB David Greene, Georgia; RB Artose Pinner, Kentucky; RB Fred Talley, Arkansas

Defense: DL David Pollack, Georgia; DL Kindal Moorehead, Alabama; DL Kenny King, Alabama; OLB Boss Bailey, Georgia; OLB Karlos Dansby, Auburn; ILB Bradie James, LSU; ILB Eddie Strong, Ole Miss; ILB Hunter Hillenmeyer, Vanderbilt; DB Ken Hamlin, Arkansas; DB Corey Webster, LSU; DB Travaris Robinson, Auburn; DB Matt Grier, Ole Miss; DB Julian Battle, Tennessee; DB Rashad Baker, Tennessee

Special Teams: P Glenn Pakulak, Kentucky; PK Billy Bennett, Georgia; RS Derek Abney, Kentucky

SEC

SEC Summary 2003

EASTERN DIVISION

Conference					Overall			
School	W-L-T	Pct.	Pts.	Opp.	W-L-T	Pct.	Pts.	Opp.
Georgia	6-2	.750	215	102	10-3	.769	337	176
Tennessee	6-2	.750	260	170	10-2	.833	351	212
Florida	6-2	.750	178	152	8-4	.667	373	234
South Carolina	2-6	.250	164	227	5-7	.417	268	314
Vanderbilt	1-7	.125	126	261	2-10	.167	235	358
Kentucky	1-7	.125	198	244	4-8	.333	328	321

WESTERN DIVISION

Conference					Overall			
School	W-L-T	Pct.	Pts.	Opp.	W-L-T	Pct.	Pts.	Opp.
LSU	7-1	.875	228	90	12-1	.923	454	140
Ole Miss	7-1	.875	218	150	9-3	.750	411	257
Auburn	5-3	.625	190	148	7-5	.583	314	198
Arkansas	4-4	.500	247	223	8-4	.667	409	291
Mississippi State	1-7	.125	93	329	2-10	.167	225	471
#Alabama	2-6	.250	216	237	4-9	.308	331	333

#On probation, banned from bowls

SEC Championship Game:
LSU 34, Georgia 13

Bowls: Music City (Auburn, 28, Wisconsin 14), Independence (Arkansas 27, Missouri 14), Outback (Iowa 37, Florida 17), Capital One (Georgia 34, Purdue 27, OT), Cotton (Ole Miss 31, Oklahoma State 28), Peach (Clemson 27, Tennessee 14) Sugar (LSU 21, Oklahoma 14).

All-SEC

Offense: TE Ben Troupe, Florida; OL Shawn Andrews, Arkansas; OL Max Starks, Florida; OL Antonio Hall, Kentucky; OL Wesley Britt, Alabama; C Scott Wells, Tennessee; WR Michael Clayton, LSU; WR Chris Collins, Ole Miss; QB Eli Manning, Ole Miss; RB Carnell Williams, Auburn; RB Cedric Cobbs, Arkansas

Defense: DL David Pollack, Georgia; DL Chad Lavalais, LSU; DL Antwan Odom, Alabama; OLB Karlos Dansby, Auburn; OLB Derrick Pope, Alabama; ILB Dontarrious Thomas, Auburn; ILB Odell Thurman, Georgia; DB Keiwan Ratliff, Florida; DB Corey Webster, LSU; DB Ahmad Carroll, Arkansas; DB Tony Bua, Arkansas; DB Sean Jones, Georgia

Special Teams: P Dustin Colquitt, Tennessee; PK Jonathan Nichols, Ole Miss; RS Derek Abney, Kentucky

SEC Summary 2004

EASTERN DIVISION

Conference					Overall			
School	W-L-T	Pct.	Pts.	Opp.	W-L-T	Pct.	Pts.	Opp.
Tennessee	7-1	.875	215	199	9-3	.750	340	288
Georgia	6-2	.750	231	133	9-2	.818	311	177
Florida	4-4	.500	251	187	7-4	.636	372	226
South Carolina	4-4	.500	185	190	6-5	.545	243	229
Kentucky	1-7	.125	106	253	2-9	.182	173	341
Vanderbilt	1-7	.125	133	213	2-9	.182	212	286

WESTERN DIVISION

Conference					Overall			
School	W-L-T	Pct.	Pts.	Opp.	W-L-T	Pct.	Pts.	Opp.
Auburn	8-0	1.000	247	96	12-0	1.000	401	134
LSU	6-2	.750	220	131	9-2	.818	319	175
Arkansas	3-5	.375	196	215	5-6	.455	328	270
Alabama	3-5	.375	152	149	6-5	.545	279	169
Ole Miss	3-5	.375	142	200	4-7	.364	215	278
#Mississippi State	2-6	.250	125	237	3-8	.273	173	280

#On probation, banned from bowl games

SEC Championship Game:
Auburn 38, Tennessee 28

Bowls: Music City (Minnesota 20, Alabama 16), Peach (Miami, Fla., 27, Florida 10), Outback (Georgia 24, Wisconsin 21), Cotton (Tennessee 38, Texas A&M 7), Capital One (Iowa 30, LSU 25), Sugar (Auburn 16, Virginia Tech 13).

All-SEC

Offense: TE Leonard Pope, Georgia; OL Wesley Britt, Alabama; OL Marcus McNeill, Auburn; OL Max Jean-Gilles, Georgia; OL Mo Mitchell, Florida; OL Andrew Whitworth, LSU; C Ben Wilkerson, LSU; WR Fred Gibson, Georgia; WR Reggie Brown, Georgia; QB Jason Campbell, Auburn; RB Carnell Williams, Auburn; RB Ronnie Brown, Auburn

Defense: DL Marcus Spears, LSU; DL David Pollack, Georgia; DL Jeb Huckeba, Arkansas; LB Kevin Burnett, Tennessee; LB Travis Williams, Auburn; LB Cornelius Wortham, Alabama; LB Channing Crowder, Florida; LB Moses Osemwegie, Vanderbilt; LB Odell Thurman, Georgia; LB Lionel Turner, LSU; DB Jason Allen, Tennessee; DB Thomas Davis, Georgia; DB Carlos Rogers, Auburn; DB Junior Rosegreen, Auburn

Special Teams: P Jared Cook, Mississippi State; PK Brian Bostick, Alabama; RS Carnell Williams, Auburn

SEC Summary 2005

EASTERN DIVISION

School	Conference				Overall			
	W-L-T	Pct.	Pts.	Opp.	W-L-T	Pct.	Pts.	Opp.
Georgia	6-2	.750	209	134	10-2	.833	349	175
South Carolina	5-3	.625	175	193	7-4	.636	253	241
Florida	5-3	.625	205	178	8-3	.727	312	202
Vanderbilt	3-5	.375	223	271	5-6	.455	299	321
Tennessee	3-5	.375	147	138	5-6	.455	205	205
Kentucky	2-6	.250	160	277	3-8	.273	239	375

WESTERN DIVISION

School	Conference				Overall			
	W-L-T	Pct.	Pts.	Opp.	W-L-T	Pct.	Pts.	Opp.
LSU	7-1	.875	214	114	10-2	.833	343	182
Auburn	7-1	.875	262	122	9-2	.818	376	162
Alabama	6-2	.750	159	87	9-2	.818	250	118
Arkansas	2-6	.250	173	169	4-7	.364	283	271
Mississippi State	1-7	.125	78	211	3-8	.273	153	259
Ole Miss	1-7	.125	97	208	3-8	.273	148	245

SEC Championship Game:
Georgia 34, LSU 14

Bowls: Independence (Missouri 38, South Carolina 31), Chick-fil-A (LSU 40, Miami, Fla. 3), Outback (Florida 31, Iowa 24), Cotton (Alabama 13, Texas Tech 10), Capital One (Wisconsin 24, Auburn 10), Sugar (West Virginia 38, Georgia 35).

All-SEC

Offense: Leonard Pope, TE, Georgia; Marcus McNeill, OL, Auburn; Max Jean-Gilles, OL, Georgia; Andrew Whitworth, OL, LSU; Tre' Stallings OL, Ole Miss; Arron Sears, OL, Tennessee; Mike Degory, C, Florida; Sidney Rice, WR, South Carolina; Earl Bennett, WR, Vanderbilt; Jay Cutler, QB, Vanderbilt; Kenny Irons, RB, Auburn; Kenneth Darby, RB, Alabama; Darren McFadden, RB, Arkansas

Defense: Willie Evans, DL, Mississippi State; Quentin Moses, DL, Georgia; Claude Wroten, DL, LSU; DeMeco Ryans, LB, Alabama; Patrick Willis, LB, Ole Miss; Moses Osemwegie, LB, Vanderbilt; Sam Olajubutu, LB, Arkansas; Greg Blue, DB, Georgia; Roman Harper, DB, Alabama; LaRon Landry, DB, LSU; Ko Simpson, DB, South Carolina.

Specialists: Kody Bliss, P, Auburn; Brandon Coutu, K, Georgia; Skyler Green, RS, LSU

SEC Summary 2006

EASTERN DIVISION

School	W-L-T	Pct.	Pts.	Opp.	W-L-T	Pct.	Pts.	Opp.
Conference					Overall			
Florida	7-1	.875	178	126	13-1	.929	416	189
Tennessee	5-3	.625	212	172	9-4	.692	362	254
Kentucky	4-4	.500	163	207	8-5	.615	347	369
Georgia	4-4	.500	185	168	9-4	.692	327	229
South Carolina	3-5	.375	147	146	8-5	.615	346	243
Vanderbilt	1-7	.125	131	206	4-8	.333	264	284

WESTERN DIVISION

Conference					Overall			
School	W-L-T	Pct.	Pts.	Opp.	W-L-T	Pct.	Pts.	Opp.
Arkansas	7-1	.875	221	134	10-4	.714	404	256
Auburn	6-2	.750	162	133	11-2	.846	322	181
LSU	6-2	.750	220	131	11-2	.846	438	164
Alabama	2-6	.250	133	175	6-7	.462	298	250
Ole Miss	2-6	.250	123	182	4-8	.333	188	275
Mississippi State	1-7	.125	127	222	3-9	.250	221	309

SEC Championship Game:
Florida 38, Arkansas 28

Bowls: Independence (Oklahoma State 34, Alabama 31); Music City (Kentucky 28, Clemson 20); AutoZone (South Carolina 44, Houston 36; Chick-fil-A (Georgia 31, Virginia Tech 24); Outback (Penn State 20, Tennessee 10); Cotton (Auburn 17, Nebraska 14); Capital One (Wisconsin 17, Arkansas 14); Sugar (LSU 41, Notre Dame 14); BCS Championship (Florida 41, Ohio State 14).

All-SEC

Offense: TE Martrez Milner, Georgia; TE Jacob Tamme, Kentucky; OL Arron Sears, Tennessee; OL Zac Tubbs, Arkansas; OL Tim Duckworth, Auburn; OL Tony Ugoh, Arkansas; C Jonathan Luigs, Arkansas; C Steve Rissler, Florida; WR Robert Meachem, Tennessee; WR Dwayne Bowe, LSU; WR Dallas Baker, Florida; QB JaMarcus Russell, LSU; RB Darren McFadden, Arkansas; RB Kenny Irons, Auburn

Defense: DL Glenn Dorsey, LSU; DL Quentin Groves, Auburn; DL Jamaal Anderson, Arkansas; DL Ray McDonald, Florida; LB Patrick Willis, Ole Miss; LB Quinton Culberson, Mississippi State; LB Sam Olajubutu, Arkansas; LB Earl Everett, Florida; LB Wesley Woodyard, Kentucky; DB Reggie Nelson, Florida; DB Tra Battle, Georgia; DB

SEC

Simeon Castille, Alabama; DB LaRon Landry, LSU

Special Teams: P Britton Colquitt, Tennessee; PK John Vaughn, Auburn; PK James Wilhoit, Tennessee; RS Mikey Henderson, Georgia

SEC Summary 2007

EASTERN DIVISION

School	W-L-T	Pct.	Pts.	Opp.	W-L-T	Pct.	Pts.	Opp.
Conference					**Overall**			
Tennessee	6-2	.750	243	246	10-4	.714	455	382
Georgia	6-2	.750	228	171	11-2	.846	424	262
Florida	5-3	.625	305	224	9-4	.692	552	331
South Carolina	3-5	.375	205	227	6-6	.500	313	282
Kentucky	3-5	.375	249	276	8-5	.615	475	385
Vanderbilt	2-6	.250	198	203	5-7	.417	260	271

WESTERN DIVISION

School	W-L-T	Pct.	Pts.	Opp.	W-L-T	Pct.	Pts.	Opp.
Conference					**Overall**			
LSU	6-2	.750	298	215	12-2	.857	541	279
Auburn	5-3	.625	156	138	9-4	.692	315	220
Arkansas	4-4	.500	274	249	8-5	.615	485	345
Mississippi State	4-4	.500	157	215	8-5	.615	279	301
Alabama	4-4	.500	212	190	7-6	.538	352	286
Ole Miss	0-8	.000	131	252	3-9	.250	241	342

SEC Championship Game:
LSU 21, Tennessee 14

Bowls: Liberty (Mississippi State 10, Central Florida 3); Independence (Alabama 30, Colorado 24); Music City (Kentucky 35, Florida State 28); Chick-fil-A (Auburn 23, Clemson 20, OT); Cotton (Missouri 38, Arkansas 7); Outback (Tennessee 21, Wisconsin 17); Capital One (Michigan 41, Florida 35); Sugar (Georgia 41, Hawaii 10); BCS Championship (LSU 38, Ohio State).

All-SEC

Offense: TE Jacob Tamme, Kentucky; OL Robert Felton, Arkansas; OL Andre Smith, Alabama; OL Anthony Parker, Tennessee; OL Herman Johnson, LSU; OL Michael Oher, Ole Miss; OL Chris Williams, Vanderbilt; C Jonathan Luigs, Arkansas; WR Kenny McKinley, South Carolina; WR Earl Bennett, Vanderbilt; QB Tim Tebow, Florida; RB Darren McFadden, Arkansas; RB Knowshon Moreno, Georgia

Defense: DL Glenn Dorsey, LSU; DL Wallace Gilberry, Alabama; DL Quentin Groves, Auburn; DL Greg Hardy, Ole Miss; DL Eric Norwood, South Carolina; LB Ali Highsmith, LSU; LB Wesley Woodyard, Kentucky; LB Jerod Mayo, Tennessee; LB Brandon Spikes, Florida; DB Craig Steltz, LSU; DB Chevis Jackson, LSU; DB Simeon Castille, Alabama; DB Rashad Johnson, Alabama; DB Jonathan Hefney, Tennessee; DB Captain Munnerlyn, South Carolina

Special Teams: PK Colt David, LSU; P Patrick Fisher, LSU; RS Felix Jones, Arkansas

SEC Summary 2008

EASTERN DIVISION

| Conference | | | | | Overall | | | |
School	W-L-T	Pct.	Pts.	Opp.	W-L-T	Pct.	Pts.	Opp.
Florida	7-1	.875	359	100	13-1	.929	611	181
Georgia	6-2	.750	215	214	10-3	.769	409	319
Vanderbilt	4-4	.500	144	174	7-6	.538	249	255
South Carolina	4-4	.500	163	186	7-6	.538	270	274
Tennessee	3-5	.375	129	149	5-7	.417	208	201
Kentucky	2-6	.250	143	238	7-6	.538	294	279

WESTERN DIVISION

| Conference | | | | | Overall | | | |
School	W-L-T	Pct.	Pts.	Opp.	W-L-T	Pct.	Pts.	Opp.
Alabama	8-0	1.000	255	115	12-2	.857	422	200
Ole Miss	5-3	.625	208	149	9-4	.692	417	247
LSU	3-5	.375	207	254	8-5	.615	402	314
Arkansas	2-6	.250	167	248	5-7	.417	263	374
Auburn	2-6	.250	93	149	5-7	.417	208	216
Mississippi State	2-6	.250	97	204	4-8	.333	183	296

SEC Championship Game:
Florida 31, Alabama 20

Bowls: Music City (Vanderbilt 16, Boston College 14), Chick-fil-A
(LSU 38, Georgia Tech 3), Outback (Iowa 31, South Carolina 10),
Capital One (Georgia 23, Michigan State 12), Cotton (Ole Miss 47,
Texas Tech 34), Liberty (Kentucky 25, East Carolina 19), Sugar (Utah
31, Alabama 17), BCS Championship (Florida 24, Oklahoma 17).

All-SEC

Offense: QB Tim Tebow, Florida; RB Knowshon Moreno, Georgia; RB Charles Scott, LSU; WR Percy Harvin, Florida; WR Mohamed Massaquoi, Georgia; TE Jared Cook, South Carolina; C Antoine Caldwell, Alabama; OL Michael Oher, Ole Miss; OL Andre Smith, Alabama; OL Herman Johnson, LSU; OL Phil Trautwein, Florida

Defense: DE Antonio Coleman, Auburn; DE Robert Ayers, Tennessee; DT Terrence Cody, Alabama; DT Peria Jerry, Ole Miss; LB Brandon Spokes, Auburn; LB Rennie Curran, Georgia; LB Eric Norwood, South Carolina; LB Rolando McClain, Alabama; LB Micah Johnson, Kentucky; DB D.J. Moore, Vanderbilt; DB Trenard Lindley, Kentucky; DB Eric Berry Tennessee; DB Rashad Johnson, Alabama

Special Teams: PK: Colt David, LSU; P: Tim Masthay, Kentucky; RS Brandon James, Florida

SEC

Robert Ayers was named All-SEC in 2008, and also won the Andy Spiva Award, given to UT's most-improved defensive player.

The 2008 Volunteers were not a factor in the SEC or national championship picture, finishing a dismal 5-7. They did manage to send Phillip Fulmer out a winner, beating Kentucky for the 24th straight time.

THE RIVALRIES

Although every college football program in the country has a rival of some sort, Tennessee is a perfect example of how a team can have numerous, and different kinds of, rivalries. Tennessee has the neighborhood rivalry (Kentucky), the big-brother rivalry (Alabama), the intrastate/public vs. private rivalry (Vanderbilt), and the division rivalry (Florida).

Of them, Alabama is considered the traditional rival, although the Crimson Tide doesn't quite see it that way, due to intrastate foe Auburn. That's more of a blood feud.

However, there is something to be said about the intensity of the Southeastern Conference, where fans can be beyond serious when it comes to football.

For example, in the 2000 game between Florida and Tennessee, the Gators had the ball at the 3-yard line with 14 seconds remaining when Jesse Palmer found Jabar Gaffney in the end zone for the controversial game-winning touchdown, with the receiver only momentarily having possession. He also made a throat-slashing gesture to the Tennessee fans in celebration.

After the game, Steve Spurrier acknowledged that it probably shouldn't have been a touchdown. The official who made the call, Al Matthews, received death threats.

Of course, none of that prevented Lane Kiffin from stoking the fires after being introduced by athletics director Mike Hamilton in December 2008, even though Florida's Urban Meyer had yet to lose to the Vols.

"Singing 'Rocky Top' all night long after we beat Florida next year, it's going to be a blast," Kiffin said with a smile. "That line was Mike's idea, by the way, all right, Urban?"

Tennessee vs. Alabama

Alabama and Tennessee have seemingly always had an interesting relationship, like in 1913 when, after numerous injuries, the game lasted into the night and spectators were asked to encircle the field and turn on their headlights so play could continue. Host Alabama won, 6–0.

The rivalry, known as the "Third Saturday in October," intensified in 1928, when the coaches met at midfield beforehand and Robert Neyland asked Wallace Wade if the game could be shortened if it got out of hand. Tennessee's Gene McEver returned the opening kickoff 89 yards for a touchdown and the Volunteers held on for a 15–13 victory that was considered a huge turning point in program history.

It was against Tennessee in 1935 that Paul W. "Bear" Bryant played his famous game with a broken leg, and later particularly enjoyed beating the Volunteers as a coach. It was after one of those wins in the 1950s that victory cigars were passed out in the locker room, a tradition both teams adopted (though considered an NCAA violation concerning extra benefits and tobacco products).

Earlier this decade, the intensity flared up again when Philip Fulmer turned in Alabama for recruiting violations, and then refused all efforts to be questioned under oath about what he knew and when.

Alabama is the only SEC team with a better overall record, and has a clear and distinct lead in their series. While Tennessee had three consensus national championships, Alabama can claim 12. Consequently, the games never lack in intensity, because it is usually the benchmark game each season for both teams.

"You never know what a football player is made of until he plays against Alabama," Neyland said.

The Rivalries

Tennessee
vs. Alabama

(Alabama leads series 46-38-7)

Year	Location	Winner	Score
1901	Birmingham	Tied	6-6
1903	Birmingham	Alabama	24-0
1904	Birmingham	Tennessee	5-0
1905	Birmingham	Alabama	29-0
1906	Birmingham	Alabama	51-0
1907	Birmingham	Alabama	5-0
1908	Birmingham	Alabama	4-0
1909	Knoxville	Alabama	10-0
1912	Birmingham	Alabama	7-0
1913	Tuscaloosa	Alabama	6-0
1914	Knoxville	Tennessee	17-7
1928	Tuscaloosa	Tennessee	15-13
1929	Knoxville	Tennessee	6-0
1930	Tuscaloosa	Alabama	18-6
1931	Knoxville	Tennessee	25-0
1932	Birmingham	Tennessee	7-3
1933	Knoxville	Alabama	12-6
1934	Birmingham	Alabama	13-6
1935	Knoxville	Alabama	25-0
1936	Birmingham	Tied	0-0
1937	Knoxville	Alabama	14-7
1938	Birmingham	Tennessee	13-0
1939	Knoxville	Tennessee	21-0
1940	Birmingham	Tennessee	27-12
1941	Knoxville	Alabama	9-2
1942	Birmingham	Alabama	8-0
1944	Knoxville	Tied	0-0
1945	Birmingham	Alabama	25-7
1946	Knoxville	Tennessee	12-0
1947	Birmingham	Alabama	10-0
1948	Knoxville	Tennessee	21-6

1949	Birmingham	Tied	7-7
1950	Knoxville	Tennessee	14-9
1951	Birmingham	Tennessee	27-13
1952	Knoxville	Tennessee	20-0
1953	Birmingham	Tied	0-0
1954	Knoxville	Alabama	27-0
1955	Birmingham	Tennessee	20-0
1956	Knoxville	Tennessee	24-0
1957	Birmingham	Tennessee	14-0
1958	Knoxville	Tennessee	14-7
1959	Birmingham	Tied	7-7
1960	Knoxville	Tennessee	20-7
1961	Birmingham	Alabama	34-3
1962	Knoxville	Alabama	27-7
1963	Birmingham	Alabama	35-0
1964	Knoxville	Alabama	19-8
1965	Birmingham	Tied	7-7
1966	Knoxville	Alabama	11-10
1967	Birmingham	Tennessee	24-13
1968	Knoxville	Tennessee	10-9
1969	Birmingham	Tennessee	41-14
1970	Knoxville	Tennessee	24-0
1971	Birmingham	Alabama	32-15
1972	Knoxville	Alabama	17-10
1973	Birmingham	Alabama	42-21
1974	Knoxville	Alabama	28-6
1975	Birmingham	Alabama	30-7
1976	Knoxville	Alabama	20-13
1977	Birmingham	Alabama	24-10
1978	Knoxville	Alabama	30-17
1979	Birmingham	Alabama	27-17
1980	Knoxville	Alabama	27-0
1981	Birmingham	Alabama	38-19
1982	Knoxville	Tennessee	35-28
1983	Birmingham	Tennessee	41-34
1984	Knoxville	Tennessee	28-27

The Rivalries

1985	Birmingham	Tennessee	16-14
1986	Knoxville	Alabama	56-28
1987	Birmingham	Alabama	41-22
1988	Knoxville	Alabama	28-20
1989	Birmingham	Alabama	47-30
1990	Knoxville	Alabama	9-6
1991	Birmingham	Alabama	24-19
1992	Knoxville	Alabama	17-10
1993	Birmingham	Tied –x	17-17
1994	Knoxville	Alabama	17-13
1995	Birmingham	Tennessee	41-14
1996	Knoxville	Tennessee	20-13
1997	Birmingham	Tennessee	38-21
1998	Knoxville	Tennessee	35-18
1999	Tuscaloosa	Tennessee	21-7
2000	Knoxville	Tennessee	20-10
2001	Tuscaloosa	Tennessee	35-24
2002	Knoxville	Alabama	34-14
2003	Tuscaloosa (5OT)	Tennessee	51-43
2004	Knoxville	Tennessee	17-13
2005	Tuscaloosa	Alabama	6-3
2006	Knoxville	Tennessee	16-13
2007	Tuscaloosa	Alabama	41-17
2008	Knoxville	Alabama	29-9

x-Game later forfeited to Tennessee as a result of NCAA sanctions.

The Rivalries

Tennessee vs. Kentucky

Although the border battle has mostly been a mismatch over the years, it used to be a unique trophy game. The original "Battle for the Beer Barrel" was conceived by a Kentucky booster club in 1925, with the aim of drawing the same kind of attention as Minnesota and Michigan's Little Brown Jug. The first game for the Barrel resulted in a rare victory for the Wildcats, 23–20, keeping the blue, white, and orange–painted keg in Lexington for its first year.

But in 1998, the annual postgame celebration was canceled out of respect for the victims of a car crash one week earlier that killed Kentucky transfer player Arthur Steinmetz and Eastern Kentucky student Scott Brock, the best friend of then-Kentucky standout quarterback Tim Couch.

The driver and sole survivor of the wreck, Kentucky football player Jason Watts, had a blood alcohol content above the legal limit following the November 15 crash. He pled guilty to two counts of reckless homicide and was sentenced to 10 years in prison. After serving nearly four months, he was a released early and sentenced to five years probation.

Consequently, the Beer Barrel was permanently retired, with Tennessee holding a 60-23-9 edge in the series.

One of the most exciting games in series history was 2007, a 52–50 Tennessee victory in four overtimes to clinch the division title and a spot in the SEC Championship Game. Although Kentucky trailed 31–14 late in the third quarter, it missed a chance to win in regulation. Meanwhile, quarterback Erik Ainge set a school record with seven touchdowns. The win also extended UT's winning streak in the series to 23 games, the longest active winning streak in an uninterrupted series.

The Rivalries

Tennessee vs. Kentucky

(Tennessee leads series 72-23-9)
Note: Kentucky was known as Kentucky A&M
through 1907, Kentucky State from 1908-16.

Year	Location	Winner	Score
1893	Knoxville	Kentucky A&M	56-0
1899	Knoxville	Tennessee	12-0
1901	Knoxville	Tennessee	5-0
1906	Lexington	Kentucky A&M	21-0
1907	Knoxville	Tied	0-0
1908	Knoxville	Tennessee	7-0
1909	Lexington	Kentucky State	17-0
1910	Knoxville	Kentucky State	10-0
1911	Lexington	Kentucky State	12-0
1912	Knoxville	Kentucky State	13-6
1913	Lexington	Tennessee	13-7
1914	Knoxville	Tennessee	23-6
1915	Lexington	Kentucky State	6-0
1916	Knoxville	Tied	0-0
1919	Lexington	Kentucky	13-0
1920	Knoxville	Tennessee	14-7
1921	Lexington	Tied	0-0
1922	Knoxville	Tennessee	14-7
1923	Lexington	Tennessee	18-0
1924	Knoxville	Kentucky	27-6
1925	Lexington	Kentucky	23-20
1926	Knoxville	Tennessee	6-0
1927	Lexington	Tennessee	20-0
1928	Knoxville	Tied	0-0
1929	Lexington	Tied	6-6
1930	Knoxville	Tennessee	8-0
1931	Lexington	Tied	6-6
1932	Knoxville	Tennessee	26-0
1933	Lexington	Tennessee	27-0
1934	Knoxville	Tennessee	19-0

1935	Lexington	Kentucky	27-0
1936	Knoxville	Tennessee	7-6
1937	Lexington	Tennessee	13-0
1938	Knoxville	Tennessee	46-0
1939	Lexington	Tennessee	19-0
1940	Knoxville	Tennessee	33-0
1941	Lexington	Tennessee	20-7
1942	Knoxville	Tennessee	26-0
1944	Knoxville	Tennessee	26-13
1944	Lexington	Tennessee	21-7
1945	Lexington	Tennessee	14-0
1946	Knoxville	Tennessee	7-0
1947	Lexington	Tennessee	13-6
1948	Knoxville	Tied	0-0
1949	Lexington	Tennessee	6-0
1950	Knoxville	Tennessee	7-0
1951	Lexington	Tennessee	28-0
1952	Knoxville	Tied	14-14
1953	Lexington	Kentucky	27-21
1954	Knoxville	Kentucky	14-13
1955	Lexington	Kentucky	23-0
1956	Knoxville	Tennessee	20-7
1957	Lexington	Kentucky	20-6
1958	Knoxville	Kentucky	6-2
1959	Lexington	Kentucky	20-0
1960	Knoxville	Tied	10-10
1961	Lexington	Tennessee	26-16
1962	Knoxville	Kentucky	12-10
1963	Lexington	Tennessee	19-0
1964	Knoxville	Kentucky	12-7
1965	Lexington	Tennessee	19-3
1966	Knoxville	Tennessee	28-19
1967	Lexington	Tennessee	17-7
1968	Knoxville	Tennessee	24-7
1969	Lexington	Tennessee	31-26
1970	Knoxville	Tennessee	45-0
1971	Lexington	Tennessee	21-7
1972	Knoxville	Tennessee	17-7

The Rivalries

1973	Lexington	Tennessee	16-14
1974	Knoxville	Tennessee	24-7
1975	Lexington	Tennessee	17-13
1976	Knoxville	Kentucky	7-0
1977	Lexington	Kentucky	21-17
1978	Knoxville	Tennessee	29-14
1979	Lexington	Tennessee	20-17
1980	Knoxville	Tennessee	45-14
1981	Lexington	Kentucky	21-10
1982	Knoxville	Tennessee	28-7
1983	Lexington	Tennessee	10-0
1984	Knoxville	Kentucky	17-12
1985	Lexington	Tennessee	42-0
1986	Knoxville	Tennessee	28-9
1987	Lexington	Tennessee	24-22
1988	Knoxville	Tennessee	28-24
1989	Lexington	Tennessee	31-10
1990	Knoxville	Tennessee	42-28
1991	Lexington	Tennessee	16-7
1992	Knoxville	Tennessee	34-13
1993	Lexington	Tennessee	48-0
1994	Knoxville	Tennessee	52-0
1995	Lexington	Tennessee	34-31
1996	Knoxville	Tennessee	56-10
1997	Lexington	Tennessee	59-31
1998	Knoxville	Tennessee	59-21
1999	Lexington	Tennessee	56-21
2000	Knoxville	Tennessee	59-20
2001	Lexington	Tennessee	38-35
2002	Knoxville	Tennessee	24-0
2003	Lexington	Tennessee	20-7
2004	Knoxville	Tennessee	37-31
2005	Lexington	Tennessee	27-8
2006	Knoxville	Tennessee	17-12
2007	Lexington (4OT)	Tennessee	52-50
2008	Knoxville	Tennessee	28-10

The Rivalries

Running back Jamal Lewis plows throws the Kentucky defense in the 59-31 bludgeoning of the Wildcats on November 23, 1997, at Commonwealth Stadium in Lexington.

Tennessee vs. Vanderbilt

In 1926, Robert Neyland was an ROTC instructor, army captain, and former football assistant coach in Knoxville when Nathan Dougherty, dean of Tennessee's College of Engineering and faculty chairman of athletics, gave his new head coach a directive: "Even the score with Vanderbilt, do something about our terrible standing in the series."

At the time, the Commodores, coached by Dan McGugin, were a regional powerhouse, having won ten Southern Intercollegiate Athletic Association and Southern Conference championships between 1904 and 1923. Tennessee had only defeated Vanderbilt twice since the first meeting in 1892.

Since Neyland was hired, UT has all but owned the series. A notable exception was 2005, when, in the words of Coach Phillip Fulmer, Tennessee hit "rock bottom." Earl Bennett's 5-yard touchdown reception from Jay Cutler with 1:11 remaining gave Vanderbilt a 28–24 victory to snap Tennessee's 22-game winning streak in the series. It was the Commodores' first win at Neyland Stadium since 1975, and at the time the overall streak was the second longest between major teams in Division I-A (Notre Dame over Navy, 42, which ended in 2007).

"You see grown men crying and you realize how long it's been since we've won," Cutler said. "It tells us how much it means to this program."

Although Tennessee had been ranked No. 3 in the 2005 preseason, the Vols missed out on the postseason for the first time since 1988.

Three years later, Vanderbilt played in a bowl game while Tennessee did not, for the first time since 1955 and just the second time ever.

Tennessee
vs. Vanderbilt
(Tennessee leads series 69-27-5)

Year	Location	Winner	Score
1892	Knoxville	Vanderbilt	12-0
1892	Nashville	Vanderbilt	22-4
1900	Nashville	Tied	0-0
1901	Nashville	Vanderbilt	22-0
1902	Knoxville	Vanderbilt	12-5
1903	Nashville	Vanderbilt	40-0
1904	Nashville	Vanderbilt	22-0
1905	Knoxville	Vanderbilt	45-0
1908	Nashville	Vanderbilt	16-9
1909	Nashville	Vanderbilt	51-0
1910	Nashville	Vanderbilt	18-0
1913	Nashville	Vanderbilt	7-6
1914	Nashville	Tennessee	16-14
1915	Nashville	Vanderbilt	35-0
1916	Knoxville	Tennessee	10-6
1919	Nashville	Tied	3-3
1920	Knoxville	Vanderbilt	20-0
1921	Nashville	Vanderbilt	14-0
1922	Knoxville	Vanderbilt	14-6
1923	Nashville	Vanderbilt	51-7
1925	Nashville	Vanderbilt	34-7
1926	Nashville	Vanderbilt	20-3
1927	Knoxville	Tied	7-7
1928	Nashville	Tennessee	6-0
1929	Knoxville	Tennessee	13-0
1930	Nashville	Tennessee	13-0
1931	Knoxville	Tennessee	21-7
1932	Nashville	Tied	0-0
1933	Knoxville	Tennessee	33-6
1934	Nashville	Tennessee	13-6
1935	Knoxville	Vanderbilt	13-7
1936	Nashville	Tennessee	26-13
1937	Knoxville	Vanderbilt	13-7

The Rivalries

275

1938	Nashville	Tennessee	14-0
1939	Knoxville	Tennessee	13-0
1940	Nashville	Tennessee	20-0
1941	Knoxville	Tennessee	26-7
1942	Nashville	Tennessee	19-7
1945	Knoxville	Tennessee	45-0
1946	Nashville	Tennessee	7-6
1947	Knoxville	Tennessee	12-7
1948	Nashville	Vanderbilt	28-6
1949	Knoxville	Tennessee	26-20
1950	Nashville	Tennessee	43-0
1951	Knoxville	Tennessee	35-27
1952	Nashville	Tennessee	46-0
1953	Knoxville	Tennessee	33-6
1954	Nashville	Vanderbilt	26-0
1955	Knoxville	Tennessee	20-14
1956	Nashville	Tennessee	27-7
1957	Knoxville	Tennessee	20-6
1958	Nashville	Tennessee	10-6
1959	Knoxville	Vanderbilt	14-0
1960	Nashville	Tennessee	35-0
1961	Knoxville	Tennessee	41-7
1962	Nashville	Tennessee	30-0
1963	Knoxville	Tennessee	14-0
1964	Nashville	Vanderbilt	7-0
1965	Knoxville	Tennessee	21-3
1966	Nashville	Tennessee	28-0
1967	Knoxville	Tennessee	41-14
1968	Nashville	Tennessee	10-7
1969	Knoxville	Tennessee	40-27
1970	Nashville	Tennessee	24-6
1971	Knoxville	Tennessee	19-7
1972	Nashville	Tennessee	30-10
1973	Knoxville	Tennessee	20-17
1974	Nashville	Tied	21-21
1975	Knoxville	Vanderbilt	17-14
1976	Nashville	Tennessee	13-10
1977	Knoxville	Tennessee	42-7
1978	Nashville	Tennessee	41-15

1979	Knoxville	Tennessee	31-10
1980	Nashville	Tennessee	51-13
1981	Knoxville	Tennessee	38-34
1982	Nashville	Vanderbilt	28-21
1983	Knoxville	Tennessee	34-24
1984	Nashville	Tennessee	29-13
1985	Knoxville	Tennessee	30-0
1986	Nashville	Tennessee	35-20
1987	Knoxville	Tennessee	38-36
1988	Nashville	Tennessee	14-7
1989	Knoxville	Tennessee	17-10
1990	Nashville	Tennessee	49-20
1991	Knoxville	Tennessee	45-0
1992	Nashville	Tennessee	29-25
1993	Knoxville	Tennessee	62-14
1994	Nashville	Tennessee	65-0
1995	Knoxville	Tennessee	12-7
1996	Nashville	Tennessee	14-7
1997	Knoxville	Tennessee	17-10
1998	Nashville	Tennessee	41-0
1999	Knoxville	Tennessee	38-10
2000	Nashville	Tennessee	28-26
2001	Knoxville	Tennessee	38-0
2002	Nashville	Tennessee	24-0
2003	Knoxville	Tennessee	48-0
2004	Nashville	Tennessee	38-33
2005	Knoxville	Vanderbilt	28-24
2006	Nashville	Tennessee	39-10
2007	Knoxville	Tennessee	25-24
2008	Nashville	Tennessee	20-1

The Rivalries

Tennessee vs. Florida

Although the teams first met in 1916, it took years for the Tennessee-Florida rivalry to develop, until 1992 Southeastern Conference expansion placed them in the same division.

Previously, the only real spark came at the 1969 Gator Bowl, when two days before kickoff word leaked out that Tennessee coach and former Florida quarterback Doug Dickey would return to his alma mater after the game to replace Ray Graves. Florida won, 14–13. (Dickey eventually returned to Tennessee in 1984; he served as athletics director from 1986 through 2002.)

What undoubtedly turned up the intensity was Florida coach Steve Spurrier, who after losing the 1992 match-up came back to win the following year, 41–34, with Danny Wuerffel as quarterback. With national title implications on the line for most of the subsequent meetings, the dislike between fans only grew as the Gators regularly came out on top.

Before long, the focus was on quarterback Peyton Manning, who took over for injured Todd Helton as a freshman in 1994. He went 39–6 as a starter, but lost all four meetings with Florida, the only blemish on an otherwise stellar collegiate career.

Manning set 33 school, seven SEC, and two NCAA passing records, with 89 touchdown passes and more than 11,000 career yards and just 33 interceptions in 1,381 attempts, but only placed second in Heisman Trophy voting to Michigan's Charles Woodson.

With Tennessee a second-place fixture in the division, a spot that frequently means an invitation to the Florida Citrus Bowl, Spurrier quipped: "You can't spell Citrus without UT."

Tennessee vs. Florida

(Series tied 19-19)

Year	Location	Winner	Score
1916	Tampa	Tennessee	24-0
1921	Knoxville	Tennessee	9-0
1928	Knoxville	Tennessee	13-12
1930	Jacksonville	Tennessee	13-6
1932	Jacksonville	Tennessee	32-13
1933	Knoxville	Tennessee	13-6
1940	Knoxville	Tennessee	14-0
1944	Knoxville	Tennessee	40-0
1952	Knoxville	Tennessee	26-12
1953	Gainesville	Tennessee	9-7
1954	Knoxville	Florida	14-0
1955	Gainesville	Tennessee	20-0
1969	Jacksonville	Florida	14-13
1970	Knoxville	Tennessee	38-7
1971	Gainesville	Tennessee	20-13
1976	Knoxville	Florida	20-18
1977	Gainesville	Florida	27-17
1984	Knoxville	Florida	43-30
1985	Gainesville	Florida	17-10
1990	Knoxville	Tennessee	45-3
1991	Gainesville	Florida	35-18
1992	Knoxville	Tennessee	31-14
1993	Gainesville	Florida	41-34
1994	Knoxville	Florida	31-0
1995	Gainesville	Florida	62-37
1996	Knoxville	Florida	35-29
1997	Gainesville	Florida	33-20
1998	Knoxville OT	Tennessee	20-17
1999	Gainesville	Florida	23-21
2000	Knoxville	Florida	27-23
2001	Gainesville	Tennessee	34-32
2002	Knoxville	Florida	30-13
2003	Gainesville	Tennessee	24-10
2004	Knoxville	Tennessee	30-28
2005	Gainesville	Florida	16-7
2006	Knoxville	Florida	21-20
2007	Gainesville	Florida	59-20
2008	Knoxville	Florida	30-6

The Rivalries

TRADITIONS

The traditions and pageantry of Tennessee football are rich and deep. They are passed down from generation to generation: a sense of duty, Southern pride, and, of course, an undying love for Tennessee football.

The Colors

Orange and white. The unusual pairing tells you plenty about a streak of independence common to Tennesseans. Most schools using orange as a school color go with a darker shade not occurring in nature. The majority of those will pair their "orange" with a darker color because graphic designers will tell you orange and white don't offer enough contrast. Television commentators hate white numerals on orange jerseys because it makes for a long day for even the most eagle-eyed spotter. Tennessee fans will offer up some choice words for all the naysayers—and then rush to the store to brighten up their closet with some more orange and white garb.

It's a good thing the Volunteers are known for a physical, rough-and-tumble style of football because their school colors pay homage to a flower. The orange and white pairing was selected by Charles Moore, a member of Tennessee's first football team in 1891, because it reminded him of the common American daisy that graced the Hill in his day, just a Hail Mary from the north end zone. The football team first donned the famous orange jersey against Emory and Henry in 1922, a game the Vols won 50–0.

The Nickname

The proud legacy of the Volunteer calls Tennessee student-athletes to compete at an elevated standard when the stakes are highest. A Volunteer is the bravest breed of human from the boldest nation on Earth, fiercely proud to call Tennessee home, whether the battle lies within its borders or in a land far away.

The Volunteers rose to defeat the British early in our nation's history, from the Overmountain Men in the Revolutionary War to Andrew "Old Hickory" Jackson's skillful defense of New Orleans in the War of 1812. No matter how fearsome the foe, whether outnumbered like Davy Crockett and his courageous Volunteers at the Alamo or Sergeant Alvin York's individual heroics against the Germans in World War I, a Volunteer is always ready when his homeland calls.

From the nation's birth to this very day, when the U.S. needs an extraordinary effort to brush back the dark curtain of hopelessness, the Tennessee Volunteers have been available. The bravery, heroism, wisdom, and ferocity of the Volunteers place them on a pedestal of great American legends.

Traditions

Tennessee is one of only two schools in the country to maintain separate athletic departments for men and women. The only other school is Texas.

Neyland Stadium

If Col. W.S. Shields were alive today, he'd almost certainly be shocked to see what now stands at the bank of the Tennessee River. Shields, president of Knoxville's City National Bank and a UT trustee, provided the initial funds for a university football field, which was completed in 1921 and named Shields-Watkins after he and his wife, Alice Watkins-Shields (previously, the team played on the corner of 15th Street and Cumberland). The facility's capacity was just 3,200.

The massive structure that developed around that field, having been expanded 16 times over the years, now seats 104,079.

In 1962, shortly after the program's most successful coach—General Robert R. Neyland—died, the stadium was renamed in his honor on the day of the Alabama game (a 27–7 victory for the Crimson Tide). That same season, the new upper deck on the west side opened, increasing capacity to 52,227, and broadcaster George Mooney became the father of the Volunteer Navy by traveling down the Tennessee River to get to a game.

Not surprisingly, Tennessee has been immensely successful playing at home, enjoying a 30-game winning streak there (1928–1933), and a 55-game streak without a loss (1925–1933).

The Volunteers switched to artificial turf in 1968 (before returning to natural grass in 1994), and with the 1972 expansion night football came to Knoxville in time for the season opener against Penn State.

Although fans would almost certainly like to do something about the narrow seating, school officials like to boast that it's the largest football stadium in the South, and the third-largest college stadium in the country.

The single-game attendance record is 108,768 for Florida in 2000.

Traditions

THE EVER-EXPANDING NEYLAND STADIUM

YEAR	ADDITION	CHANGE	CAPACITY
1921	Original West Stands	3,200 seats	3,200
1926	East Stands	3,600 seats	6,800
1929	West Stands	11,060 seats	17,860
1937	North Section X	1,500 seats	19,360
1938	East Stands	12,030 seats	31,390
1948	South Stands	15,000 seats	46,390
1962	West Upper Deck	5,837 seats, press box	52,227
1966	North Stands	5,895 seats	58,122
1968	East Upper Deck	6,307 seats	64,429
1972	Southwest Upper Deck	6,221 seats	70,650
1976	Southeast Upper Deck	9,600 seats	80,250
1980	North Stands	10,999 seats	91,249
1987	West Executive Suites	42 suites	91,110
1990	Student Seating Adjust	792 seats	91,902
1996	North Upper Deck	10,642 seats	102,544
1997	ADA Seating Adjust	310 seats	102,854
2000	East Executive Suites	78 suites	104,079
2006	East Executive Suites	Club level	102,037

Neyland Stadium, even with its slight reduction in seats, is the fourth largest stadium in the country and seventh largest in the world.

The Helmet

Like its peers at the top of the college football world, Tennessee's familiar football helmet is iconic. Not unlike Notre Dame's golden glow or Michigan's eye-catching design, the T emblazoned on the side of the Vols' headgear leaves no doubt as to affiliation. Love them or hate them, it doesn't take long to recognize when the Volunteers are on TV again.

With the orange power T logo affixed to both sides of a white helmet and an orange stripe down the center, the basic design hasn't changed much since 1964, when head coach Doug Dickey arrived in Knoxville. Before 1964, the design featured white helmets with an orange stripe down the middle, with just two exceptions: in 1962, orange numerals were added to the sides of the helmets, and in 1963, the design remained the same except black numerals were used.

Marching Band

The Pride of the Southland Marching Band adds to Tennessee's considerable reputation as a state richly marinated in musical history. Dr. Gary Sousa, director of bands, heads a program employing the services of more than 400 musicians in all bands. The Pride of the Southland Marching Band marks the best-known unit in the program. The band is known for its precision pregame and halftime formations—and for its numerous renditions of "Rocky Top."

First organized after the conclusion of the Civil War, the band offered war-weary Knoxvillians a welcome change from musket balls to music. In time, the Pride of the Southland Band became one of the state's most respected musical ambassadors, and it has represented the state of Tennessee for the last 40 years at 10 con-

Traditions

secutive presidential inaugurations. From Dwight D. Eisenhower to George W. Bush, the Pride of the Southland Band has provided pomp and pageantry befitting such a ceremony.

VolWalk

Tennessee spirit and pageantry is on display each Saturday two and a half hours before kickoff when the Volunteers make their march amid thousands of orange-and-white clad fans who line the trail. The Tennessee players walk in loose ranks from the Neyland-Thompson Sports Center, down Volunteer Boulevard, through Peyton Manning Pass, and finally into Neyland Stadium where the day's opponent awaits them.

The band leads the way, blasting "Rocky Top" and stepping high, whetting the appetite of the early arriving fans who can't bear to prolong the anticipation of another Volunteer victory.

The heroes follow the band, most dressed in suits or ties, carrying their uniforms in a duffel bag as they head for the locker room.

In addition to the goodwill, the VolWalk produces by allowing fans an up-close look at the players without helmets and shoulder pads.

Traditions

Vol Navy

George Mooney, a former Tennessee broadcaster, first navigated his small runabout vessel down the Tennessee River before a 1962 Volunteers football game. It quickly caught on, and thus was born the Volunteer Navy, a floating tailgate party that crowds the Tennessee River in the shadow of Neyland Stadium. Thousands of Tennessee football fans arrive at Neyland Stadium via the river, docking their boats along Neyland Drive before hiking the final two blocks on foot.

The Tennessee River provides a scenic background at Neyland Stadium, but it's also a popular spot for "sailgating." Two hundred boats regularly make up the "Vol Navy," a tradition unique in college football.

Traditions

"Rocky Top"

Wish that I was on ol' Rocky Top
Down in the Tennessee hills;
Ain't no smoggy smoke on Rocky Top,
Ain't no telephone bills.
Once I had a girl on Rocky Top,
Half bear, other half cat;
Wild as a mink, but sweet as soda pop,
I still dream about that.
(chorus)
Rocky Top, you'll always be
Home sweet home to me;
Good ol' Rocky Top—
Rocky Top Tennessee, Rocky Top Tennessee.
Once two strangers climbed ol' Rocky Top,
Lookin' for a moonshine still;
Strangers ain't come down from Rocky Top,
Reckon they never will.
Corn won't grow at all on Rocky Top,
Dirt's too rocky by far;
That's why all the folks on Rocky Top
Get their corn from a jar.
(chorus)
I've had years of cramped-up city life,
Trapped like a duck in a pen;
All I know is it's a pity life
Can't be simple again.
(chorus)

Traditions

"Rocky Top"

The foot-stompin' jingle rouses Tennessee fans each time it's played, be it at Neyland Stadium, Thompson-Boling Arena, Lindsey Nelson Stadium, or perhaps even your local pub. Felice and Boudleaux Bryant wrote the song in 10 minutes at the Gatlinburg Inn in 1967. The song features just five basic chords, and the title is repeated 19 times in the song. It was first played as part of a country music show at the 1972 Tennessee-Alabama game.

Checkerboard End Zones

The orange and white checkerboard end zones first appeared in 1964, the first year of current athletics director Doug Dickey's coaching tenure. They disappeared in 1968, with the introduction of an artificial playing surface, then reappeared in 1989, where they remain to this day.

Smokey the Bluetick Coonhound

Serving as mascot for the Volunteer football team since 1953 is Smokey the bluetick coonhound. The late Reverend Bill Brooks' prizewinner served as Smokey I in 1953 and 1954. Smokey VIII was the winningest Smokey, sporting a record of 91–22 (.805), with two SEC titles and the 1998 national championship. The Tennessee-bred canine currently leading the Vols through the T prior to each home game and stalking the sidelines is Smokey IX.

Traditions

Smokey VIII was the most successful Smokey in school history, presiding over 91 wins, two conference championships, and one national title. He passed away in 2003.

Fight Song

No, the official fight song is not the infectious "Rocky Top." That honor belongs to "Here's to Old Tennessee (Down the Field)." The official fight song captures much about the character of campus and the state's military heritage. The marriage of Gwen Sweet's words and Chas. Fielder's arrangement was copyrighted in 1939, a year that saw the Vols take the SEC title and hold all 10 regular-season opponents scoreless. A model of efficiency, "Down the Field" pays tribute to Tennessee football, fighting, orange and white, marching, the Spirit of the Hill, courage and loyalty in a mere 78 words. The Pride of the Southland Band gives the song an honored place in its pregame show before every home game.

"Here's to Old Tennessee (Down the Field)"

Here's to old Tennessee

Ne'er shall we sever

We pledge our loyalty

For ever and ever

Backing her football team

Faltering never

Cheer and fight with all your might

For Tennessee!

Traditions

Running through the T

In the culmination of a pregame spectacle unrivaled in college athletics, Tennessee's football team piles into a crowded tunnel as the Pride of the Southland Band wraps up its pregame show. The players are unable to see their rivals or the hysteria building to a fever pitch around them. But they can hear it building louder and louder. And they can feel it, as the venerable House that Neyland Built shakes and rumbles its steel skeleton as the fanatics await their entry. With 107,000 fans whipped into a frenzy, The Pride of the Southland Band forms the giant T that serves as a runway as the players sprint onto the field bathed in the admiration of the Volunteer nation. With mascot Smokey up front sniffing out a true trail, head coach Phillip Fulmer leads his charges up the base of the T and hangs a left to take up residence on the Tennessee sideline.

The T was one of head coach Doug Dickey's innovations. In 1965, Dickey moved the Tennessee bench from the east sideline, its current location, to the west sideline. The move allowed the Vols to make the ceremonious entry from their dressing room, which then exited at the 50-yard line on the east side, through the T formed east to west, and onto the west sideline. In 1983, a new dressing room was built underneath the north end zone stands. In response, the T, thankfully a flexible letter, was moved to its current location, running north to south, though players took a right to the west sideline. When the home bench returned to the east sideline, the only change necessary was a left turn instead of a right.

Traditions

John Ward

More than a play-by-play announcer, John Ward earned his position as a Tennessee institution by painting a vivid picture of Appalachia's grandest autumn drama for 31 seasons. From 1968 to 1998, Ward and color analyst Bill Anderson dutifully took their positions in the press box and brought fall's action into living rooms across the Volunteer State. Ward's delightful descriptions proved accurate, colorful, and endearing.

Ward began his football announcing career when there was precious little college football television coverage. It's quite a rarity today not to be able to watch the football Vols on television, but that wasn't always the case. For those unfortunates unable to attend the game, Ward served as the eyes and ears of Volunteer fans far and wide. He was so esteemed that even when television games became commonplace, families across the state preferred to turn down the television sound and turn up Ward and Anderson to tell the story of the day with substance and style. His oft-imitated signature phrases—"Give Him Six!" and "It's Football Time in Tennessee!"—testified that Ward's hero status was alive and well in countless ragtag backyard games from Mountain City to Memphis. To millions of Tennessee fans, Ward *was* Tennessee football, even more than some of the legendary coaches who cast a long shadow stalking Tennessee's sideline in his tenure. His last football game befitted his charmed run. On January 4, 1999, as the sun sank low in the Arizona desert, televisions across the Volunteer State were silenced and radios crackled to life as Ward masterfully detailed Tennessee's Fiesta Bowl win over Florida State to capture the national championship.

"Alma Mater"

Verse I

On a hallowed hill in Tennessee
Like a beacon shining bright
The stately walls of old U.T.
Rise glorious to the sight.

Refrain

So here's to you, old Tennessee
Our alma mater true.
We pledge in love and harmony
Our loyalty to you.

Verse II

What torches kindled at that flame
Have passed from hand to hand.
What hearts cemented in that name
Bind land to stranger land.

Refrain

So here's to you, old Tennessee
Our alma mater true.
We pledge in love and harmony
Our loyalty to you.

Verse III

O, ever as we strive to rise
On life's unresting stream
Dear Alma Mater, may our eyes
Be lifted to that gleam.

Refrain

So here's to you, old Tennessee
Our alma mater true.
We pledge in love and harmony
Our loyalty to you.

Traditions

THE GREAT TEAMS

The 1951 and 1998 national championship teams certainly weren't the only great teams in Vol history. Here's a quick sampling of some of the other great units to grace the Hill.

1914 (9–0)

Had there been wire service polls in 1914, coach Zora Clevenger's 1914 Tennessee team might have been national champs. Prior to that season, UT had been winless against Vanderbilt in 12 tries, but the Vols pulled off a 16–14 win in Nashville that year on the way to a perfect 9–0 slate, outscoring their opponents by a total of 374–37. Tennessee captured its first championship in football that season, finishing atop the Southern Intercollegiate Athletic Association standings.

1916 (8–0–1)

John R. Bender took over as Tennessee coach in 1916 and finished the year undefeated, though a scoreless tie with Kentucky in the season finale marred the record. As a result, the SIAA title was awarded to Georgia Tech. A 16–6 win over Vanderbilt brought UT's record against its cross-state rival to 2–12–1.

1938 (11–0), 1939 (10–1), 1940 (10–1)

From 1938 through 1940, Bob Neyland's Tennessee teams enjoyed three straight perfect regular seasons. From midseason 1938 until midseason 1940, the Vols didn't surrender a regular-season point.

The Great Teams

The 1939 Tennessee team is the last in college football history to finish a regular season unscored upon. The record over those three years, counting bowl games: 31–2.

1950 (11–1)

The Big Orange posted a 10–1 regular-season mark in 1950, dropping only Game 2 to Mississippi State. The biggest win of the year was a 7–0 decision over Bear Bryant's undefeated and top-ranked Kentucky team, which featured SEC Player of the Year Babe Parilli at quarterback. The Vols went on to upset Texas 20–14 in the Cotton Bowl, keyed by a scintillating 75-yard run by Hank Lauricella. Two of the three teams ranked ahead of Tennessee—Oklahoma and Texas— lost their bowl games, and second-ranked Army had lost to Navy on December 2. But the polls were closed.

1951 (10–1)

Tennessee's first consensus national championship came in the second-to-last year of Robert Neyland's coaching tenure. The 1951 Vols featured tailback Hank Lauricella, who finished second in that year's Heisman voting, and Doug Atkins, arguably the greatest defensive end who ever played the game. UT outscored its opponents 386–116 and finished the regular season 10–0 before losing the Sugar Bowl to Maryland 28–13.

The Great Teams

1956 (10-1)

With former Vol end and Hall of Fame coach Bowden Wyatt in his second season at the helm in Knoxville, Tennessee won the 1956 SEC Championship with a 10-0 regular-season record before dropping the Sugar Bowl to Baylor 13-7. The Vols' 6-0 win over Georgia Tech that year is an all-time college football classic. Tailback Johnny Majors finished second in the Heisman voting, and Tennessee finished second nationally in the final rankings.

1967 (9-2)

The 1967 Volunteers, with All-Americans Bob Johnson at center and Richmond Flowers at wingback, won the SEC and a share of the national championship. In between losses to UCLA and Heisman Trophy winner Gary Beban in the opener and to third-ranked Oklahoma in the Orange Bowl, the Vols were perfect. The highlight of the season was a 23-14 win at Alabama, which ended a six-year string of futility against the Tide.

1970 (11-1)

The Volunteers finished with a fourth-place national ranking in 1970, Bill Battle's inaugural season as head coach. The only smudge on the record was a three-point loss to Auburn in Game 2. Guard Chip Kell, defensive back Bobby Majors, and linebacker Jackie Walker were All-Americans. The season was capped by a 34-10 rout of Air Force in the Sugar Bowl.

1989 (11-1)

The Vols won the second of coach Johnny Majors' three SEC Championships and ranked fifth in the final wire service polls with an 11-1 campaign in 1989. The only setback was a 47-30 shootout at Alabama.

Antone Davis and All-American Eric Still were the
most dominating guard duo in Knoxville since Bob
Suffridge and Ed Molinski in the glory years of 1938–
1940. Chuck Webb rushed for 1,236 yards gaining just
under six per carry and added 250 rushing yards in a
31–27 Cotton Bowl victory over Southwest Conference
champion Arkansas.

1998 (13–0)

Tennessee posted its second consensus national
championship, and sixth overall, in 1998. Tee Martin
took over for the graduated Peyton Manning at quarterback and led his team to the promised land.
Tailback Jamal Lewis was lost for the season with a
knee injury in Game 4, but Travis Henry answered
the challenge and finished the season just 30 yards
shy of a 1,000-yard rushing campaign. Wide receiver
Peerless Price contributed 61 pass receptions to the
cause. Linebackers Al Wilson and Raynoch Thompson
cemented the defense, with placekicker Jeff Hall
becoming the SEC's all-time leading scorer. It took
three fourth-quarter rallies to finish the regular season unscathed, but these Vols were on a mission. After
a resounding 23–16 victory over Florida State in the
Fiesta Bowl, Tennessee stood at 13–0 as the undisputed
national champion.

The Great Teams

2001 (11-2)

The 2001 Tennessee Vols came within half a game of playing for the national championship, falling to LSU in the SEC Championship Game. Instead, UT closed the season with one of the most impressive bowl victories in school history, trouncing Michigan 45–17 in the Citrus Bowl behind Casey Clausen's 26-of-34, 393-yard, three TD passing performance.

Indeed, it was one of the most prolific offensive squads to wear Orange and White, as future NFL receivers Dante Stallworth and Kelley Washington flanked future NFL All-Pro tight end Jason Witten. Travis Stephens, a speedy jitterbug back, provided an explosive burst out of the backfield.

Defensively, twin towers John Henderson and Albert Haynesworth thwarted the run from their tackle positions, and the tireless Will Overstreet provided a blind-side rush. Kevin Burnett ranked as one of the fiercest hitters in the nation in the linebacking corps, sidelining no fewer than three QBs during a season that included triumphs at Alabama (35–24), Notre Dame (28–18), and Florida (34–32).

The Tennessee win over Michigan in the 2001 Citrus Bowl was the first bowl win for the team since they won the National Championship over Florida State.

THE GREAT GAMES

Tennessee 15, Alabama 13
October 20, 1928

Tennessee and Alabama hadn't played each other for 14 years, and the Crimson Tide had won eight of the previous 11 meetings. But this was the first game with Bob Neyland at the helm for the Volunteers. Neyland's first two teams had posted records of 8–1 and 8–0–1, an accomplishment scarcely known outside of Knoxville. The Volunteers needed a win over a big-name team, and nobody was bigger than Alabama, which was coming off consecutive Rose Bowl trips under coach Wallace Wade. Tennessee sophomore halfback Gene McEver's 98-yard touchdown on the opening kick-off opened the festivities, and the Vols won 15–13. The win focused national attention on Tennessee and its "Hack, Mack, and Dodd" backfield of Buddy Hackman, McEver and Bobby Dodd.

Tennessee 17, Oklahoma 0
January 2, 1939

Tennessee finished the 1938 regular season 10–0 and ranked second in the nation behind TCU and Heisman Trophy winner Davey O'Brien. The Vols' first-ever bowl game—in the Orange Bowl against fourth-ranked Oklahoma—ensued. The Sooners were also 10–0 and had won their last 14 games. The game was billed as one of speed (Tennessee) versus power (Oklahoma). Speed won. It is remembered as one of the most vicious football games ever played. One journalist referred to the contest as the "Orange Brawl." Players were knocked out of the game with startling regularity. A block by Tennessee All-American George Cafego finished OU All-American Waddy Young for the day. UT center Joe Little was ejected from the game for retali-

The Great Games

ating after a Sooner cheap shot. Touchdowns by Bob
Foxx and Babe Wood, a Bowden Wyatt field goal, and
a shutout by a typically impenetrable Neyland defense
rendered a final tally of 17–0.

Tennessee 7, Kentucky 0
November 25, 1950

Many observers felt the 1950 Tennessee team was
superior to the 1951 national champions. After dropping Game 2 to Mississippi State, the 1950 Vols rolled
over seven straight opponents before their matchup
with Bear Bryant's undefeated, top-ranked Kentucky
team. The Wildcats, led by Southeastern Conference
MVP Babe Parilli at quarterback, had already clinched
the SEC crown. The Vols weren't given much of a
chance entering the contest, but their defense, spear-
headed by Bill Pearman, Ted Daffer, Bud Sherrod and
Doug Atkins, kept Parilli on the run most of the day. A
27-yard touchdown pass from Hank Lauricella to Bert
Rechichar was all the scoring the Tennessee needed.

Tennessee 20, Texas 14
January 1, 1951

Had the final polls been taken after the post season in 1950, as they are today, Tennessee would have
been national champions. Neyland's Vols, 10–1 and
ranked fourth nationally, traveled to Dallas to take on
the 9–1, third-ranked Texas Longhorns in the Cotton
Bowl on New Year's Day, 1951. The Volunteers scored
first on a short pass from Herky Payne to John Gruble.
The score was set up by a memorable 75-yard run by
All-American Hank Lauricella. The Horns stormed
back to lead 14–7 at intermission, but the Vols owned
the second half. Neyland's troops, using the single wing
formation that had been ditched by all but one or two
other teams in favor of the T formation, stormed back

for 13 fourth-quarter points on a pair of touchdown plunges by fullback Andy Kozar. Tennessee's speed won over Texas' bulk to the tune of a 20–14 final score. With top-ranked Oklahoma falling to Kentucky in the Sugar Bowl that same day, a post-bowl poll could have crowned Tennessee champion.

Tennessee 6, Georgia Tech 0
November 10, 1956

In 1956, Bowden Wyatt enjoyed the best campaign of his eight-year coaching regime in Knoxville. Tennessee and then-SEC foe Georgia Tech, coached by former UT Vol Bobby Dodd, were each 6–0 entering their classic matchup. Wyatt and Dodd had both trained as players under Neyland, and now they coached the two finest teams in the Southeastern Conference.

A pair of third-quarter passes from Johnny Majors to Buddy Cruze set up the game's only score, a 1-yard plunge by Tommy Bronson.

The Vols held on for the win in what was to be Tech's only loss of the season.

Tennessee 14, LSU 13
November 7, 1959

In 1959, LSU was the defending national champion, with Paul Dietzel as coach and Heisman Trophy winner Billy Cannon as its star halfback. The Tigers brought a 19-game winning streak and No. 1 ranking into Knoxville on November 7 to face the 4–1–1 Vols. Cannon and Johnny Robinson ran wild in the first half for LSU, but the Tigers could only manage to squeeze out seven points by halftime. In the third quarter, Tennessee's Jim Cartwright intercepted a Warren Rabb pass and returned it 59 yards for a game-tying touchdown. The Vols took a 14–7 lead

The Great Games

on a 14-yard Neyle Solle run. A fumbled punt at the 2-yard line led to LSU's final touchdown and brought the score to 14–13. But Cannon was stopped short on the two-point conversion try in one of the greatest moments in Tennessee football history, preserving the huge upset win.

Tennessee 35, Miami 7
January 1, 1986

Miami finished the 1985 regular season on a 10-game winning streak, having not lost since dropping its opener to Florida 35–23. Coach Jimmy Johnson brought his Hurricanes into the Sugar Bowl to face Johnny Majors' SEC champion Tennessee squad. The 'Canes took a 7–0 lead on an 18-yard pass from Vinny Testaverde to Michael Irvin to end the first quarter, but after that it was all UT. A 6-yard touchdown pass from Daryl Dickey to Jeff Smith in the second quarter knotted the score at 7–7 and sent the game spiraling out of Miami's control. The Vols led 14–7 at the half, tacked on two more TDs in the third period, including a 60-yard punt return by Jeff Powell, and another in the fourth. The defense produced seven sacks and six turnovers, sending the highly partisan crowd into a frenzy that spilled onto Bourbon Street. The final tally: Tennessee 35, Miami 7. It was the resounding exclamation point on one of the truly magical seasons in Tennessee history.

Tennessee 35, Notre Dame 34
November 9, 1991

It was the greatest come-from-behind win in Tennessee history and the greatest comeback ever at Notre Dame Stadium. On November 9, 1991, at South Bend, Notre Dame jumped out to a 21–0 first-quarter lead and led 31–7 in the second quarter. Just before halftime, Darryl Hardy blocked a field goal attempt by ND's

Craig Hentrich. Floyd Miley scooped up the ball and took off on an 85-yard touchdown jaunt to bring the score to 31–14 at intermission. The Volunteers scored three TDs in the second half, including two by Aaron Hayden, to take the lead 35–34. Irish walk-on kicker Rob Leonard, subbing for an injured Hentrich, came in for a 27-yard field goal as time expired, but Jeremy Lincoln blocked the attempt and the Vols came away winners.

Tennessee 20, Florida 17
September 19, 1998

Tennessee's 34–33 win over Syracuse in the 1998 season opener could qualify for greatest-game status, but it was the Vols' next game, two weeks later against Florida, that fans remember most fondly. After a Florida field goal, Shawn Bryson scored on a 57-yard run for a 7–3 Tennessee lead in the first quarter. The first half ended in a 10–10 deadlock. After three quarters the score was knotted at 17, and the final period was scoreless. Jeff Hall kicked a 41-yard field goal in the first-ever overtime period for both schools, and UT led 20–17. Jeff Chandler came up empty on his 32-yard attempt to end the Gators' overtime possession, and the Vols were off and running to a national title. Deon Grant's fourth-quarter interception and linebacker Al Wilson's nine tackles and school-record three forced fumbles were keys to the win. And the Neyland Stadium goal post enjoyed a late-night parade through the town as Knoxville celebrated like never before.

Tennessee 34, Florida 32
December 1, 2001

Steve Spurrier appeared to have the Vols right where he wanted them in the final moments, but UT reserve defensive back Buck Fitzgerald blanketed star receiver Jabar Gaffney on a two-point conversion pass attempt from Rex Grossman, and helped to secure a 34–32 victory. The Gators were on their heels all game long. A Vols receiving corps that included Donte Stallworth, Kelley Washington, and tight end Jason Witten left Florida in defensive sets that were susceptible to the run, and Travis Stephens took full advantage with a 19-carry, 226-yard, two-TD performance.

Tennessee 51, Alabama 43 (5 OT)
October 25, 2003

The Vols' defense stepped up at the end of regulation, stopping the Tide on three consecutive plays when all Alabama needed was 2 yards to run out the clock. Once with the ball, Casey Clausen orchestrated an 86-yard touchdown drive in the final two minutes to tie the game at 20–20 and send the battle into overtime.

From the final drive of regulation to the end of the fifth overtime, Clausen was at his best, going 10-for-17 for 146 yards and four touchdowns, and rushing for the game-winner. Clausen also completed a fourth-and-19 pass to C.J. Fayton in overtime to keep the game alive.

"There's not a tougher-minded quarterback in the country than Casey Clausen," UT coach Phillip Fulmer said. "He's as tough physically and mentally as I've ever been around."

The win boosted Clausen's mark to 3–0 in overtime games, 12–1 on the road, and gave him his sixth fourth-quarter comeback win.

Tennessee 10, Miami 6
November 8, 2003

A near-scuffle in the pregame warm-ups set the tone for one of the hardest-hitting games in Tennessee history as the Vols battled a Hurricanes team riding a 26-game home win streak.

"This game was about respect," said UT linebacker Kevin Burnett, whose team certainly earned it by holding Miami without a touchdown in the Orange Bowl for the first time in 19 years. For all the big plays, which included Corey Campbell's head-splitting shot on 'Canes All-America tight end Kellen Winslow—which later led to Winslow's infamous locker room "soldier" tirade—the biggest play of all came at the UT 9-yard line. There free safety Mark Jones pressured Brock Berlin into an errant pass that strong safety Gibril Wilson picked off to secure the win. It was one of four turnovers the Vols forced on that day.

Tennessee managed just one touchdown drive, a 15-play 73-yarder that featured one of the biggest play-call gambles of Phillip Fulmer's career. Facing a fourth-and-goal at the 'Canes' 2-yard line, there was time for just one more play. Fulmer shocked Miami and the Vol Nation by abandoning his conservative ways, eschewing a field goal attempt and calling an end-around to Derrick Tinsley, of all things. Tinsley beat Miami All-America safety Sean Taylor to the corner of the end zone to provide all the scoring Tennessee needed in its biggest win of the new millennium.

Tennessee 30, LSU 27
September 26, 2005

The brightest moment of the otherwise downtrodden 5–6 2005 season was provided by Rick Clausen, who returned to the school he transferred from and made magic with a storybook comeback finish amid curious circumstances.

Hurricanes Katrina and Rita forced the game to be moved back to Monday night at Tiger Stadium, and a lack of hotel rooms forced the Vols to fly in the day of the game.

Early on, the delay appeared to benefit LSU, as the Tigers jumped out to a 21–0 lead by harassing on sophomore Erik Ainge, who was clearly not having his best night.

The Tigers were up 24–7 entering the fourth quarter before Clausen gave LSU fans reasons to wonder how they'd ever let him get away. Clausen led Tennessee on a 13-play, 75-yard drive that he capped with a 1-yard QB sneak to draw the Volunteers within 10.

Cornerback Jonathan Hefney provided the next big life on LSU's ensuing drive, stepping in front of a JaMarcus Russell pass and returning it 24 yards to the Tigers' 2-yard line. Tailback Gerald Riggs scored on a 2-yard run, and suddenly it was 24–21 and the Volunteers were back in a game that had appeared hopeless just one hour earlier.

The Tennessee defense held firm, forcing a punt, and a 22-yard Riggs run set up James Wilhoit's game-tying 28-yard field goal.

LSU drew first blood in overtime with a field goal, but Riggs and the Volunteers countered. Riggs caught a 10-yard pass and rushed for 14 yards on a carry. Finally, Riggs bulled through Tiger defenders for a 1-yard game-winning touchdown that left the hurricane-ravaged state of Louisiana in further shock.

Who would have believed that the same Rick Clausen who wasn't good enough to start for the Bayou Bengals three years earlier could return with a 21-of-32, 196-yard passing performance?

THE GREAT MOMENTS

Punt, Beattie, Punt

The 1932 Tennessee-Alabama game was the scene of the greatest punting duel in college football history. The backdrop was rainy, mud-soaked Legion Field in Birmingham. Tennessee coach Bob Neyland and Alabama coach Frank Thomas both decided to play conservatively and await the other team's mistakes. Vol halfback Beattie Feathers averaged 48 yards on 21 punts. His Crimson-clad counterpart, fullback Johnny Cain, punted 19 times at 43 yards per boot. 'Bama blinked first. Punting from his own end zone in the fourth quarter, Cain had to leap for a high pass from center. His hurried kick traveled only to the Tide 12-yard line. Three plays later, Feathers slashed into the end zone for the game's only touchdown, and Tennessee won 7–3.

Butler's Run

The most memorable play ever in Neyland Stadium, known at the time as Shields-Watkins Field, was achieved by a sophomore second-string halfback. In the 1939 Alabama game, Johnny "Blood" Butler eluded every player on the Alabama defense in a twisting, darting, 56-yard touchdown run. They all had a shot at him, but no one laid a hand on him. Legendary sportswriter Grantland Rice, in attendance in the press box that day, termed Butler's run the greatest he had ever seen. Tennessee won 21–0.

The Artful Dodger

Condredge Holloway's artistic escape acts became legendary during the little quarterback's tenure at Tennessee and resulted in some memorable victories. But the most remarkable performance by the man they called the Artful Dodger may have come in a game the Volunteers didn't win. In the 1974 season opener against UCLA, Holloway led Tennessee to a 10–0 first-quarter lead before injuring his shoulder. Holloway was rushed to a nearby hospital for X-rays, which proved negative. Returning to Neyland Stadium to deafening roars, Holloway reentered the game over the objections of coach Bill Battle. With Tennessee facing a 17–10 deficit, the Huntsville Houdini rallied the Vols to a tying touchdown, leaping over defenders into the end zone at the end of a 12-yard fourth-quarter run.

"I'm Going to Stay…"

When Peyton Manning walked to the podium for a press conference in March 1997, many people were prepared for the worst. Manning had rewritten the Tennessee record books during his three years as the unofficial president of Vol Nation, and the riches of professional football that were seemingly his birthright beckoned him to leave The Hill after his junior season.

But Manning, the type of kid for whom the phrase student-athlete was seemingly coined, had other ideas. The following nine-word statement thrilled fans all across Rocky Top and stunned others who were certain he was leaving:

"I'm going to stay at the University of Tennessee."

The packed house erupted as fellow players, media, athletic department officials, friends, and family reveled in the news. "I've had an incredible experience at the University of Tennessee with all the people I've met, learned from, and become friends with here," Manning explained. "College football has been great to me, so have the people, and the coaches, and players I've played with the past three years. I wanted to come back and be a college student one more year and enjoy the entire experience."

Said coach Phillip Fulmer: "Today we are blessed with the ultimate return of loyalty and commitment... Peyton's decision makes a huge statement, I think, for Peyton Manning and his character, putting team and program and alumni and fans and friends and teammates ahead of immediate financial gains and the limelight of the National Football League."

11,201

Career passing yards at Tennessee for Peyton Manning, the most in school history.

Acknowledgements, Thanks, and Sources

Thank you to my family for your love, support, and patience. The same goes for my extended family around the country and world. You all know who you are, and how important you are to me (even when I ignore your emails, phone calls, and instant messages while doing things like writing books).

Thank you Tom Bast for green-lighting this project and everyone at Triumph Books who worked on it.

Thank you, fans. Without you, this project never would have happened.

The sources for this book are essentially too numerous to list, but most of the accumulated information simply came from years of being a sportswriter, along with the numerous official team sources. That means more media guides, Internet sites, press conferences, interviews, transcripts, and press releases than you can imagine – and from numerous bowls, conferences, services, and teams.

Some additional sources deserve special mention:

- University of Tennessee 2004 Media Guide
- University of Tennessee 2008 Media Guide
- 2008 Tennessee Football Record Book
- UTSports.com
- ESPN.com
- The Association Press
- The Official 2008 Division I and Division I-AA Football Records Book
- The College Football Hall of Fame website
- The Pro Football Hall of Fame website
- "*ESPN College Football Encyclopedia: The Complete History of the Game*," by Michael Maccambridge, 2005
- 2008 SEC Football Media Guide
- NCAA.com
- NFL.com
- "*Sugar Bowl Classic: A History*," by Marty Mule, 2008.

About the Author

Christopher Walsh has been an award-winning sports-writer since 1990, and currently covers the University of Alabama football program for the *Tuscaloosa News*. He's been twice nominated for a Pulitzer Prize, won three Football Writers Association of America awards, and received the 2006 Herby Kirby Memorial Award, the Alabama Sports Writers Association's highest honor. Originally from Minnesota and a graduate of the University of New Hampshire, he currently resides in Tuscaloosa.

His previous books include:

" *100 Things Crimson Tide Fans Need to Know & Do Before They Die*," 2008.

"*Who's No. 1? 100-Plus Years of Controversial Champions in College Football*," 2007.

"*Where Football is King: A History of the SEC*," 2006.

"*No Time Outs: What It's Really Like to be a Sportswriter Today*," 2006.

"*Crimson Storm Surge: Alabama Football, Then and Now*," 2005.

"*Return to Glory: The Story of Alabama's 2008 Season*," 2009 (contributing writer).

The "Huddle Up" series will remain a work in progress. To make comments, suggestions, or share an idea with the author, go to http://whosno1.blogspot.com/. Check out other 2009 editions: Alabama, Auburn, Michigan Notre Dame, Ohio State, Oklahoma, Tennessee, Texas, and the New York Giants.

Dedication

To Ian and Leah—congratulations

Triumph Books and colophon are registered trademarks of Random House, Inc.

This book is available in quantity at special discounts for your group or organization. For further information, contact:

Triumph Books
542 South Dearborn Street
Suite 750
Chicago, Illinois 60605
(312) 939-3330
Fax (312) 663-3557
www.triumphbooks.com

Printed in U.S.A.
ISBN: 978-1-60078-188-9

Design by Mojo Media Inc.

Photos courtesy of AP Images except where otherwise noted